Viktor E. Fra
— Life with Meaning —

Viktor E. Frankl
— Life with Meaning —

William Blair Gould
University of Dubuque

Brooks/Cole Publishing Company
Pacific Grove, California

 A CLAIREMONT BOOK

Brooks/Cole Publishing Company
A Division of Wadsworth, Inc.

Printed in the United States of America

10 9 8 7 6 5 4 3 2 1

Library of Congress Cataloging-in-Publication Data
Gould, William Blair.
    Viktor E. Frankl : life with meaning / William Blair Gould.
      p.   cm.
    Includes bibliographical references and index.
    ISBN 0-534-19470-2
    1. Frankl, Viktor Emil—Contributions in philosophy.
2. Logotherapy. 3. Psychoanalysis and philosophy. 4. Humanistic
psychotherapy. I. Title.
RC489.L6F734   1992
616.89'14—dc20   92-16809
                                               CIP

Sponsoring Editor: *Claire Verduin*
Editorial Associate: *Gay C. Bond*
Production Editor: *Marjorie Z. Sanders*
Manuscript Editor: *Lorraine Anderson*
Permissions Editor: *Carline Haga*
Interior Design: *Vernon T. Boes*
Cover Design: *Vernon T. Boes and Susan Haberkorn*
Cover Photo: *Evan Golden*
Typesetting: *BookPrep*
Printing and Binding: *Malloy Lithographing, Inc.*

To

Viktor E. Frankl

   —PATRIARCH

Joseph B. Fabry

Stephen S. Kalmar

Vera Lieban-Kalmer

   —PIONEERS

Natalie R. Gould

   —PARTNER

   IN THE SEARCH FOR MEANING

Preface

Viktor E. Frankl: Life with Meaning has four goals.

The first is to explore Frankl's role as a philosopher and to show how his philosophy affects his theories and practice of meaning analysis. Theodore McConnell highlights Frankl as a philosopher and writes that "among contemporary models for selfhood Viktor Frankl is one of the most metaphysical and speculative." Frankl is also one of the most existential and pragmatic. One of the primary tasks of this book is to show how and why this philosophical mix has made Frankl a unique and especially compelling voice for meaning.

The second goal is to examine the contribution of meaning analysis to the study and practice of philosophical psychology and Frankl's role in helping to heal the institutional split between philosophy and psychology. It is my contention that whether readers approach this book as philosophers or as psychologists they face the same questions: What is the nature of the self? How is a person motivated? What is the relation between how one perceives and how one acts? What are the dimensions of freedom and responsibility? The following chapters discuss how Frankl, as a philosopher and psychiatrist, answers these and other questions about the self in relation to other humanistic and existential writers in both disciplines.

Third, using Frankl's meaning analysis as a catalyst, this book aims to rethink what being fully human means at the end of the 20th century.

Fourth, this book shows how Frankl's philosophy and therapy can be a resource for discovering meaning in life.

The eight chapters of this book are arranged to help the reader examine critically Frankl's philosophical psychology. They are aimed at stimulating dialogue in classrooms, conferences, clinics, and as Frankl might say, with "the person in the street." While the chapters follow a particular sequence from psychological issues to philosophical developments, each can be read independently or in reverse order if the needs and interests of the reader are better served.

I strongly recommend that the reader become familiar with the writings of Frankl, especially *Man's Search for Meaning, The Doctor and the Soul,* and *Psychotherapy and Existentialism.* Two books by Joseph Fabry are invaluable:

The Pursuit of Meaning, an excellent overview of the thought of Frankl; and *Guideposts to Meaning*, which provides practical examples of the use of meaning analysis in a variety of situations. The Munich-based logotherapist Elisabeth Lukas continues to make a valuable contribution through her discussion and expansion of Frankl's therapeutic techniques. Her two books, *Meaningful Living* and *Meaning in Suffering*, are worthwhile resources and provide excellent material for discussions of Frankl's methods. Further, the publications of the Frankl Institute of Berkeley, California, especially the *International Forum for Logotherapy*, provide up-to-date information on developments and directions in meaning analysis.

    Viktor E. Frankl: Life with Meaning invites discussion, and there are as many ways to discuss Frankl's life and his influence as there are to conduct a choral work or a symphony. Frankl is like a composer whose work is being increasingly performed, so that both appreciation and criticism of his contributions are being assessed and recognized by a growing audience of psychologists, philosophers, theologians, educators, and laypersons.

William Blair Gould

Acknowledgments

This book is a tribute to Viktor E. Frankl's witness to meaning and an expression of appreciation for what I have gained through knowing him and by exploring his writings. I am especially grateful to my friends in the Frankl Institute of Logotherapy for the exchange of ideas through international congresses and publications. Special thanks is due Joseph B. Fabry, founder of the Frankl Institute and editor of its publications, and to Stephen S. Kalmar and Vera J. Lieban-Kalmar, the guiding spirits of the institute's educational program and outreach for more than ten years. Their encouragement and friendship helped me to exercise "the defiant power of the human spirit" and finish the book. The teaching and writings of Elisabeth Lukas, director of the South German Institute of Logotherapy in Munich, were valuable resources. The students in my graduate classes on Frankl were a testing ground for most of the material that appears in these chapters. They helped to keep me at my task of writing by asking, "When will be able to read the book?"

The personal love and editing skills of my wife Natalie made *Viktor E. Frankl: Life with Meaning* a special partnership. My reviewers deserve particular thanks: Robert C. Leslie, dean emeritus of the Pacific School of Religion, curator of the Frankl Library in Berkeley, and Fellow and Diplomate of Viktor Frankl Institute of Logotherapy; James A. Peterson, University of Vermont; and Darrell Smith, Texas A&M University. Others who have been supportive include my secretary Donna Kramer; the staffs of the Graduate Theological Union Library, Berkeley; the Robertson Memorial Library, University of Prince Edward Island, Canada; the Ficke-Laird Library, University of Dubuque; the University of Iowa Library; Wartburg Theological Seminary Library; and the University of Dubuque for sabbatical leave. For her confidence in this book, I thank Claire Verduin, publisher of Brooks/Cole. I am also indebted to Gay Bond and Marjorie Sanders at Brooks/Cole and to Lorraine Anderson for their seeing the manuscript through to its completed form.

Introduction

THE AREA WE HAVE ENTERED WITH OUR LOGO-
THERAPY, AND ABOVE ALL, WITH EXISTENTIAL ANALY-
SIS, IS A BORDERLAND BETWEEN MEDICINE AND
PHILOSOPHY.

—VIKTOR FRANKL

Viktor Frankl invites us to enter a borderland between medicine and existential philosophy that will help us to find meaning in life. Frankl's psychiatric practice began as a medical ministry that focused on the *homo patiens* (the suffering person); it is now also a *ministry humane* that is concerned for the *homo possedens* (the person who wishes to take hold of life). In her tribute to Frankl's *The Unheard Cry for Meaning*, the internationally known psychiatrist Elisabeth Kübler-Ross writes that this book "emphasizes the importance of helping people to find meaning in their lives, and thus to live at their fullest potential." The *ministry humane* of Frankl enters borderlands between the psychological and the philosophical, the secular and the sacred, the meditation of the East and the activism of the West, the needs of the poor and the needs of the affluent, those just starting life's journey and those reaching life's end. And as he enters each borderland, he focuses on the same task: to help others find meaning in life.

Frankl's Terminology

Frankl's modesty kept him from using his own name to describe his psychiatric philosophy and method. Aware that Ludwig Binswanger had already introduced the term *existential analysis*, which he would have favored, Frankl coined the word *logotherapy* to describe his philosophy and method: *logos*, or meaning, and *therapie*, or healing—that is, healing through meaning. This coined word has not worn well over the years. The use of *logos* is one stumbling block. The secular person identifies *logos* with an advertising symbol or slogan. The religiously oriented person thinks of *logos* as the theological concept of the Divine Word, as defined by the Gospel of John in the New Testament. The philosopher associates *logos* with its use by the Sophists as an argument or the content of an argument, or with Heraclitus's description as a kind of nonhuman intelligence that organizes the world into a coherent whole. Such conflicting perceptions of *logos* do not help a person to recognize Frankl's definition from the Greek of *logos* as meaning. The word *therapy* does not fare any better than *logos* in the marketplace, although it is more easily identified. *Therapy,* which is commonly understood as treatment for the mentally ill, frightens away some persons who don't want to be identified as part of a "program for sickies." It is difficult for any group—including the followers of Frankl—to agree on a common title for his philosophy and method. I will use the term *meaning analysis* as the primary reference and the term *logotherapy* when such use is unavoidable.

The Search for Meaning

The search for meaning is our central quest as humans. Meaning in life enables us to make sense of our existence despite guilt, suffering, injustice, seeming chaos, and the inevitability of death. It also gives us new perspectives for a time in which values are on the decline and the cults of success and hedonism dominate. Meaning analysis focuses our attention on the human spirit as the key resource for recapturing the health, wholeness, and caring of the fully human person. It emphasizes the importance of our being value-bearers, of being able to learn from the past, to live responsibly in the present, and to plan hopefully for the future.

The Central Affirmations of Meaning Analysis

These are the central affirmations of meaning analysis:

> Life has meaning.
> We have the will to meaning, our central motivation for living.
> We have the freedom to find meaning in how we think and in what we do.
> We are mind, body, and spirit. These dimensions of the self are inter-dependent. The key is the spirit (*noös*); it enables us to exercise our will to meaning, to envisage our goals, and to move beyond our instinctual and sexual needs to self-transcendence.

The Viennese psychiatrist Viktor Frankl teaches that meaning in life cannot be dictated or invited. It can only be discovered by the searching self in each person's own existential situation. The human goal, he believes, is not to find peace of mind, nor even peace of soul, but to experience meaning in a healthy striving by who we are now toward who we can become in the future. Meaning in life comes through the individual's using the unconscious and the conscious power of the human spirit in freedom that is linked to responsibleness.

Contents

Chapter Three

The Kantian Dimension
— 48 —

Chapter Four

Pragmatism Redux:
The Humanism of James and Frankl
— 62 —

Chapter Five

Phenomenological Perspectives
— 81 —

Chapter Six

The Existentialist Posture
— 102 —

Chapter Seven

Frontiers of Humanistic Psychology
— *124* —

Chapter Eight

Healing the Shattered Self
— *142* —

Appendix

A Comparison of Socrates' and Frankl's Philosophical Fundamentals and Methods
— *159* —

— 1 —

Witness

to

Meaning

THE CONCEPT OF MEANING IN ALL OF ITS VARIETIES
IS THE DOMINANT PHILOSOPHICAL CONCEPT OF
OUR TIME.
                        —SUZANNE LANGER

Although a philosophy of life is more than one person's story, Viktor Frankl's witness to meaning is one of the significant philosophical testimonies of the 20th century. The account of his experiences in the Nazi concentration camps, which was first published in Vienna in 1946 and subsequently translated into many languages and in several editions as *Man's Search for Meaning,* is a moving story of how one person exercised the last human freedom—the ability to "choose one's attitude in a given set of circumstances" or, as Frankl writes, "to find meaning in every situation, even the most miserable." Frankl entered the concentration camps as a young, innovative psychiatrist whose work focused on the search for meaning. He left the last camp as a person whose philosophy of meaning had been tested for two and a half years of suffering as a victim of the most bestial kind of behavior. But Frankl's understanding of life as meaning began long before he entered the death camps. It started when he was a teen-age boy experiencing the harsh deprivation of the Austrian people after the 1918 armistice.

Young Frankl in Vienna

Frankl still remembers how he and his family had to beg for food at the farmers' market in Vienna. He tells of stealing corn from the fields when he and his family visited relatives in Moravia. Thus, as a boy entering his teens, he identified with the social and economic needs of the poor. It is understandable that in later years the young Frankl was attracted by the work of Sigmund Freud (1856–1939), who considered himself a world reformer as well as a leader of a new science of the self called psychoanalysis. At the same time, Frankl especially identified with the works of Alfred Adler (1870–1937) in the *Volkshochschule* (people's free schools) for the unemployed and working classes. In 1920, as a schoolboy of 15, Frankl enrolled in a philosophy class in one of the schools. This aroused his interest in philosophy and led eventually to his receiving a Ph.D. in 1949. Frankl became a spokesman for a philosophy of freedom and responsibility at an early age. He recalls that as a teenager, speaking to youth clubs, he gave lectures that were based on the thesis that "life asks us questions that we have to answer not only by what we say, but how we act." Frankl was caught up and deeply influenced by the psychological, political, and philosophical controversies of Vienna between the two world wars as a schoolboy and later as a medical student. It has been said that Freud, Adler, and Frankl could have come out of any European city, but Vienna provided a unique intellectual and emotional climate for the psychological developments that took place.

In the latter part of the 19th century and the first decade of the 20th, Vienna was the old Imperial city, the seat of the Austro-Hungarian Empire and, after Paris, the second largest city of the continent. It was a Germanic political stronghold, a cultural mecca for thousands in the provinces, a center of science, and a major economic capital. A variety of notable immigrants came to Vienna, including Theodor Herzl, the founder of Zionism; the composers Gustav Mahler and Johannes Brahms; the architect Josef Hoffman; the educator Franz Cizek; and the Nobel Prize winner for literature Elias Canetti. In addition, hundreds of thousands of the poor and unknown immigrated to Vienna, among these in 1860 a family named Freud with their 4-year-old son, Sigmund. According to Bruno Bettelheim, Vienna's uniqueness came about through a quirk of history in which the greatest flowering of Austrian culture was accompanied by the withering of its political power:

> Things had never been better, but at the same time they had never been worse: this strange simultaneity, in my opinion, explains why psychoanalysis, based on the understanding of ambivalence, hysteria, and neurosis, originated in Vienna and probably could have originated nowhere else. And psychoanalysis was but one of the major intellectual developments of a time when a pervasive awareness of political decline led Vienna's cultural elite to abandon politics as a subject to take seriously, to withdraw their attention from the wider world and turn inwardly instead.[1]

The decline of the empire, which began coincidentally at about the same time as the Freud family's arrival in Vienna, reached its nadir in 1918, after its defeat in World War I. By 1920, the 64-year-old Freud dominated the psychological scene internationally and had managed to gain the reluctant respect of the Austrian state and of the University of Vienna. He was awarded the title of full professor, without, however, a seat on the board of the faculty. During this same period, the young Frankl was caught up in the multiple ideas and events occurring in Vienna. He and his classmates discussed a variety of topics as they walked in the Prater—politics, philosophy, and especially Freudian and Adlerian psychology. The teenage Frankl explored psychoanalysis by taking courses with two exceptional followers of Freud: Eduard Hitschmann, the psychoanalyst most sympathetic to Adler's theories, and Paul Schilder, who disagreed with Freud on the nature of training in analysis. Although Frankl had begun to have theories that contradicted Freud's central theme of the pleasure principle, he almost joined that psychoanalytic circle. He changed his mind, however, deciding that its philosophy was nihilistic. Instead he turned to the Adlerians. As Frankl comments on this period, "All this from a boy who had just started his medical studies."[2]

Frankl was a precocious thinker and conversationalist whose actions matched his thoughts and words. Still a teenager himself, he lectured to hundreds of other young people in youth clubs on the relationship between sexual problems and meaning. He read Freud's epochal work *Beyond the Pleasure Principle* shortly after its publication in 1920. In this book, Freud argues that we are motivated not only by the desire for happiness but also by earlier events in our lives that we replay. Freud concludes that while we may think that we are growing toward a life unified by love (eros), we are actually being driven toward the disintegrating powers of decay or death (thanatos). This battle between the life drive and the death drive had been informally discussed by Freud, before 1914, with the Russian analyst Sabina Spielrein, Alfred Adler, and Carl Jung (1875–1961) who were at the time all members of Freud's psychoanalytic circle.

Freud wrote *Beyond the Pleasure Principle* as a corrective to Jung's attempt to resolve the life-death dualism through a monistic theory of the libido. Thus Frankl, in reading the book, could assess the arguments of both Freud and Jung. Two years after the publication of Freud's *Beyond the Pleasure Principle,* Frankl conceived the importance of ultimate meaning for the self; and as Frankl states 60 years later, "this concept accompanied me throughout my life and stood the test of the concentration camp."[3] Frankl agrees with *Beyond the Pleasure Principle* that life does indeed have a death drive, but Frankl believes that the life drive is ultimately victorious. Freud's publication of *The Ego and the Id* (1923) and *Inhibitions, Symptoms, and Anxiety* (1926) gave the young Frankl further opportunity to see Freud's system as a whole and to compare it with Adler's theories. It was during this same period that Frankl was caught up in the battle of the psychiatrists and in an atmosphere that made Vienna a city of couches as much as a city of dreams.

Frankl joined the Adlerians in 1926, 14 years after Adler had been expelled from Freud's circle. Although Freud had caused Adler to leave, it is possible that the split was not caused only by Freud. Adler said later that he had seen himself too much in Freud's shadow and that he feared he would be held accountable for Freudian theories that he had begun to question. Of equal importance to Adler was his feeling that his own work would be either ignored or destroyed by

Freud's followers.[4] Dr. Vera Lieban-Kalmar explains the central aspect of Adler's thinking that caused the break:

> Adler . . . sees the underlying forces in the formation of the personality as the individual need to master the environment. This need for social assertion is usually called "the will to power," an incorrect translation of the term *Geltungsstreben*. Adler used the term to describe the individual's attempt to overcome the handicaps of biological inferiorities. . . . Adler's early studies about human inferiorities brought him to postulate that every individual has the ability to overcome inferiority handicaps through the use of his/her free will and free choice of actions. This theory of freedom and action was strongly opposed by Freud and perpetuated Adler's separation from Freud's school of psychoanalysis.[5]

Frankl agreed with Adler's viewpoint. Adler saw a person's freedom of choice as central in the decision-making process, and as Lieban-Kalmar emphasizes, freedom of choice became the starting point for the development of Frankl's own theories. It is ironic that Adler, after going through the pain of being rejected by the Freudian psychoanalytic society, should force Frankl, the youngest of his followers, out of the Adlerian movement. It began when two Adlerians— Oswald Schwartz, who later became the leader of psychosomatic medicine, and Rudolph Allers—criticized Adler's idea of *Gemeinschaftsgefühl* (community spirit) as being too rigidly structured and disregarding the individual's unique ability to use his or her will to change. After Schwartz presented these views before Adler and the others, Adler turned to Frankl and another listener and demanded, "*Ihr Helden bekennt Euch!* What sort of heroes are you? Show that you are courageous enough to speak up! Do you take my side or theirs?" Frankl replied that he was of the same opinion as Schwartz and Allers but believed that what they had said was in essential agreement with Adler, that there should be room in the society for differences of opinion, and that there was no cause for them to leave. But Adler forced all three to leave and never forgave Frankl. In turn, Frankl came to believe that Freud and Adler, each in his own way, were dictators. Their dictatorial attitudes caused gossip, betrayals of friendships, and uneasiness within their respective schools. Early in his career, Freud established a secret committee of seven to help him keep political control and to expel rebels.[6] This may, however, have been a prudent move because, according to J. A. C. Brown, "one is led to believe that Freud, like D. H. Lawrence, was surrounded by a group of egocentric primadonnas whose highly ambivalent devotion to the Master was only equalled by their dislike of each other and the abnormal volubility which manifested itself in their writings."[7] While Adler never forgave Frankl, Frankl did establish a friendly relationship with Adler's daughter, Dr. Alexandra Adler, in the 1970s. She once reminisced about Frankl's joining the scientific meetings with her father: "Frankl's remarks were original and gave rise to many discussions . . . [it is probable that Frankl] the youngest of Adler's followers was more spirited than docile."[8]

Frankl's insistence that meaning analysis is a *supplemental* therapy allows for cooperation with other contemporary psychiatric methods. For instance, Frankl recognizes that the depth psychology of the psychoanalysts may be necessary, but he points out that it should be supplemented by what he calls height psychology, a dimensional ontology that utilizes the ideals and aspirations of the self. Further, while Frankl agrees with Adler that biological, sociological, and psychological factors are important, he insists that the self still has areas determined primarily by the noetic dimension, which allows personal freedom and responsibleness. In addition, though Freud and Adler were aware of the existential perspective, Frankl's meaning analysis is one of the first therapies to develop a psychologically oriented existential analysis of the self. Meaning analysis is also one of the first therapies originating in Europe to provide a bridge between existential psychotherapy and humanistic psychology. It redefines the existential emphases on choice, freedom, and responsibleness while maintaining the humanistic appreciation of rationality and the fundamental assertion that the self is more than the sum of its parts.

Freud, Adler, and Frankl were nurtured by the humanistic tradition as part of their training in medicine. They were aware of existentialist literature, especially the works of Friedrich Nietzsche (1844–1900) and Fëdor Dostoevski (1821–1881). Of greater importance, they lived in a time when the rise of totalitarianism challenged their understanding of the reliability of human reason and also increased their own experience of existential anxiety. Although there were obvious differences in Freud's and Frankl's age, how each man responded to the rise of Hitler and the Nazi takeover of Austria reveals much about how each man personally faced that crisis.

Frankl, Freud, and the Nazi Takeover

Sandor Ferenczi wrote one of his last letters to his old friend Freud in March 1933 in which he begged Freud to leave Austria. Freud wrote back that he was too ill from cancer of the mouth and jaw and too dependent on his physicians and his comforts to do so. Freud was also ambivalent about the invasion of Austria by Hitler, saying at one time that he did not think the Germans would come and at another time that if they did, things in Austria "will not reach the height of brutality they have in Germany."[9] In February 1938, less than a month before the German *Anschluss,* Freud wrote to another friend, "At present our government, upright and brave in its way, is more energetic in fending off the Nazi than ever before" and described Chancellor Kurt von Schuschnigg, who had given way to Germany's demands, as "decent, courageous and a man of character."[10] Yet at other times, Freud admitted that the Austrians were no less brutal than the Germans; a judgment that was verified within months as the Austrians outdid their German mentors in destroying the weak and helpless. Only on March 12, 1938, the day of the *Anschluss* when Nazi troops paraded through the streets to the cheers of the Viennese populace, did Freud finally admit *finis Austriae* (Austria is finished). But he still stubbornly refused to leave, though he knew that his books had been burned and that the Nazis called him degenerate.

Two days after the *Anschluss,* Freud's offices and his home were searched by the Nazi brownshirts for "evidence of an international conspiracy." On March 15, 1938, his passport was confiscated; he still would not budge. Only Freud's international fame, his conscientious friends, and the personal intervention of President Franklin D. Roosevelt saved Freud and his followers from the terrors experienced by Frankl and his family. The most troublesome player in this difficult period was Freud himself, who argued with his English friend and disciple Ernest Jones that "he [Freud] could not leave his native land; it would be like a soldier deserting his post." Jones had an appropriate answer, telling Freud about a man named Lightoller, the second officer of the doomed *Titanic.* Lightoller was blown to the surface when the ship's boiler exploded as it was sinking. When Lightoller was later asked when he left the ship, he answered, "I never left the ship, Sir; she left me."[11] Freud then allowed Jones to arrange visas for him and for his family to go to England. But then Freud requested that not only his family but also his staff, 16 persons in all, accompany him.[12] On March 22, in the midst of red tape and obstruction by the Viennese officials considering Freud's request for permission to leave with his family and staff, his daughter Anna was arrested, questioned by the Gestapo, and finally released that night. It was this event that finally convinced Freud that they must leave Austria. After having all his assets confiscated, Freud received a passport and left Vienna at last on June 4, 1938. But just before the Nazis let him go, they forced him to sign a statement that he had not been ill-treated by them. He signed, adding the comment "*Ich kann die Gestapo jedermann auf das beste empfehlen* [I can most highly recommend the Gestapo to everyone]."[13]

We are aware that Freud did not want to leave Vienna, for he said that his "abandoning his post would give a signal for the complete dissolution of the analytic group," an eventuality that he wanted to avoid.[14] Freud's worry about the dissolution of the analytic group may account in great part for his rationalization of political events, including his ambivalence toward his fellow Austrians. After arriving in England, the threats he perceived against psychoanalysis, whether from "untrustworthy America," or far worse, from Nazi-dominated Europe, weighed on his mind. Although 82 years old, Freud continued his intellectual battles, this time against Jewish critics who disagreed with his lengthy *Moses and Monotheism,* which he was determined to complete and did. In July 1938, he began his *Outline of Psychoanalysis,* which embodied his last message to his colleagues: do not let psychoanalysis stagnate. He remained a professional to the end, but he was ambivalent about where he truly belonged as a person. After his long fight to remain in Vienna, less than a year before his death he wanted to become a British citizen—possibly because of his long affection for England and his reception there as an emigrant but more probably because of his final rejection of Austria. As in so many of his personal relationships, love had turned to hate.

There are obvious differences between Freud and Frankl: Freud was a man in his late 70s with a grown family, internationally recognized as the founder of psychoanalysis; Frankl was a man in his late 20s, still unmarried and just beginning his career as a psychiatrist. But their reasons for remaining in Austria at a time of personal danger provide clues to the nature of their selves and, especially, to how they chose to use their personal freedom.

Frankl and his family correctly read the signs of the times as anti-Semitism increased in Vienna and the annexation of Austria by Germany became imminent. One member of the family, Frankl's sister, had already emigrated to Australia. After discussing the situation with his family, Frankl applied for a visa to come to the United States. While he believed that as a psychiatrist he could protect his family, they urged him to leave. At this time he writes that he had a dream "that belongs to my deepest experience in the realm of dreaming. I dreamed that people were lined up—psychotics, patients to be taken to the gas chambers. And I felt so deep a compassion that I decided to join them."[15]

The day that his visa was approved by the United States, he agonized over whether he should accept the visa with the hope that his parents and his fiancée would be able to follow him. Covering the yellow star that he was compelled as a Jew to wear, he entered Saint Stephen's Church in the center of Vienna, where an organ concert was taking place. He sat in a pew and prayed silently, "O God, give me a sign." Should he stay with his family with the hope that they could be saved, or should he go to the United States, where he believed he could continue his pioneer work in psychology? When he came home he found his father in tears. When Frankl asked his father what had happened, his father replied, "Viktor, the Nazis have destroyed the synagogue" and showed him a fragment of marble he had salvaged. The fragment of the Torah his father held in his hands had one letter engraved on it, the beginning of the commandment "Honor thy father and thy mother." Frankl called the American embassy and canceled his visa. He had received his sign.

Frankl's decision to remain was a symbolic act of self-transcendence. He explains that "self-transcendence . . . is equally implied whether a man transcends himself by *meaning fulfillment* or *loving encounter*: in the first case, an impersonal logos is involved; in the second, a personal logos (a sense of meaning)—an incarnate logos, so to speak."[16] Essentially, Freud symbolizes the impersonal logos with his desire for meaning fulfillment centered in his vocation; Frankl symbolizes a personal logos. Frankl became an incarnate logos of love to his family, to his friends, and when the time came, to his fellow prisoners in the concentration camps.

The presence of a personal logos gave Frankl the strength to survive the concentration camps for two and a half years. Self-transcendence helped him to find meaning in significant ways. In the midst of severe physical pain, he would think back to incidents from his childhood that illustrated the love between his family and himself. He began to become aware that everything preserved in the past could be rescued from the past, that the past was not irretrievably lost but could be reclaimed to help the self in times of suffering and despair. He quoted to himself the psalm, "You, Lord, have preserved my tears in a vessel." He also self-transcended by projecting, or even fantasizing, the future: the reunion that would occur with those he loved and the time when he would resume his psychiatric practice. He also used his memory as a constructive agent of time to rewrite and to revise his completed manuscript *Ärztliche Seelsorge* (*Medical Ministry,* renamed *The Doctor and the Soul* over Frankl's objection), which he had sewn into the lining of his overcoat before he entered the first concentration camp and which was taken from him and destroyed. At first, this appeared to him as a terrible defeat, as he thought of the long hours he had spent spelling out the transition from psychotherapy to meaning analysis, but he began to reconstruct the book in his mind. When he completed it for the second time, he cried with relief at being able to communicate from the past to the future.

Frankl's primary expression of self-transcendence in the camps was in reaching out to others, especially to the mentally and physically ill. He recognized that there were only two kinds of human beings in a camp, the decent and the indecent. He tried in every way possible to help the decent and to encourage them to keep their humanity in the midst of so much inhumanity. Almost 50 years after his concentration camp experience, Frankl recalls signs of humanness from unexpected sources: a warden who gave him a piece of bread, though that was forbidden; an SS man who brought him needed medicine; a former Viennese gangster who as a capo (a collaborator put over other prisoners by the Nazis) saved Frankl from extreme violence; a German doctor who kept Frankl from being placed on a truck full of prisoners who were executed. So Frankl found decency among the indecent. He concluded that an individual may block the noös (spirit) but that it remains the basic resource that enables the self to remain human. This conviction has remained the cornerstone of his therapy. When he was asked after the war when he had resumed his psychiatric practice, "How did you get your strength back after the concentration camps?" Frankl replied, "By dealing with the task at hand; listening to those across the desk, to those who had had 'crimes' committed against them by other psychologists."[17] By "crimes" he meant and means those reductionistic and deterministic therapies that dehumanize the patient.

The Third Viennese School of Psychotherapy

In 1946, Frankl became head of neurology at the Poliklinik Hospital in Vienna. *Man's Search for Meaning* (first published in Austria in 1946 as *Ein Psycholog erlebt das Konzentrationslager*), which is Frankl's own story of his life in the concentration camps and a brief explanation of meaning analysis, marked the beginning of his international fame and his recognition as the founder of the third Viennese school of psychotherapy, in succession to Freud and Adler.

What accounts for the fact that millions of copies of *Man's Search for Meaning* have been sold and that Frankl's other books, including *The Doctor and the Soul* (in its 57th edition and published in nine languages) are critically acclaimed by laypersons as well as those in the medical and psychiatric professions? I suggest as reasons five interdependent factors: (1) the personal witness of Frankl, (2) his holistic understanding of the self, (3) his conviction of the centrality and power of the noös as evidenced in self-transcendence, (4) the use of his meaning analysis as a supplement to other therapies, and (5) the openness of meaning analysis to future developments.

Frankl's witness to meaning stands out as a symbol of human integrity and caring. His concentration camp imprisonment remains the most dramatic form of his witness; but during the 45 years since his release, he has carried on his therapeutic ministry, helping people to rehumanize themselves, through counseling, writing, and lecturing. He reaches out to them not only in his official psychiatric practice but also through letters and personal visits, especially to prisoners. In 1985, he dedicated a lecture to Professor Edith Weisskopf-Joelson, who had personally overcome mental illness to become an internationally recognized pioneer in meaning analysis. In this lecture, Frankl explains what he means by "tragic optimism": a way of saying yes to life in the face of suffering, guilt, and death.[18] Elisabeth Lukas comments that "there is today a disease more infectious and deadly than AIDS: the disease of the denial of life."[19]

The need for a holistic understanding of the self—the interaction of body, mind, and spirit—is as imperative today as it was when Freud started his psychiatric practice a century ago. But the focus has shifted from a priority of treating psychosexual problems to dealing with what Frankl calls the noögenic neurosis, a failure of the self to find meaning. He believes that this failure has resulted in an existential vacuum leading to an existential neurosis that has replaced sexual dysfunction as the primary malaise of humankind. Frankl sees these symptoms leading to a despair that often results in self-destruction, particularly among young people. In 1980, he commented on this publicly.

> I gladly and readily confess that as a young man I had to go through the hell of despair over the apparent meaninglessness of life, through total and ultimate nihilism. But I wrestled with it like Jacob with the angel did until I could say "yes to life in spite of everything," until I could develop *immunity* against nihilism.[20]

His immunity from nihilism began with his understanding of the self holistically, especially in seeing the key to our humanness as the spirit, or noetic dimension.

The noös of the self is an existential instrument rather than an instinctual factor. Unlike the mind and the body, the noös cannot become ill, but it may become blocked. The noös does not force its way into our consciousness; we must choose it. The spiritual nature of the noös is one of the most debated aspects of Frankl's thought. As Irvin Yalom points out, "though he [Frankl] claims to present a secular approach to meaning (he states that as a physician who has taken the oath of Hippocrates, he is obliged to develop treatment methods that apply to all patients, atheists and devout alike), it is clear that Frankl's approach to meaning is fundamentally religious."[21] Dr. Stephen Kalmar disagrees with such a conclusion:

> Frankl is aware that his thoughts about the human dimension of the spirit could be mistaken as religious in nature. . . . In German there is a clear distinction between *geistig* and *geistlich,* the latter, but not the first, having religious connotations. Both are rendered in English as "spiritual." Frankl puts logotherapy into the *geistige* (nonreligious) sphere of scholastic systems. Because the words spirit and spirituality have religious connotations, Frankl prefers to call the *geistige* dimension the noo-sphere, to avoid a religious interpretation.[22]

Kalmar is careful to note that logotherapy must stay apart from religion, and that Kalmar does not mean "logophilosophy" and its relation to religion. A review of the written accounts of the use of the noetic dimension by various meaning analysts indicates that whether a secular or religious interpretation is used depends on the religious orientation, or lack of it, of either the therapist or the patient as well as on the existential situation itself. This is seen especially in how one defines self-transcendence, the key to meaning analysis. Howard Slaatte's discussion of self-transcendence illustrates the confusion that results in defining the noetic dimension as secular in one place and as religious in another. In the same article he writes first, "The self-transcendence or noölogical dimension of the human being involves elements of free will, reflection, self-detachment, humor, conscience, and the will to meaning." But in his final paragraphs Slaatte concludes (using Tillichian language), "Frankl's intention is to keep the mentally healthy person open to God above all finite concepts of God," based on the premise that "at times unconscious religiousness needs to become conscious."[23] Frankl's priority is defining the role of self-transcendence as the dimension of the self that enables persons to become aware of what it means to be fully human.

Frankl's concept of intuitive conscience is that it is the key element of self-transcendence, which helps the self to discover unique meanings and ethical values in a variety of existential situations that demand choice. The strength of Frankl's concept of conscience is in its ability to avoid both the rigidity of a Kantian deontologically structured imperative of duty and the constriction of value bearing to a reductionistic and moralistic view of life. While intuitive conscience is an essential element of self-transcendence, it is nevertheless a human phenomenon; and this conscience, which can lead us to meaning, can also lead us astray. Thus, in listening to our intuitive conscience, we must still be alert, ready to discern not only what is but what ought to be. Frankl's emphasis on meaning in life encourages us not to be tied to one system or method. His commonsense approach to life offers a type of therapy that can be an effective and needed supplement to physical, mental, and spiritual care.

Meaning Analysis and Judaism

Once one realizes that Frankl does not claim to have all the answers but rather aims to provide a dimensional approach, one can build on the three tenets of meaning analysis's understanding of human existence. These are that (1) humans have freedom of the will, (2) there is a human will to meaning, and (3) even suffering has meaning. As I mentioned earlier, the debate continues as to whether Frankl's psychological philosophy is essentially religious or secular. Thus far, Frankl seems to attract more favorable attention from those who possess a religious dimension than from those who are agnostic or atheistic, and this factor turns attention to Frankl's own theism. Reuven Bulka, a Canadian rabbi, writes that "all similarities and affinities notwithstanding, there is no system with which Logotherapy shows a greater rootedness and similarity than Judaism."[24] This is illustrated, as Bulka shows, by equating Biblical and Talmudic principles with the three tenets of meaning analysis: (1) freedom of the will, (2) the will to meaning, and (3) the unconditioned meaning of life.

Freedom of the will asserts that we are free to choose those values and purposes that can lead to a sense of meaning. This is in harmony with the Hebrew covenant and with the Talmudic principle that "everything is foreseen, but freedom of choice is given."[25] The will to meaning, the principal motivating force of the self, points out the reductionistic nature of the will to pleasure and the will to power. The Bible witnesses to how the pursuit of power, happiness, and self-aggrandizement ends in frustration and defeat. The Talmud states, "Let all thine actions be for [the sake of] the name of Heaven."[26] By substituting the word *meaning* for "the name of Heaven," the dictum becomes an aphorism of meaning analysis. Meaning analysis addresses the entire scope of the unconditioned meaningfulness of life, including the formation of values, facing the tragic triad (pain, guilt, and death), and the relation of freedom to responsibleness. Its prototype is the Biblical story, found in the Old and New Testaments, of the relation of humankind to its Creator.

Frankl's concept of ultimate meaning is, however, essentially a declaration of faith, not a dogma. In his desire to address the secular as well as the religious thinker, Frankl is careful to allow the individual to decide whether he or she interprets ultimate meaning as being responsible to an intuitive conscience, to the needs of another person, to the expectations of society, or to the commands of God. For some persons, Frankl realizes, ultimate meaning may refer to an ultimate concern or have a supermeaning significance; for others, the concept of ultimate meaning may be incomprehensible or a sheer mystery. While Frankl sees in religion an important ingredient of human life that expresses the search for ultimate meaning, even this orientation toward ultimate meaning remains for him a *human* phenomenon, not something divine. Our sense of a super-human dimension is a human trust in something we hope to be real though unseen. This trust is in harmony with St. Paul's aphorism that "faith is the substance of things hoped for, the evidence of things not seen."

Whether couched in religious or secular terms, our perception of ultimate meaning demands transcendence. "As Rabbi Hillel asked, 'But if I am for my own self only, what am I?' It is this very quote which Frankl himself employs quite skillfully in projecting the notion of self-transcendence as basic to the human condition."[27]

Self-transcendence enables us to have what Frankl sees as an encounter with the *logos* (meaning) of life. Biblical religion describes this encounter, and Martin Buber expresses it as the I-Thou relationship. Both the Bible and Frankl underscore dynamic understanding of the self that links freedom to respon-sibleness: the Scriptures through a covenant relationship; Frankl through what he calls the demand, or expectation, quality of life. This approach brings to mind the Talmudic dictum, "It is not incumbent upon you to finish the task, but neither are you free to desist from it."[28] Neither the Biblical faith nor Frankl expect perfection; rather, we are *expected* to develop an awareness of the essential tasks that have been entrusted to us and a willingness to perform them. For Scriptural faith and for Frankl, such responsibleness is not relegated to a person who is just task-oriented but to one who acts from an integrated world view (*Weltanschauung*).

Bulka points out that Judaism and Frankl have correlative world views. He cites Frankl's suggestion that monotheism, belief in one God, should be balanced by monanthropism, belief in the oneness of humankind.[29] As an example of the correlation of Biblical faith with Frankl's suggestion, Bulka refers to the per-sonality of Abraham:

> It turns out that Abraham's kindness was directly related to, even an emanation of, his monotheistic credo. If God is one and all human beings are equally God's children, then it is incumbent upon Abraham as the espouser of this notion to show an uncompromising caring for all of humankind. Therefore kindness, which is founded on the principle of concern for the welfare of others, is an absolute necessity within the mono-theistic framework.[30]

Because Frankl's therapeutic philosophy comes from concern for the oneness of humankind, including caring, he is, as Bulka suggests, carrying on the best of the Abrahamic tradition of universal concern. Both the Jewish faith and Frankl's philosophy of the self are integrative, looking inwardly to find harmony of mind, body, and spirit, and looking outwardly to a world that has meaning despite its contradictions, disappointments, and pain. Self-transcendence is the essential human dynamic. It is expressed in theological terms by the Jewish faith and in psychological terms by the faith of the logotherapist. In Judaism, revelation is the handing down to the human race of the means of human power and values.[31] In Frankl's view, human power and awareness of values come through the power of the noös. For both, our ethical values are tested in the crises of life.

Frankl does not moralize, but his philosophy embraces a moral sense of being that is energized by an intuitive conscience. Because we are free to obey or disobey moral promptings, we are subject to guilt. Frankl points out that each individual has a right to think of himself or herself as guilty. The issue is not whether or not a person is guilty, but how the individual uses guilt. This parallels traditional Judaism's tracing guilt to finiteness, disobedience, and the evasion of responsibleness. While Frankl states that we are free to become guilty, he also tells us that we are responsible for facing the guilt and overcoming it. We can use guilt as a learning process, either by understanding what has caused the guilt or by dismissing it if we are not responsible for it. If we are responsible, we can stop the thought or action that causes the guilt; when this occurs, guilt plays a positive role in a life of meaning. When we realize that we deserve the guilt, we follow a Biblical pattern: awareness, remorse, change of mind and habit, and restitution when possible. But there is a key difference between Frankl's secular solution and the religious solution: for Frankl, we have the power to ask and receive forgiveness from each other, while the religious tradition requires the forgiveness of God as well.

The nature of suffering is misunderstood by many who read Scripture as well as by those acquainted with meaning analysis. The Jewish Scriptures teach that a person draws closer to God through suffering.[32] Frankl sees suffering as a basic component of life but never teaches that suffering is *necessary* to find meaning. Frankl escapes the dilemma of the Book of Job, and its justification of innocent suffering, by concentrating on how suffering can be used as a tool for achieving meaning. Meaning may be found through suffering but not because of it. In this respect, Frankl's view is close to that of Rabbi Harold S. Kushner, author of *When Bad Things Happen to Good People*. Rabbi Kushner comments that Archibald MacLeish's play *J-B*, which deals with the innocent suffering of Job, is better theology than the original account. The play parallels Frankl's and Kushner's thinking that we should not ask "Why?" when tragedy strikes but ask instead "What should I do?"[33] When Frankl had to surrender his clothes at Auschwitz, he was given those of a former inmate who had been sent to the gas chamber. He found in a pocket a page ripped out of a Hebrew prayer book, containing the most important of all Jewish prayers, *Shema Yisrael* (Deut. 6:4-5).[34] He took it as a challenge to live his belief that life has meaning, even under the most miserable circumstances. When suffering is unavoidable, we can change ourselves even if the situation cannot be changed. The noetic power of the self can enable us to find meaning in the midst of pain. In the Scriptures, the God of strength and the God of suffering are one and the same. Similarly, for meaning analysis, "the reality of joy and the reality of suffering are both basic components of a human life lived to the full,"[35] but fullness is found through affirmation of life's meaning, not through denial and tears. Frankl's tragic optimism is optimism at its deepest level. It is teleologically optimistic because it affirms that the essential outcome of life is meaning, not nothingness; it is the triumph of love, not death.

Frankl writes of love as grace, enchantment, and above all as a miracle, "for true love is its own warrant of permanence."[36] Love's essence is not contingent upon existence, he explains:

> That is why love can outlast the death of the beloved; in that sense we can understand why love is "stronger" than death. The existence of the beloved may be annihilated by death, but his essence cannot be touched by death.... The "idea" of a person—which is what the lover sees—belongs to a realm beyond time.[37]

Frankl admits that this argument goes back to scholastic or Platonic philosophy, but he also points out that it is empirically proven by our recognition of its intellectual validity and its testing by life. Frankl is translating love from the emotional to the intentional act. He gives as an example the instance of a concentration camp inmate whose love of his mother helped him to stay alive for her sake. In essence, we are loved and recalled for our deeds, not for our physical forms. What we do out of love has value; all else fades away.

Whereas there is mutual action between meaning analysis and Biblical Scriptures, Judaic and Christian, Frankl's analysis of meaning crosses religious boundaries. Meaning analysis stands, so to speak, firmly on its own philosophical and psychological feet, but its secular, humanistic foundation has been built upon by persons of diverse religious backgrounds and by those who have none. Bulka is correct when he writes, "Paradoxically, Logotherapy belongs, at once, to no one and to everyone."[38] One of the significant developments in the last decade is the fact that the existential witness of Frankl has crossed national, ethnic, philosophical, religious, and psychological boundaries. One man who uses Frankl's philosophical psychology is the eminent Japanese psychiatrist Hiroshi Takashima (1912–   ), who is a respected physician in his own land and a fellow of the Frankl Institute.

Meaning Analysis and Eastern Thought

A comparison of Takashima's and Frankl's philosophies offers an opportunity to explore two major points: first, the significance of the development of an effective philosophical psychology; second, the similarities and differences between an Eastern and a Western understanding of the dimensions of the self.

The life histories of Takashima and Frankl are integrally related to their philosophies. There are striking similarities in their lives as well as in their professional commitments. Joseph Fabry summarizes these similarities in his foreword to Takashima's book *Humanistic Psychosomatic Medicine*:

Frankl as well as Takashima are "graduates of three schools": The school of medicine, the school of philosophy, and the school of life at its lowest. Both have MDs and PhDs, and both have gone through periods of suffering. Frankl has lived through German concentration camps, Takashima through wartime Japanese jails (he was suspected of spying) and through a near fatal bout with tuberculosis that cost him a lung and several ribs. Both are medical doctors who reach beyond science into philosophy and humanness . . . both men have a deep regard for each other and their work.[39]

Takashima's and Frankl's pioneering work in philosophical psychology shows the scope and depth of the interdependence of philosophy and psychology. Their philosophical psychology is based on four basic premises: (1) a person equals humanity, (2) the self must be understood holistically, (3) the noetic dimension is the key to the self, and (4) wisdom, which includes a moral core, is the basis of medical ministry. Takashima's and Frankl's medical ministry—whether it is called psychosomatic medicine by Takashima or meaning analysis (logotherapy) by Frankl—includes the insights of key philosophers as well as developments in psychotherapy in the Western world. Whereas the Western philosophical tradition is part of Frankl's intellectual heritage and education, for Takashima it represents a special quest for meaning, as it often is for other Japanese intellectuals. As T. P. Kasulis points out in Yuasa's book *The Body: Toward an Eastern Mind-Body Theory,*

> . . . many Japanese intellectuals know quite well the major works of Western philosophy, especially those of the modern Continental tradition. . . . Furthermore, living in one of the most advanced technological nations of the world, the Japanese philosopher is generally as knowledgeable about scientific developments as are European or American philosophers. In short, Japan is at the crossroads of many great intellectual traditions and movements.[40]

Takashima is a scientist-philosopher who transmutes Western philosophical psychology through his knowledge of Eastern philosophy and Buddhism.

Takashima's understanding of the dimensions of the self illustrates his position at the crossroads of contemporary thought. He starts with a critique of the two-dimensional view of psychosomatic medicine: the somatic and the psychological. (He and Frankl see this model as reductionistic and giving only a partial picture of the nature of being human.) He then turns to Frankl's three-dimensional model (mind, body, spirit) and agrees that the key dimension of the self is the spiritual (noetic), which he locates in the metaphysical field. He also follows Frankl in identifying the psychological dimension (mind), which he places in the scientific field. Where he differs from Frankl is in dividing the physical dimension (body) into two parts: the physiological (functional) and the somatological (structural). According to Takashima, the Japanese think of the self as *tai* (body), *shin* (spirit), and *gi* (technique). What Takashima adds to Frankl's view is the concept of *gi*. The *gi* has two interrelated functions: "One is the function of nerves with no mind, as discussed by the physiologists, the other is the function of the brain—the psyche, as referred to by experimental psychologists . . . this mind is a brain function—the psyche that can be *measured, analyzed,* and *reproduced* by scientific techniques."[41]

Although agreeing with Frankl that the spiritual dimension is the key factor in understanding the self, Takashima is more comfortable in recognizing a religious form of the spiritual dimension. He affirms the noetic dimension as a universal quality of the self that is available to all persons, but "human beings can also open up to the *religious dimension* within their spiritual dimension."[42] Takashima's distinction between the spiritual and the religious is important for two reasons: (1) he affirms that the spiritual (noetic) dimension is fundamental in maintaining the openness of meaning analysis, but (2) he welcomes meaning analysis as foundation for religionists who wish to build on its spiritual premises and methods. Frankl is clear, however, on the issue of maintaining meaning analysis's independence from religious dogma: "Whoever tries to make psychotherapy into an *ancilla theologiae,* a servant to theology, not only robs it of the dignity of an autonomous science but also takes away the potential value it might have for religion. Any fusion of the respective goal of religion and psychiatry must result in confusion."[43]

The independence of Frankl's spiritual dimension from religious dogma makes meaning analysis attractive to Takashima and to those within the Buddhist tradition because of its compatibility with Eastern thought.

As Takashima's writings indicate, the Japanese do not distinguish between religion and philosophy; and as Hajime Nakamura notes, the acceptance of reality (or actuality) is one of the key features of Japanese philosophy. It is in this area of acceptance of reality that Takashima and others combine traditional Eastern thought and Western thought, especially in relation to Frankl's understanding of the self. Four of the six factors in the acceptance of actuality cited by Nakamura are featured as well in meaning analysis: (1) a this-worldliness, (2) an acceptance of natural human qualities, (3) a spirit of tolerance, and (4) an apprehension of the Absolute in a phenomenal world. The two other factors, however, are in sharp contrast to Frankl's thought: an acceptance of cultural stratification and a reluctance to receive direct criticism.[44]

While meditation is still an essential aspect of Buddhism, its emphasis has shifted, it seems, from concerns with the otherworldly to contemporary goals that can be attained in this life; and in the process, the focus of its attention has widened from the monastery to the marketplace.

A growing priority is being given to a philosophy that identifies with what is known as the Middle Way. Hideki Yukawa explains that "the Middle Way is a practical principle of life which sees the living value of things themselves in their rightful place and at their opportune moment. Based on an open point of view, it makes possible an infinite range of insight."[45] While the Western mind would tend to see the Middle Way as purely intuitive, the Eastern philosophers believe, "In order to grasp the changing real moment, the rational analysis of the

whole, *an untiring activity of the will* continued with fortitude and persever-
ence is of absolute necessity."[46] The Middle Way's emphasis on the primary role
of the will is evidenced in Takashima's synthesis of Buddhist thought and the
radical empiricism of meaning analysis. Frankl's explanation of the will also
harmonizes with what Yukawa and others say about the Middle Way:

> What I call the "will to meaning" is even to be regarded as "man's primary
> concern." . . .[47] I speak of a will to meaning to preclude a misinterpretation
> of the concept in terms of a drive to meaning . . . will cannot be demand-
> ed, commanded, or ordered. One cannot will to will. And if the will to
> meaning is to be elicited, meaning itself has to be elucidated.[48]

Frankl does not follow Western methodology by intellectualizing the will. Rather,
he agrees with Eastern thought that the will is existential and that thought
involves the body as the expression of the will. Meaning analysis is in harmony
with Suzuki's conclusion: "The body, the will, and the individual self are concepts worked out by the analytical *vijñāna* [discursive understanding], but the
inner creative life as it creates all these concepts through *vijñāna* is immediately
apprehended only by *prajñā* [intuition]."[49]

Frankl's approach to the self avoids the traditional split between Eastern
and Western thought regarding freedom and creativity. T. P. Kasulis points out
that "we find the Japanese emphasis on *achieving* freedom, rather than the
Western focus on the universal *presence* of freedom or determinism."[50] Frankl
sees a place for both the achievement of freedom and the presence of freedom
in a life of meaning. Thus meaning analysis agrees with Yasuo Yuasa that the
question is "not about whether human beings are intrinsically free, but about
how freedom can be psychophysically attained."[51] Yuasa and Frankl ask not only
what the relation between the mind and the body *is* but also what it may *become*.
While his vocabulary may differ from Frankl's, Yuasa's emphasis is the same:

> In the East one starts from the experiential assumption that the mind-body
> modality changes through the training of the mind and body by means of
> cultivation (*shugyo*) or training (*Keiko*) . . . the mind-body issue is not simply
> a theoretical speculation but it is originally a practical lived experience
> (*taiken*), involving the mustering of one's whole mind and body.[52]

When Yuasa and others speak of the intuitive mind, they are not talking about it
in the Western sense of bare cognition; rather, for them, intuition is "a creative
function which appears, as it were, in almost all fields of human experience,
including moral practice, artistic creativity, and religious awakening."[53]

Both Takashima's humanistic psychosomatic medicine and Frankl's
meaning analysis center on the cultivation and training of the self. How this
cultivation is to be accomplished reflects where they agree and disagree. Zeami's
(1363-1443) understanding of the relation of mind to body provides the framework for understanding Takashima's approach to psychosomatic medicine:

Initially, the body's movements do not follow the dictates of the mind. The body is heavy, resistant to the mind's movement; in this sense, the body is an object opposing the living subject's (*shutai*) mode of being. . . . To harmonize the mind and body through training is to eliminate this ambiguity in practice; it amounts to subjectivizing the body, making it the lived subject. ˙ . . . The "mind" here is not the surface consciousness, but is the "mind" that penetrates into the body and deeply subjectivizes it.[54]

An essential goal of the mind (or the *logos*) in logotherapy is to help a person trapped by the ego to escape through dereflection. Buddhism has the same goal, which is accomplished by *anattan. Anattan* has two meanings:

The first meaning, namely, "that which is not mine," teaches us to detach ourselves from the egoism directed toward all things, including the self itself. . . . The second meaning, "that which does not have an ego," indicates the state of being free from the just-mentioned kind of egoism . . . [It] also means that in such a state, we will be able from the first time, to see that which is true.[55]

Buddhism and existential analysis use self-detachment in achieveing self-transcendence. The Buddha believed that "what is most necessary for humanity is not theoretical speculation, but, rather, the practice that eliminates delusions from one's own soul and detaches one from egoism."[56] This helps to bring about nirvana (*satori*).

Although Frankl speaks of human existence instead of enlightenment, his description of the purpose of self-transcendence mirrors Eastern thought: "Only as a man withdraws himself in the sense of releasing self-centered interest and attention, will he gain an authentic mode of existence."[57] Dereflection and self-transcendence help a person accept life, an essential mark of humanness shared by Buddhism and meaning analysis. Charles A. Moore, quoting Nakamura, observes that "the Japanese simply accept life as it is, with all its confusions, incompatibilities, contradictions."[58] Acceptance, in the Eastern view, does not mean resignation; acceptance, for the Buddhist, comes from a well-formed philosophy of action, "the well-known Eightfold Path of the noble (*ārya*), i.e., right view; right thought; right speech; right action; right remembrance; right effort; right liveliness; right contemplation."[59]

Takashima lists four differences between Western thought and Buddhism that influence attitudes toward ourselves and our world:

(1) In Western religions, God resides in the supernatural dimension while man and the rest of nature . . . dwell in the natural dimension which humans can explore and use. In Japanese Buddhism, Buddha, man, animals, plants, and non-living matter . . . are all united in one dimension.

(2) In the Judeo-Christian tradition, the main separation is made between creatures which have emotional feelings and the things which have not.

(3) Western religions emphasize "teleological awareness" (concerned with purpose) and Japanese Buddhism emphasizes "axiological awareness" (concerned with awareness).

(4) Western religions emphasize "reflection" and Japanese Buddhism emphasizes "thankfulness."[60]

He concludes his comparison of the two ways of approaching life by writing, "It may be useful to point out the difference in Western and Japanese philosophies so that we can take the best from both in order to develop an ethic that will help us create an environment in which we not only can survive but also lead a meaningful life."[61]

Takashima sees meaning analysis as a means of achieving this goal, especially through what Frankl and Takashima call a medical ministry. Meaning analysts are helping persons to increase their awareness of their human and physical environment, reflecting the Eastern way of encouraging individuals to appreciate and participate in the fine arts or in the beauty of nature. Thankfulness, another Eastern quality, also plays a major role in meaning analysis counseling. Dr. Elisabeth Lukas, a leading European logotherapist, stimulates thankfulness in despondent persons by having them list experiences that reflected instances of meaningful living.

Takashima and Frankl show that there can be agreement between Eastern and Western thought on what are the essential dimensions of the self: a holistic view (mind, body, spirit); a recognition and use of the spirit (noös) as the key to meaning; a balance of purpose and awareness; thankfulness as well as reflection; and an affirmation of a life of meaning for the future as well as the present. Their lives and medical ministries attest that science must be completed by philosophy. As Takashima observes, "Medicine without science is powerless, medicine without philosophy is meaningless, and medicine without humanity is soulless."[62]

The parallels between Frankl's existential psychology and the classical teachings of the Chinese are easily discerned, especially in relation to what Frankl calls the existential vacuum. Both Taoism and Confucianism deal with this problem, and both recognize that the existential vacuum involves a crisis in moral and cultural values. As Sandra Wawrytko explains, Chuang Tzu, representing Taoism, seeks a return to instinctual awareness, and Confucius calls for a dynamic rethinking of tradition. According to Wawrytko, awareness of creative, experiential, and attitudinal values is present in the teachings of Chuang Tzu and Confucius, as it is in Frankl's, but their emphases are different. While Chinese teachings emphasize the first two, Frankl stresses attitudinal values, especially in relation to the tragic triad—pain, guilt, and death.

Frankl outlines the aspects of existential neurosis as follows: aimlessness, fatalism, conformism, and fanaticism. Wawrytko cites a quotation from Confucius that could have been written by Frankl himself: "All around I see Nothingness pretending to be Something, Emptiness pretending to be Fullness, Penury pretending to be Affluence . . . concern merely for the superficialities of life, for expedient rather than moral values."[63] In addition to aimlessness, fatalism (as a form of reduction) has been a concern of Chinese philosophy as has conformism, which Chuang Tzu describes as the height of foolishness.[64] Fanaticism is countered with dimensional ontology by Confucius as well as Frankl: "Confucius contrasts the *chun-tzu,* who 'can see a question from all sides without bias,' with the 'small men' limited to a single side of the question."[65]

Freedom, common sense, intuitive conscience, and responsibleness toward one's self and others are common hallmarks of the value-oriented radical empiricism shared by Chuang Tzu, Confucius, and Frankl. Each, however, has a different emphasis: Chuang Tzu, the power of spirituality; Confucius, morality; and Frankl, a life of meaning. But their emphases complement each other because each seeks to correct the dehumanization of the self and to help the inquirer to be more fully a person. Confucius's follower Tzu-hsia writes, "Disciples may indeed be compared to plants and trees. . . . They have to be separately treated according to their kinds";[66] and Douglas Fox writes, "Whatever else its tasks and virtues, Logotherapy is committed to helping persons find meaning and value intrinsic to themselves."[67]

Douglas Fox shows how Confucius's principle of *chen ming (chen =* rectification; *ming =* name) harmonizes with logotherapy.[68] Confucius's goal is to help persons recognize names and use them accurately and fully, for how we name something determines our response. This perception is fully shared by Frankl, which can be seen in his criticism of psychoanalysts who name persons and conditions in a reductionistic way. He recognizes, as does Confucius, that when we think or speak inaccurately about ourselves and others we deny ourselves the chance to find meaning. Frankl points out the reductionistic habit many of us have when we speak about ourselves as an "only"—for example, I am *only* a student," "I am *only* a housewife." The accuracy and completeness of our definitions are tested daily in the effect our concepts have on our values, our actions, and our relationships to others. When we accept a name, we must also take on the values and obligations attached to that name. Thus, it is vital to know as fully as possible what we mean by the name, how others define the name, and what they expect from it.

Fox reminds us that Confucius evolved the rectification of names in response to the despair of his own age, and the task seems just as applicable to our age. So many in our society ask, What's in it *for* me? rather than the question Frankl sets us, which is What does life demand (or expect) *of* me? We need to ask ourselves, Frankl says, What does the name I bear expect of me in terms of responsibleness? If the name or title (physician, Congress member, president, and so on) its seen only as a ladder to success or power, then—as we see daily in the press—betrayal of self and others is a result. Confucius and Frankl agree that if we seek a particular name (including husband, wife, father, or mother), we must be taught to be accountable for understanding what the name implies and what it demands of us. Confucius and Frankl are empirical realists: *chen ming* and meaning analysis share the common task of helping us to see things as they are.

Meaning Analysis and the Native American

The effect of Frankl's teaching on disparate religions and cultures is being recognized by an increasing number of scholars who see meaning analysis as a valuable dialogical tool. Frankl's witness is ecumenical in the widest sense of the word. For him, we are not fully human until we reach out to another person with empathy in a common search for meaning. Some of the recent discussions of the connection between Frankl's thought and non-Western cultures, while brief and exploratory, hold promise for further dialogues. The Hindu priest Sitansu Chakravarti strongly agrees with Frankl's view that the noögenic neurosis is a universal neurosis, and he relates Frankl's use of self-transcendence and freedom to the central teachings of Hinduism.[69] Further, an article written by W. G. Jilek and L. Jilek-Aall on the relation of logotherapy to the Native American shows the extent of Frankl's ecumenical appeal.

It is unfortunate that so far so little has been written about the uses of meaning analysis for the Native American, for those from the Native American community whom I have known see meaning analysis as a major spiritual and therapeutic resource for their people. One student told me that a reason that he could so easily identify with Frankl's concentration camp experiences was that his people had been concentrated in camps for generations. But while Native American students have been impressed by Frankl's personal experiences, their feeling is for his philosophy and understanding of the human self, which they see as complementing their native beliefs. The Native Americans enrolled in my graduate courses in meaning analysis have a sense of urgency about Frankl's therapy, seeing it as an effective way to combat the existential vacuum so prevalent among their people. The result among Native Americans of the noögenic neurosis generated by an existential vacuum is startling and grave.

While Native American youths are the fastest growing ethnic population in North America, their suicide rate is increasing at an alarming rate. In contrast to suicide rates for Europeans and European North Americans, Native American suicide rates are highest among late teenagers, especially males. Yet this suicidal behavior is the opposite of traditional Native American societal values in which suicides were rare occurrences. Two Canadian anthropologists believe that these suicides should be seen in the context of the sociocultural changes imposed on the Native Americans during the last hundred years.[70] They cite such factors as rapid and enforced acculturation, disintegration of Native American mores, and the suppression by an outside authority of the rituals, language, and beliefs essential to the Native Americans' identity and well-being. Further, Native Americans have experienced in their past, and experience in their present, financial and cultural exploitation and rejection by the so-called Christian and democratic societies, who did invade and have invaded not only their living space but, as well, their families and their minds. It is little wonder that a noögenic neurosis—a sense of helplessness, existential frustration, and dehumanizaton—characterizes so much of Native American society.

A Salish Native American consultant to the Canadian Department of Health and Welfare writes that he is talking about the death of his people, "not only the deaths by accident, suicide and violence, but also the death of the soul which lies beyond the environment of self-destruction and despair in which Indian people exist."[71] This cry from the heart illustrates his thesis: "In our people, it's been a continuous pain, it's a continuous painful existence for the Indian . . . many of them say I don't belong anywhere. *Where am I going, what is my purpose?* I'm existing that's all."[72] The same student who identified Frankl's experience in the concentration camps with the experiences of Native Americans was faced with the dilemma of how to remain loyal to his ethnic heritage while bringing to it his new understanding of the human self. He came to realize that the neuroses of the Native American were not psychosexual, environmental, or even ethnic, but universally noögenic. Thus his first help came from Frankl's explanation that it is important to establish an atmosphere of trust and through Socratic dialogue to help his brothers and sisters gain self-understanding and then meaning. Further help came from Frankl's perception that we must approach truth from various sides and sometimes from opposite directions. If we cannot attain truth, we can at least encircle it. This determination to encircle truth with love and understanding helped the young man better to understand the emotional, psychological, and above all, the spiritual needs of his community.

In large measure, Frankl's appeal comes from a growing awareness that the central need of humankind is to find a sense of meaning. While the search for meaning is as old as the start of philosophy itself and has been pursued by a galaxy of thinkers over the generations, the need for a sense of meaning has taken on a new urgency in the last 50 years in a world of increased violence and dehumanization of all kinds, including the breakdown of decency and values individually and socially. Frankl's existential witness to our world challenges us to face and overcome the dis-eases of hedonism, nihilism, pandeterminism, and reductionism.

— 2 —

From Freud

to

Frankl

I AM NOT A MAN OF SCIENCE AT ALL, NOT AN OB-
SERVER, NOT AN EXPERIMENTER, NOT A THINKER. I
AM NOTHING BUT A CONQUISTADOR BY TEMPERA-
MENT, AN ADVENTURER IF YOU WANT TO TRANSLATE
THIS TERM, WITH ALL THE INQUISITIVENESS, DARING,
AND TENACITY OF SUCH A MAN.
                                    —SIGMUND FREUD

FREUD WAS NOT HIS OWN BEST JUDGE.
                                    —PETER GAY

Just as Socrates is the key seminal mind of Greek philosophy, Sigmund Freud is
the formative genius of psychoanalysis. Freud himself was among the first to
assign his place in history; he assessed that he was a great master and should be
placed somewhere between Copernicus and Darwin. Viktor Frankl acknowledges Freud as a master but at the same time reminds us that Freud also said that
"reverence before the greatness of a genius is certainly a great thing, but our
reverence before facts should exceed it."[1] As Frankl and others have discovered,
the facts about Freud and his work are not easily discerned. This is due to three
factors: the tumultuous time in which he lived; the tangled web spun by those
within the psychoanalytic movement; and the volume of literature about Freud
since his death. Each factor is complicated by the personality of Freud himself.

Doktor Freud

First, Freud must be seen in relation to his time, for often *when* Freud said
something is as important as *what* he said. He was a volatile man in an equally

volatile time. The 19th century has been described as the psychological century par excellence.[2] As I shall discuss more fully in outlining Freud's and Frankl's formal training, the 19th century was a time of both dissolution and building. The old forms of humanism and *Naturphilosophie* of the previous century were challenged by interpreters of the new science such as Charles Darwin (1808–1882), author of *On the Origin of Species.* The young Freud wrestled with the conflicting positions in his efforts to develop his own *Weltanschauung* (world view), just as Frankl would a half century later.

Freud often found himself involved in controversy and relished it. In an early letter to his future wife he writes, "One would hardly know how to look at me, but already in school I was always a bold man of the opposition, was always where one could avow an extreme and, as a rule, had to atone for it."[3] He never modifies this early stance. He is a pioneer, sometimes urging his followers up trails that are not always clearly marked. As a result his work contains failures as well as successes as he explores everything he reads to see if it will meet his professional and personal needs. His reading is widespread, ranging from Mark Twain to Nietzsche. He refers to himself as a Sherlock Holmes, engaged also in detective work; at other times he compares his work as a psychiatrist to that of an archaeologist uncovering layer after layer of what is hidden from view. His eclecticism, his iconoclastic spirit, and his conscious desire sometimes to obscure and mislead make him difficult to understand—heightened by the fact that Freud declares that only *he* can correctly interpret psychoanalysis. These characteristics account in part for the fact that from its beginning in 1902 as Freud's Wednesday night group, the psychoanalytic movement has been marked by strife.

The psychoanalytic movement itself is the second factor hindering an accurate appraisal of Freud's work. Not only did the major schools of psychological thought originate in Vienna, but all their founders were part of the Jewish community as well. (Indeed, Freud feared that psychoanalysis would be identified as a Jewish science.) Thus he welcomed the Swiss Protestant psychologist Carl G. Jung as a favorite son. Writing in 1910 to Sandor Ferenczi, Freud admonishes, "Now don't be jealous and include Jung in your calculations. I am more convinced than ever that he is the man of the future."[4] It is significant that Freud warns about jealousy, for infighting became a major disturbance within the psychoanalytic movement and one that, despite his warnings, Freud did little to correct. Another of Freud's gentile disciples, the Englishman Ernest Jones, brought his own psychological understanding and jealousies to the movement; so much so that his credibility as an interpreter of Freud has become a matter of debate among psychoanalysts. The turmoil within the original psychoanalytic circle spread during Freud's lifetime across the Atlantic. This is especially noticeable in the work of American and other neo-Freudians whose translations and conclusions regarding Freud have been challenged by Bruno Bettelheim and others active in psychology.

The third factor is that the immense amount of literature that has grown up around Freud since his death has become overwhelming. Peter Gay remarks, "Some of this avalanche is revealing, much of it is useful, more of it provocative; an astonishing share is malicious or downright absurd."[5] Even the international authority, the *Standard Edition of the Complete Psychological Works of Sigmund Freud,* under the general editorship of James Strachey in collaboration with Freud's daughter Anna Freud, while a monumental work, needs revision that should include translation. As Gay notes in his own brilliant study *Freud: A Life for Our Time,* present and future scholars seeking the facts will have a formidable task of selection and evaluation as long as psychoanalysis is debated.

Each of the facts I have mentioned—the times in which Freud lived, the psychoanalytic movement, and the voluminous literature about Freud—needs to be measured in conjunction with his personality. Abram Kardiner says candidly that "Freud was a different man to everyone who knew him."[6] Freud is also a different person to everyone who reads him. He is a master of an intricate style and his ego dominates every presentation. As Viktor von Weizsaecker says of him, "There is still another thing . . . a charm which verges on seduction, a noncommital attitude which might be put down for modesty or for decadence."[7] Freud was neither modest nor decadent, however; nor was he, as Erich Fromm charges, cold, unloving, remote, or unable to enjoy life.[8] He had a good memory for persons, events, and places. Frankl recounts that as a young man he met Freud on the street and told him who he was. Freud immediately responded that he did indeed know of him and named exactly where young Frankl was living in Vienna. As one reads of Freud's friendships, he appears too involved in the lives of others (he enjoyed personal intrigue) rather than remote and unloving.

Viktor von Weizsaecker gives some insightful impressions of Freud from long conversations he had with him in 1926 when Freud was 70 years old. Three aspects of Freud's personality emerge from these interviews: his evasiveness and even deceptiveness, his opinion of others, and his relation to his followers. Von Weizsaecker questioned Freud about the possible conflict between psychoanalysis and "binding ties" of patients, especially the tenets of Roman Catholicism. Freud replied that he felt that psychoanalysts had "always found the way to respect and to spare these spheres in the patient."[9] This answer puzzled von Weizsaecker when a year after this conversation, Freud in *The Future of an Illusion* contradicted what he had said by attacking religion as illusionary and neurotic. Freud refused to answer von Weizsaecker's further questions on the subject. Freud's opinion of others' intelligence is contained in a rhetorical remark: "You surely agree that most people are stupid."[10] He thought of most of his disciples as being "neuroticized," and as von Weizsaecker concludes, "There was more benevolence than respect in the way he spoke of his followers. On the whole, he seemed weary of his school and not in need of it any longer."[11] Von Weizsaecker's impression of Freud agrees with Erich Fromm's conclusion that Freud was essentially a solitaire. Until the Freudian archives are opened at the end of this century, we will not have a full picture regarding these appraisals and facts regarding Freud. Yet we can agree with Alfred Kazin's comment that "Freud, a tough old humanist with a profoundly skeptical mind, would have been shocked or amused by the degree to which everything is sometimes explained by 'Freudian doctrines.' "[12]

Freud's initial impetus does not come from a set doctrine but from his mission to free persons from those unconscious forces that tear them apart; he wants to restore them to humanness. Frankl, also a tough old humanist, shares the same mission as Freud, but he disagrees with Freud in defining what it means to be fully human and in suggesting the way humanness can be restored or achieved through psychology.

The Viennese Milieu

Vienna is an important clue for understanding the origin of the humanism of Freud and Frankl and its expression in liberal social causes. While the schools of psychology at the turn of the century might have originated in any city, it is significant that they began in Vienna. Whereas some think romantically of 19th-century Vienna as the "city of dreams," it has been more realistically described as the "home of the sensitive but weak-willed *Nervenmenschen* and a city of grandiose illusions."[13] "It was an age of Hamlets," Peter Gay comments, noting Ralph Waldo Emerson's thought that "the young men were born with knives in their brain, a tendency to introversion, self-dissection, anatomizing of motives."[14]

Nineteenth-century Vienna nevertheless became a mecca for the Jews of Eastern Europe, possibly because conditions elsewhere were even more un-favorable. From 1865 to 1873, when Freud was in the gymnasium, the Jewish enrollment grew from 68 to 130, or 73% of the total school population.[15] These figures show that, as in the case of the Freud family, Jewish immigrants' sons were being educated for positions of influence. These opportunities continued to be offered through Frankl's school and university years. A Jewish boy might dream of becoming an important government official or a member of the judiciary or a medical doctor or—especially in Freud's case—a professor, the rank so highly prized in Europe. But such dreams of the educated Jew were linked to the politics of mercurial Vienna. The dreams had a chance of being realized when the liberals were in power but were frustrated or destroyed when the anti-Semitic conservatives, such as the New Right, took over. The Austrian support in recent years of the ex-Nazi Kurt Waldheim as their president indicates that the temperament of the city and the nation has not changed perceptibly since Freud's day.

Freud and Frankl were both children of a liberal Jewry that existed for over 60 years despite the entrenched anti-Semitism in Vienna. Both were proud of being Jews. Freud bragged that his parents were Jews and pointed out that he remained a Jew. (He did admit toward the end of his life, however, that his

Jewish identity had remained a problem for him.) Frankl is also proud of his Jewish heritage, pointing out that he is the descendant of a famous rabbi of Prague. But their Judaism was a Judaism of the Diaspora and reflected to some degree the middle-class morality of Vienna. Freud and Frankl, as part of the Jewish community, had the freedom to pursue professions prescribed by the Viennese hierarchy (the social stratification was rearranged with the fall of the Hapsburgs; the middle class replaced the aristocracy). However, anti-Semitism remained a time bomb, which exploded with the 1938 German *Anschluss*. As mentioned in Chapter 1, in 1938 Freud left Austria to spend the final years of his life in England; and in 1938 began the road that led Frankl to his imprisonment in the concentration camps.

As citizens of virtually two cities—the official, Roman Catholic–dominated Vienna and the Viennese ethnic community of liberal Judaism, Freud and Frankl have in common four essential experiences: (1) the classical education of the Austrian gymnasium, especially in Greek philosophy and the *Aufklärung* (German Enlightenment); (2) a medical training dominated by the changes in physical science, especially in psychology; (3) an appreciation of German romanticism; and (4) a growing awareness of the role of existentialism and phenomenology. Although Freud was 50 years older than Frankl and the differences in time and events have to be taken into account, it is vital to understand how each man used these four experiences to form his own *Lebenswelt* (life in the world) and the effect they had on his philosophy of psychology and his therapeutic methods.

The Influence of Greek Philosophy on Freud and Frankl

Two key factors dominated Freud's and Frankl's education: liberal Judaism and the humanistic curriculum prescribed by the Austrian state. Free-thinking Judaism liberated them from religious form and dogma. It affirmed a strong social morality, was realistic in the way it viewed life, encouraged an ironic sense of humor, and was marked by what has been described as a mature eroticism. The humanistically oriented state curriculum, designed for the gentile student, provided analyses of the philosophy, literature, history, and science of the Western world. The Renaissance concept of education dominated the course of study, and the humanities were considered the best preparation for the sciences.

Freud and Frankl learned Latin, because its study was the model for logic. Both men learned how to think and how to write (style accompanied content). Freud mentions that a professor commented on one of his essays, "You have an *idiotic* style," meaning, according to Freud, "the highest praise for a style at once correct and original."[16] (Later generations might disagree with Freud's interpretation and let the professor's comment stand as read.)

Although the curriculum was Germanic in spirit and content, it was grounded in Greek classical philosophy. The teachers used the metaphysics of

Plato and the epistemology of Aristotle as learning models of the person. As a result, Plato (c.428–c.348 B.C.) and Aristotle (384–322 B.C.) also became the philosophical mentors of Freud and Frankl and the key to understanding the *Lebenswelt* of psychoanalysis and logotherapy.

Plato

Plato's metaphysics centers on the functioning of the tripartite soul: the appetitive, the spirited, and the rational. The human psyche (German: *seele*; English: *soul*) is directed by a form of love described by Plato as eros. Eros is the power (*dunamis*) of the psyche moving from the love of the physical to the love of honor and finally to the love of wisdom. Plato is the first philosopher to provide a phenomenology of love and to explain it metaphysically. The Platonic process of eros is not the automatic achievement of an ideal goal but a battle with the complexitie and paradoxes of human nature to achieve a victory of the rational over the appetitive and the spirited. His analysis of the self explores the same themes used by Freud and Frankl more than 2000 years later. Plato's analysis of the self includes consideration of the nature and role of reason, irrationality, and tamed and untamed emotions; the power of sexual needs; the relation of the conscious to the subconscious; the significance of dreams; and the importance of language in describing the self. Plato strives to deal with the whole person. Although he is best known for providing the model of philosophical idealism, he also recognizes the importance of the body and emotions in arriving at a viable understanding of the human psyche.

Plato's first function of the psyche, the appetitive, is the basic and most ignoble expression. It is limited to satiating the senses, incapable of either proper perception or correct action. At best it is pleasure bent; at worst, it is hedonism, which includes an obsession with wealth that seeks its own gain at all costs. Freud and Frankl recognize the power of the appetitive, but the role each assigns to it in the final appraisal of the psyche shows how greatly they differ.

Freud expands the power of appetitive eros so that it becomes the *dominant* feature of the psyche. On these grounds he builds a "needs" psychology, focusing on how to recognize the needs of the appetitive and finding ways to control them. Freud describes the appetitive as the id. The id functions according to "the pleasure principle." When separated from the ego, the id is driven by untamed passions. Further, in most cases, the id has the upper hand over the ego when they are together. Peter Gay quotes Freud's now-famous analogy to explain this relation:

> The ego . . . resembles the rider who is supposed to rein in the superior strength of the horse, with the difference that the rider does this with his own, the ego with borrowed strength (borrowed from the id). . . . Just as there often remains nothing for the rider, if he does not want to be separated from the horse, but to lead it where it wants to go, so the ego, too, is

accustomed to translating the will of the id into action as if it were its own.[17]

This analogy is understandable if we accept Freud's assertion that the ego is primarily a bodily ego—that is, that it comes from bodily sensations. When conscience is separated from the ego to become superego, it is still subject to external pressures from the world. Essentially, the ego is beleaguered at best and victimized at worst. It remains a captive of the appetitive expression of eros.

Plato's second function of the psyche, the spirited, can be either noble or ignoble depending on how a person uses eros. The self achieves nobility of spirit when eros is used to channel energy in ways that build rather than destroy the best that is within the self. Freud speaks of this as psychic economy; the role of the spirited is to sublimate. In contrast, Plato goes beyond any simplistic sublimation formula to examine motivation. If persons are motivated by the highest goals, eros helps them achieve a sense of worth and ways to be remembered with honor. Plato's spirited persons include statesmen, military commanders, and writers or artists who hope that their works will survive them. Most people see themselves as heroes rather than as villains or as philosopher-kings; thus, they more quickly identify with Plato's spirited function than with the appetitive or the rational. The characteristics of the spirited function mirror the paradoxical nature of existence: reason and irrationality, controlled and uncontrolled emotions, external and internal moral conflicts; and underlying all, a desire to be admired and remembered, to avoid baseness while eschewing any expectation of perfection. At its lowest level, a person's moral courage seeks only to enhance the reputation of the self; at its highest level, it is, as Plato writes, concerned with "the conduct of life, the tendance of the soul, and with the good of the state."[18]

The spirited self is exhibited by Freud himself in two ways: professionally, by his developing a psychology with the courage to fight to free the self from psychic pain; personally, in his own courageous, long-time, and losing battle with cancer of the mouth and jaw. Frankl's spirited self also takes both a professional and a personal form. Professionally, when in his meaning analysis he calls on the defiant power of the human spirit to overcome the mental and physical disabilities of life; personally, when his spirited self triumphed over the pain, misery, and degradation of the concentration camps. Essentially, Freud's spirited psyche reflects classic Stoicism's indifference to pain or pleasure; in contrast, Frankl is closer to Plato, using the noble aspects of the spirited by linking it to the rational, the highest expression of eros.

Plato's third function of the psyche, the rational, is the culmination of his metaphysics, the goal of all knowledge, and the raison d'être of his ethics. As the reflection of divine reason, the rational is imperishable, promising the self harmony in this world and happiness in the next.

At first glance it may appear that Freud's triadic structure of the self may be equated with Plato's: id equals the appetitive; ego, the spirited; the superego, the rational. But the dynamics and outcomes of the two models are substantially different. Freud has no progressive energy of eros to move the psyche from the appetitive to the rational. Instead, the superego is still at the mercy of the war between the ego and the id. Further, while Freud is attracted to reason, he limits its role to that of a policeman attempting to arrest the psyche when it follows destructive drives that are either consciously or subconsciously motivated.

Yet Plato and Freud, each in his own way, are both pioneers in depth psychology. The importance and place of dreams, catharsis, and the relation of the unconscious to the conscious are all issues that were first raised by Plato and later addressed by Freud. But the two men differ radically in the way they see the self in relation to these issues. Plato is primarily a cognitive psychologist, whereas Freud substitutes a biological-mechanical explanation for the reasoning process. Freud was attracted by the place and power of reason, but his immersion in 19th-century science convinced him that a truly rational self is a chimera, not a human possibility. As a result, his break with Plato's cognitive psychology is complete. He substitutes a psychosexual-biological dependence for Plato's belief and reliance upon eros governed by reason. If Plato's metaphysics results in a teleological optimism based on the triumph of reason, Freud's ends in a teleological pessimism determined by psychosexual pathology rather than by ideals and meaning.

Fabry points out that while recognizing the value of Freud's identification of pathology, Frankl says that "all pathology . . . requires first of all a diagnosis, a 'looking through,' namely a looking through the *pathos* at the *logos* which lies beyond it, a looking through the suffering at the meaning behind it."[19] Plato's view of eros is a way of looking through to a *logos* that affirms the rationality of the human psyche. The rational is more fully explained as we move from the metaphysical emphasis of Plato to the epistemological understanding of Aristotle.

Aristotle

Aristotle may be missing titanic fire, as Bertrand Russell charges,[20] but he introduces a fundamental adherence to common sense that Plato often lacks. His emphasis on practical reason (*phronesis*) illustrates how he avoids the split between reason and experience that occurs so often in Western philosophy. His model of practical reason is composed of three interrelated elements, which he lists in order of ascending importance: theory (*theoria*), or reason in search of knowledge; action (*praxis*), or life as action; production (*poiesis*), or the achievement of a particular goal. Taken together, these elements offer both a philosophy of life and the means by which it can be achieved. Aristotle does more than purge Plato's understanding of the self of its mysticism; he develops instead a science of "education to life" in which the productive, rational goals of life are its major concern. Some scholars associate Freud more with Plato than with Aristotle, possibly because Plato's tripartite self has been linked with Freud's psychological triad of the id, ego, and superego. My contention is that Aristotle's epistemological model based on theory, action, and production is closer to Freud's and Frankl's thinking than Plato's metaphysical structure of the self.

Aristotle's understanding of practical reason is paralleled by Freud's and Frankl's aims: the unity of the self, an active life, and the realization of established goals. Freud sees the psyche as the instrument to bring unity of the self; Frankl chooses the search for meaning. Both concentrate on helping persons to live truly active lives. Freud feels that a fully active life is possible once the demons have been tamed; Frankl uses the will to meaning to achieve a life that is not only free from demons but also free to be there for others. Production, the achieving of particular aims, is a vital part of every psychiatric plan. In setting his aims, Freud was careful to select only those patients whom *he* thought could produce, or achieve, the goals he set. Frankl does not impose such a screening. Part of his counseling process is a therapeutic contract in which the conditions and goals of the treatment are mutually agreed on by the patient and the analyst.

Pleasure plays an important role in the philosophies of Plato, Aristotle, Freud, and Frankl. Aristotle's discussion begins as a reaction to Plato's view. Plato, using depth psychology, relates pleasure to the psyche, defining pleasure as basically the absence or the avoidance of pain. Pleasure functions as a catharsis and has no positive role in the formation of personality. Aristotle presents an alternative to Plato's view by posing two questions: (1) What happens to the psyche when pleasure occurs? (2) What is the nature and function of specific pleasure? In answer to the first question, Aristotle believes pleasure does more than help cleanse the psyche of its unhealthy parts. Pleasure has a positive value, affirming the healthy aspects of the self in the healing process. In response to the second question, the nature and function of pleasure, Aristotle urges that each pleasure be analyzed to see where it may do good or harm in a particular situation. Pain and pleasure have several roles, depending on how they are conceived and where they are applied in relation to the self as a whole. "Pleasure is defined as an unimpeded activity of the natural state. . . . Thus, pleasure as such is not to be evaluated, but rather the different actions with which pleasure is associated."[21]

Aristotle's disagreement with Plato regarding pleasure is a major one. It is a disagreement in both principle and practice. Plato concentrates on the person's unhealthy areas, whereas Aristotle takes into account *all* aspects of the self. He looks behind the illness to see when and how pleasure helps or injures a person. His disagreement with Plato is mirrored in the methods used by Freud and Frankl.

Essentially, Freud, like Plato, concentrates on the ill parts of the self. In Freud's view, the primary task of the psychoanalyst is to "excavate" the regions that are disturbing to the patient and identify the cause before any cure can begin. Frankl, though agreeing that the disturbing elements must be faced and treated, goes beyond them to deal with Aristotle's concern for the whole person. Frankl, too, sees that both pleasure and pain can play positive roles in life, depending on when and how they are used by the client. In logotherapy, pleasure can be an ally of the healthy aspects of the spirit in effecting a cure. As a result, symptoms can be reduced before the cause of the illness is known. While Freud concentrates on examining the map of the psyche, Frankl focuses on the map of the spirit in helping the client return to health, which includes the experience of pleasure (*eudaimonia*). Aristotle uses a network analysis to define *eudaimonia* by considering the various habits, relationships, and other lines of communication that connect human beings' ideas and actions. As Abraham Edel explains, for Aristotle, "*Eudaimonia* means faring-well, prospering, flourishing. It thus denotes a quality of living (*eu zen,* to live well) rather than a feeling assimilated to a pleasure-pain principle."[22] Frankl, like Aristotle, believes that our choices should lead toward achieving the Good, as it is defined by the Golden Mean: moderation in all things. (Although Frankl does not use Aristotle's term "the Golden Mean," his view of life in the world incorporates it.)

In contrast to Plato, Aristotle and Frankl recognize that *perfect* good is humanly unattainable. Frankl follows Aristotle by adopting moderation as the standard of duty for the soul (psyche) in order to achieve a *proportional* goal. As a result, the healthy or happy life is measured by each person's needs, place, and condition. Frankl locates such practical wisdom in what he calls the noölogical dimension, which he defines as "that dimension in which the specifically human phenomena are located."[23] In contrast, Freud rejects any spiritual dimension in life as deceiving at worst and overprotective at best. He believes that religion must go, for "man cannot remain a child forever; he must venture at last into the hostile world. This may be called '*education to reality.*' "[24] This concept of education to reality is used in different ways by Aristotle and Frankl. Aristotle, while recognizing that hostile forces exist in the world, believes that the noös allows the greatest good to be realized in this life. For him, education to reality is education to pragmatic truth, which has many dimensions that depend on the individual, his or her location, and the individual's interpretation (either as speaker or hearer) of what is meant by truth and goodness. Like Aristotle, Frankl expands the meaning of the Greek *noös* (mind) to include everything that is human and to provide a holistic understanding that avoids the unfocused mysticism of Plato and the reductionistic materialism of Freud. Frankl's Aristotelianism realizes that the validity of the noös must be tested by logic and experience.

Frankl incorporates Aristotle's coupling of practical reason with the spiritual dimension to enrich our understanding of truth and wisdom. Following Aristotle's model, Frankl describes an education to reality that combines common sense, realistic optimism, moderation, and the empirical testing of moral and spiritual (noetic) values. Freud equates education to reality with the pleasure principle and reduces the humanistic approach to a biological-mechanical formula. As Frankl notes:

> The reality principle is according to Freud's own words, a mere extension of the pleasure principle; one which serves the pleasure principle's purpose.... Ultimately, the psychodynamic concept of man presents him as being

basically concerned with maintaining or restoring his inner equilibrium, and in order to do so, he is trying to gratify his drives and satisfy instincts . . . [thus] reality, the world of beings and meanings, is debased and degraded to a pool of more or less workable instruments to be used to get rid of various stimuli such as irritating superegos or archetypes. What has been sacrificed, however, and hence totally eliminated in this view of man, is the fundamental fact . . . namely, that man is a being encountering other beings and reaching out for meanings to fulfill.[25]

The fact that we are beings encountering other beings in reaching for meanings to fulfill is a social reality affirmed by Aristotle and Frankl but almost entirely ignored by Freud. It may be, as suggested earlier, that Freud is a solitaire. Freud himself realizes this fact about himself:

> In the first place I get tired of people . . . I am not basically interested in therapy, and I usually find that I am engaged—in any particular case—with the theoretical problems with which I happen to be interested at the time. . . . I am also too patriarchal to be a good analyst.[26]

In contrast, Aristotle is deeply concerned about relationships in the city state; a great portion of his teaching is directed toward educating Alexander the Great for his responsibilities to others as a ruler. Frankl's medical ministry reaches out to include the person trying to get a handle on life (*homo possedens*) as well as the suffering person (*homo patiens*). His understanding of religion allows him to affirm, with Aristotle, the possibility of achieving the Golden Mean. Frankl remarks that it was Albert Einstein who maintained that to be religious is to have found an answer to the question of the meaning of life. If we agree, then we understand belief and faith as an essential trust in ultimate meaning. This trust in the human search for meaning is a basic part of the legacy of classical humanism that Frankl reaffirms. Freud may have been "a tough old humanist," but Frankl is a tougher one, determined to hand on intact that legacy of humanism.

The Influence of the German Enlightenment on Freud and Frankl

The gymnasium of Freud's and Frankl's times supplemented classical humanism with a grounding in the 18th-century Enlightenment, especially the *Aufklärung* or German Enlightenment, as might be expected in the strongly Teutonic Austrian capital. This educational emphasis greatly influenced both Freud and Frankl, although they responded to it in dissimilar ways. Freud has been described as a loyal son of the Enlightenment, the last of the "philosophes."[27] And so he was, embracing the entire plan of the Enlightenment—its philosophy, its language, its methods, and its prudent self-censorship. The *Aufklärung* built on the Greek aphorism "Know thyself," integrating it with the philosophical, psychological, and sociological developments of the late 18th and early 19th centuries. This provided an intellectual force that especially gripped the Germanic countries. Freud and Frankl were caught up in this intellectual ferment as they reexamined the role of philosophy and psychology in explaining the nature of human consciousness.

Much of the excitement and timeliness of the *Aufklärung* came from four of its writers: Christian Thomasius (1635-1728), Christian Wolff (1679-1754), Alexander Baumgarten (1714-1762), and its philosophical capstone, Immanuel Kant (1724-1804). While the emphasis and scope of each varies from the others, they share an understanding of the Socratic dictum "Know thyself," using the insights and scholarship of their own age. How they responded helps us to understand better Freud's and Frankl's findings of the *Aufklärung* in their philosophical psychology.

Christian Thomasius

Christian Thomasius is a thoroughgoing empiricist, rejecting metaphysics and theological speculation for a utilitarian, commonsense approach to knowledge of the self. The epistemological task is essentially psychological. Using terms later employed by Freud, Thomasius lists three basic human drives: "the desire to live as long and as happily as possible, the instinctive recoil from death and pain, and the desire for property and mastery."[28] Thus far, Thomasius's view appears to be a model for Freud's view of the self. And so it would be if Thomasius had remained within the empirical method. But he exchanges his empirical explanation of the self for a pietistic religious view that stresses inner faith and redemption by grace. In his later writings, the desire for a happy life, the reasons for pain and death, and the desire for mastery of worldly goods are brought by him to the bar of divine judgment. The call to redemption replaces a psychological approach to analysis and therapy. Thomasius's *volte-face* results in his championing the pietistic religious stance so vehemently attacked by Freud. Frankl's meaning analysis is closer to the early empiricism of Thomasius than to Thomasius's later religious advice. Although Frankl's understanding of the self combines commonsense utilitarianism with psychotherapy, his reliance upon the noetic dimension provides a transcendental element that escapes both the pietistic methods and conclusions of the later Thomasius and the atheism of Freud.

Christian Wolff

Christian Wolff, like Thomasius, wants a philosophy that is practical but desires that it also be comprehensive. Instead of starting with empiricism, Wolff begins to rethink and to enlarge the role of reason, recognizing the importance of inductive and deductive thinking in arriving at logical conclusions. He develops what is called "the science of the possible of all possible things, a possible thing being anything which does not involve a contradiction."[29] He expands the scope of philosophy to consider "becoming" as well as "being." He champions the freedom of the self without explaining how freedom takes place in a world that functions according to a preestablished harmony.

Wolff is a minor figure in philosophy compared with Descartes, Spinoza, Leibniz, or Kant; yet he is recognized as an important philosophical educator of Germany in the pre-Kantian period. Thus Wolff is valuable not only for the questions he raises during his own lifetime, but also for the philosophical and moral issues he raises that were discussed by those who came after him. Wolff poses three questions that helped Freud understand a philosophy of the self: What is the role of reason? What is the extent of freedom? and To what extent is a "philosophy of the possible" realistic?

"It may seem strange to call Freud a rationalist," Will Herberg remarks, "but David Reisman not only calls him that, but goes on to say that 'it would be difficult to find anyone in the Enlightenment who was more so.' "[30] Herberg agrees with Reisman, concluding that "reason is Freud's god, and truth—which he identifies with scientific truth—the only epiphany he recognizes."[31] Herberg explains how Freud's rationalism is exhibited in his view of conflicts within the self, which center on the battle between reason (ego) and the passions (id) with the superego acting as a referee. But, as Herberg notes, rationalism is more than a battle; it should result in some kind of victory for reason as well.

While reason may be Freud's god, as Reisman remarks, it is not a perfect god, for all intellectual reason can err. Imperfect reason allows us to make bad choices as well as good ones. Neuroses that may result from our agony over those choices are marks of our freedom. Freud believes that we are free to be neurotic! Bettelheim makes the point that the relation of freedom to change becomes clearer if we understand the German word *Trieb* as impulse instead of as instinct.[32] Impulse allows a quality of life that is flexible instead of rigid. Impulses can change, working for us or against us. The aim of the superego, as Frankl defines it, is to help us discover and use the impulses that will strengthen us in significant ways.

Although Freud discusses the types of conflict between reason and impulses or desires, he hopes for a triumph of the scientific spirit over the doubts of the mind, which will be expressed as a victory of psychological maturity rather than as an intellectual accomplishment. Thus, he reduces Wolff's rationally based metaphysics to a psychoanalytic instrument for change. In contrast, Frankl reaffirms Wolff's "science of the possible" by restoring the role of reason, including a sense of what is moral. While Frankl agrees with Freud that "unmasking the neurotic" is a major task, he sees it as the *first* step in achieving wholeness, not the last. The heart of Frankl's criticism of psychoanalysis is what he sees as Freud's failure to differentiate between the instinctual and the spiritual in his analysis of the self. Frankl explains why this is so vital:

> . . . the line between the spiritual—as the human in man—and the instinctual cannot be drawn sharply enough. In fact we may conceive of it as an ontological *hiatus* which separates the two fundamentally distinct regions

within the total structure of the human being. On one side is existence, and on the other side is whatever belongs to facticity: whereas existence . . . is in essence, spiritual, facticity contains somatic and psychic "facts," the physiological as well as the psychological.[33]

Freud never looks behind the "facts"; he dismisses the intellectual, moral, and spiritual values emphasized by Wolff and Frankl instead of assessing their role in the composition of the self. Frankl goes beyond the reductionism of Freud and even "the science of the possible" of Wolff and emphasizes the will to meaning. The will to meaning is the power of the noetic dimension that allows the self to be free inwardly from noögenic and psychogenic neuroses and to be able to look outward to use reason and morality in relation to others. As Frankl explains,

> We must go beyond both necessities and possibilities and bring in—in addition to the "I must" and "I can" aspects of the total "I am" phenomenon— that dimension which can be described as the "I ought." . . . At the moment when we bring in the "I ought," we complement the subjective aspect of human existence, *being,* with its objective counterpart, which is *meaning.*[34]

Alexander Baumgarten

Alexander Baumgarten brings added dimensions of meaning through what he calls the science of aesthetics. By the science of aesthetics he means more than thinking of the beautiful. He wants what Wolff labels the lower powers (sensation and aesthetic enjoyment) as well as the higher powers (intellect) to be used in understanding the self. Baumgarten uses aesthetics to provide a psychology of sensation, a logic of the senses, and a system for aesthetic criticism. Thus Baumgarten expands Wolff's philosophy of the possible by using aesthetics as an analogue of reason. Although Baumgarten never defines the nature of aesthetics, he describes its function as being both concrete and abstract and universal as well as personal. Aesthetics reveals special meaning for the self to those who use its special philosophy and special language to achieve sensitive knowledge.

At first glance it appears that Freud's empiricism has little or no connection with sensitive knowledge, but there is another side to Freud that shows an interest in art and literature that includes the romantic period as well as the *Aufklärung.* Freud's views on art have been debated over the years, partly because of disagreement among Freud's critics but also because of Freud's own inexplicable silences on important issues and his lack of clarity. Thus, an essential dualism runs through Freud's aesthetics. On the one hand, Freud sees art in relation to a biological, psychological model, and on the other hand, as a reflection of the romantic period and even of the occult. This dualism is a result of Freud's attempt to cope with the varied nature of his own life. While he constructs a meta-psychology in an attempt to cover every aspect of life, he never resolves the conflict between the scientist and the artist. This does not, however, vitiate Freud's attempts to relate the life and work of the artist to the ideas and methods of psychoanalysis.

In his essay "Psychotherapy, Art, and Religion," Frankl adds the spiritual as a vital element of the artistic and psychological struggles of the self. In the case study that he presents in this essay—an artist, a middle-aged woman, who complained that she was unable to complete paintings—in which the dreams of the patient play a vital role, Frankl stresses the importance of what the person under analysis calls up from the past. Some readers of this case history may be put off by the linking of the patient's creative power to the rather violent internal religious struggle that is taking place. But what Frankl is stressing is the use of the noös (not the struggle itself) in interpreting both the dreams and the waking experiences so that the patient may be enabled to achieve a fully active life filled with meaning. Frankl's use of the noetic dimension adds a vital pragmatic element to Wolff's philosophy of the possible and Baumgarten's aesthetics. At the same time, his addition of the noetic dimension to the somatic and psychic eliminates Freud's dualism between the scientific and the aesthetic and releases the self to find meaning.

Immanuel Kant

The *Aufklärung* reinterprets classical humanism in the light of the philosophical and psychological developments of its own day and—above all—sets the stage for Immanuel Kant. Kant's discussion of the relation of knowledge (What can I know?) to ethics (What ought I to do?) was a key factor in philosophy in Freud's day and remains so to the present time. While Freud himself believed that he advanced and completed Kant's epistemology, Philip Rieff feels that Freud is radically anti-Kantian because "he [Freud] has no theory of *forms* of the mind."[35] It is more accurate to say that while Freud follows Kant's lead in the need to explore the *active* mind and the horizons of science, he reaches conclusions that are radically different.

Freud has been labeled not only as a radical anti-Kantian but also as the champion of raw instincts. A great amount of the opposition that he received in the early 20th century from Rabbi Stephen Wise and other religious leaders was due to the fact that Freud's "excavation" of the psyche exposed, in their view, the sexual "sewage" that they wished would remain hidden.

Kant and Freud, each in his own way, are solitary figures isolated from others by the revolutionary nature of their ideas, by their strict discipline, and by their inability to compromise. As a result, they are also pioneers and giants: Kant as the father of modern philosophy and Freud as the father of modern psychology. Kant's explanations of the self are rooted in and guided by reason. Freud, while attracted by philosophy, uses a biological-psychic rationale to explain the self. Kant explains the self through outlining a mental development that uses pure and practical reason in the exercise of judgment. Freud reduces human development to two processes. The first he calls the " 'primary process,' . . . the collection of primitive untamed mental energies lodged in the mind from the beginning is still under the sway of the pleasure principle: it wants gratification . . . with no patience for thought or delay."[36] The second process takes reality into account. It mentally regulates feelings. It calculates how and when the desired pleasures can best be enjoyed. The effect of these two processes is best illustrated by moral philosophy. Freud's ethics pinpoints especially where he agrees with and differs from Kant. Freud's ethics is described most often, and inaccurately, as based purely on the pleasure principle. But Freud teaches that ethics must result from psychology's exploration of the dark areas of the self that are rooted deeper than the pleasure principle.[37] Freud grapples with the fundamental forces of the mind that cancel out the pleasure, or reality, principle's ability to delay instant gratification.[38]

To understand Freud's position more fully, we should remember that he sees himself as a scientist who is also a teacher of morals. As a result, his reality principle has a definite aim and a methodology. He integrates his reality principle with his therapy, which "implies an intention to convert, to criticize one way of life and to work toward another."[39] This requires an ethics of honesty to replace what Freud describes as false innocency. A person should reveal everything not only to an analyst but to society as well. In so doing, Freud feels that society's repressions will be replaced by a new tolerance. He is not arguing for a more "civilized" attitude but drifts toward what has been called a sophisticated primitivism based on a delicacy of feeling.[40] Freud argues that we must reflect a delicacy of feeling that is sensitive to the differences in human thought, emotions, and behavior. This requires honesty, tolerance, and accommodation. Thus, his reality principle restricts pleasures, and in so doing, sets the limits of freedom—not from fear and coercion, but from self-awareness and self-mastery. How persons recognize and deal with the necessities of the past determines how they can be free and responsible for the future. Freud, however, never identifies what shall be the guide for a person's or society's exercise of freedom and responsibility.

Kant and Freud both agree that moral obligation must be *chosen*, not imposed. This choice links freedom to responsibility. Kant bases his ethics on a moral law, but *it is a law given to the self by the self.* The personal choice of the moral law, and the behavior that results from it, is based on reason and is given form and substance by an a priori moral categorical imperative. Freud, on the other hand, takes into account that reason is important, but he does not see it as the central agent of the reality principle. Rather, he emphasizes that the emotions vitiate and even negate the rational process, including the prompting of conscience. Thus, "Freud shares Kant's awe and wonder at the starry heavens above; but as for the moral law within, here, Freud says, God has been guilty of 'an uneven and careless piece of work.' "[41]

The role of conscience remains a critical issue in the evaluation of psychoanalysis. If we keep in mind that Freud is a "digger" and not a "builder," the issue becomes clearer. The aim of Freud's reality principle is to show how all the mental processes—including conscience—are inhibited and distorted by unconscious forces that must be brought to light and dealt with individually but not on the basis of moral law, irrespective of how the law is recognized and accepted. Conscience often results in what may be described as moral inflation resulting in moral repression. Thus, psychoanalysis brings those corrective devices that can enable the individual and the society to mitigate or avoid repressions that enslave the self. Whereas Kant's moral categorical imperative points to an aspiration from above, Freud's reality principle uses aspiration from below. As a result, while Freud is not an antinomian, as some have charged, he reflects a philosophy of resignation at best and nihilism at worst. It is more accurate to describe his work as a *reductionistic* form of a principle of reality, rather than as an appeal to a pleasure principle. He remains resigned to the fact that while a person may gain a sense of greater awareness of the self through honesty, he or she can never gain full self-mastery. Further, the inability of the emotional or rational aspects of the self to resolve the internal battle between love (eros) and death (thanatos) leaves the self with a dualism that is essentially nihilistic. For Freud, persons may be more aware, may criticize, and may even aspire, but they cannot truly win the battle of the psyche.

Frankl goes beyond both Kant's and Freud's premises and conclusions. Later (in Chapter 3) I discuss in some detail the Kantian dimension in Frankl's thought, explaining how Frankl's use of the noetic dimension transmutes Kant's understanding of reason and morality. Frankl's analysis of Freud shows how the reality principle can be expanded in a way that builds as well as excavates to achieve a more holistic concept of the self. Frankl's reality principle centers on the noetic dimension. The use of the noetic dimension accomplishes three purposes: (1) it avoids a mind-body dualism, (2) it enlarges the concept of conscience, and (3) it focuses on the possibilities of the future rather than dwelling on the limitations of the past. The noös in relation to the *soma* (body) and the psyche does justice to both the unity and the diversity of the self.

Frankl quotes Thomas Aquinas's description of the self as *unitas multiplex* and goes on to say that "I would define man as a unity in spite of multiplicity."[42] The multiplicity that results is not chaotic. Rather, Frankl's definition of the self as body, mind, and spirit does not refer to parallel layers but to three organically interrelated and interdependent elements. The spirit (or noös) is the key to the self, allowing each person to rise above the biological and psychological levels to be fully human.[43] Frankl's focus on the noetic dimension, and its resultant dimensional ontology, allows him to avoid Kant's reduction of the self to various kinds of reasoning and Freud's dualism between mind and body. The noetic dimension preserves Kant's transcendental dimension without linking it to a strictly defined "duty imperative" and establishes an ethics of responsibleness.

The moral philosophies of Kant, Freud, and Frankl are based on how each conceives of human conscience. While they all use reason and experience in their explanations of the role of conscience, they differ in the roles they assign to rationalism and empiricism in the making of moral judgments.

For Kant, the origin and decisions of conscience come from a priori reason, not from either external circumstances or from internal psychological conditions. A priori reason is the source of the maxims and laws that guide conscience. Kant outlines a metaphysics of morals that investigates the source of the practical principles and obligations that are to be found a priori in our reason as natural beings.[44] All duty is measured by a firm, practical, and humanitarian imperative. "*So act as to treat humanity, whether in your person or in that of any other, always at the same time as an end and never as a means.*"[45] Freedom is essentially an obligation to obey or disobey a law depending on how a person chooses intelligibly, humanely, and practically. Kant's position is essentially paradoxical: the self is "noumenally free and empirically determined."[46]

Freud agrees with Kant's paradox, but he disagrees with Kant on the role of freedom and the extent of determinism. Kant's final appeal is to practical *reason*; Freud's is to practical *psychology*. Kant trusts the rational spirit; Freud relies only on the scientific spirit. Freud's mission is to establish a *science* of the self. He feels that a science of the self enables a person to distinguish between appearance and reality and, in so doing, to avoid both the God of religion and any appeal to an abstract rational principle. Instead of looking outward to a moral categorical imperative or a Golden Rule, Freud teaches that a person must look inward to the psyche for moral guidance, though Freud never defines the moral role of the psyche. A person must learn to reflect, to discriminate, and when necessary, to sacrifice: to sacrifice is to renounce all that would keep one from maintaining a healthy psychic balance. The choices remain with each individual. Thus, obligation is never externally imposed; rather, it is internally accepted. This acceptance is traced to the role of the superego in the formation of the conscience and all that it implies. Freud observes that the more a person desires to be virtuous, the greater is the sense of moral failure and guilt as each individual responds to the outward demands of authority and the inner demands of the superego. The resulting picture is both pessimistic and paradoxical, as "every renunciation of instinct now becomes a dynamic source of conscience and every fresh renunciation increases the latter's severity and intolerance."[47]

Freud's frustration in attempting to explain the origins and expressions of guilt within the empirical structure of the id, the ego, and the superego illustrates the incompleteness of his empirical method. While he urges that the self use the powers of reasoning, he cautions that both our conscious and unconscious impulses may inhibit or even destroy the rational controls needed to accomplish our purpose. Freud's aim is "the control of all passions, affects, feelings by will and reason."[48] But Freud's aim is never realized, and his philosophy of the self has as many marks of ethical bondage as it does of liberation. Frankl explains why this is so.

Frankl sees meaninglessness, or nihilism, as a more potent form of ethical bondage in today's world than sexual repression. While Freud's sexually based therapy may help persons to achieve psychic freedom, his exclusion of the spiritual dimension leaves the way open for an existential vacuum that results in what Frankl calls a noögenic neurosis. Frankl points out that "nihilism is masked by speaking of the 'nothing-but-ness of man'.... Reductionism has become the mask of nihilism."[49] In contrast to Freud's thinking of the self as nothing but the relation of the body to the psyche, Frankl's inclusion of the noetic dimension as the uniquely human dimension corrects Freud's reductionism and also gives psychological validity to Kant's philosophy of the a priori and the transcendental:

> In my opinion Kant by his transcendentalism has turned a *quaestio iuris* (a question of law) into a *quaestio facti* (a question of fact) in that the question whether or not we are justified in using certain categories, is answered by showing that we cannot do without them, and that we have been using them all along. There is no point in questioning what we must do.[50]

For Frankl, existence is basically located in the unconscious. Thus he agrees with Freud that the foundations of existence can never be fully probed or understood. Where he differs from Freud is in his insistence that there is a spiritual unconscious as well as an instinctual one. While both Freud and Frankl agree that the border between the conscious and the unconscious is permeable, Frankl insists that a sharp line must be drawn between the instinctual and the spiritual. For Frankl, the vital distinction in assessing human existence is not, as Freud holds, between the unconscious and the conscious but rather between the instinctual and spiritual. In contrast to the Freudian concept that a person is driven by his or her impulses, Frankl insists that the noetic dimension gives the self the power to choose what one will be and what one will become. A noetically empowered conscience is the key.

Frankl describes conscience as an irreducible human phenomenon. It is prelogical and premoral. For him, the premoral conscience cannot be fully explained, because each person and each situation is unique. According to Frankl, conscience has one task: "To disclose to man the *unum necesse,* the one thing that is required. . . . This one thing, however, is absolutely unique inasmuch as it is the unique possibility a concrete person has to actualize in a specific situation."[51] Thus, while conscience is a given, it cannot be reduced to a Kantian moral categorical imperative that reflects a universally valid law for all times. "Only conscience is capable of adjusting the 'eternal,' generally agreed-upon moral law to the specific situation a concrete person is engaged in."[52]

At first glance, it might appear that Frankl's emphasis on the intuitive and existential nature of conscience points toward an ethical instinct that is much like Freud's biological instinct. But as Frankl explains, "The ethical instinct is entirely different. In contrast to vital instincts, the effectiveness of the ethical instinct depends on the fact that its target is not anything general but something individual, something concrete."[53]

Frankl sees love as a parallel to conscience. Just as conscience identifies the unique possibilities latent in each life situation, so love points toward the equally unique potentialities latent in a loved person.[54]

Can love make rational decisions? Frankl says yes, essentially in the I-Thou relationship. "To be sure, the choice of a partner is only a true choice when it is not dictated by drives. . . . As long as a self is driven by an id to a Thou, it is not a matter of love. . . . In love the self is not driven by the id but rather the self chooses the Thou."[55] The reality of choice is centered in the nature of the will.

Both Kant and Frankl agree that the will is a unitary faculty for the self. Kant's definition of the will as *Willkür* (the power to choose alternatives) parallels Frankl's will to meaning. When Kant speaks of the will as *Wille* (the law of freedom), he describes the role Frankl assigns to the noös. Frankl's uniqueness, in relation to both Kant and Freud, is his ability to integrate the will into a comprehensive understanding of the self. Meaning analysis is based on three essential premises: the freedom of the will, the will to meaning, and the meaning of life. The freedom of the will denies pandeterminism. "Man's freedom is no freedom from conditions but rather freedom to take a stand on whatever conditions might confront him."[56]

Although Frankl acknowledges that Freud helps the self to recognize more accurately the conscious and unconscious conditions of life, he criticizes psychoanalysis's pandeterminism, which limits how a person takes a stand to the biological-psychological elements of the self. For Frankl, the noetic dimension—omitted by Freud and defined by Kant in purely rational terms—becomes *the* unitary agent of the self. It enables a person to recognize and use the will in achieving a life of meaning. Thus the self is neither an a priori (Kantian) nor an a posteriori (Freudian) machine. Rather, the noetic dimension enables a person to see fate in a way that still affirms that life has meaning. For Frankl, if we face a fate that cannot be changed, we can turn tragedy to triumph; we can change ourselves, even if we cannot change the situation, by going beyond ourselves. This understanding of the self involves a new look at the sciences as well as the humanities.

The Influence of the Scientific Method on Freud and Frankl

Besides a grounding in Greek philosophy and immersion in the spirit of the *Aufklärung,* the Viennese gymnasium education that Freud and Frankl shared included training in the scientific method, the development of which began in the middle of the 19th century. As mentioned earlier, the humanities were considered the best preparation for the sciences, which began to dominate the curriculum of the university and were the focus of the medical school in Freud's and in Frankl's time. The most important development in their medical training was the establishment of clinical psychiatry after the publication in 1861 of the second edition of Wilhelm Griesinger's *Die pathologie und Therapie der psychischen Krankheiten für Aertze und studirende.* This work became the Magna Charta of clinical psychiatry. What is vital in interpreting Freud's approach, according to Ludwig Binswanger, is Griesinger's belief that psychic phenomena should be interpreted by natural (that is, biological) science because of their "organicity." Freud adopted this biological model.

> To understand Freud's great ideas correctly one must *not* . . . proceed from psychology. . . . For otherwise one does not do him justice and stumbles at every point against the thoroughly unpsychological appearance of psychic *apparatus.* But if these notions are—as Freud wished—understood biologically, they then fit easily into psychiatric thought.[57]

This biological-mechanistic model is the crux of Frankl's criticism of Freud's *Lebenswelt* and methodology. Freud's basic error, according to humanistic psychology, is his narrowing his description of the psyche to fit the biological model and his belief that the drives and needs determine the essential behavior of the self. This raises the question of the relation of humanistic psychology to scientific investigation. How the development of both disciplines has progressed in the past 40 years is shown by Frankl's understanding of how they can complement each other, rather than being locked in irresolvable conflict as Freud concludes. It is important to realize that *science* has two clear meanings: a narrow meaning, reflected in controlled empirical investigation, and a broader interpretation that refers to any type of systematic scholarship. Freud and his followers use the first meaning while Frankl uses the broader interpretation in developing a human level in the use of science.

Frankl's thinking agrees with that of Maurice Merleau-Ponty (1908–1961), who defines what makes us human as our ability to overturn any given mental and emotional structure. As I shall show later in more detail, Frankl is able to understand the nature and place of structures on the basis of his studies in philosophical anthropology, phenomenology, and hermeneutics. Frankl's theory of meaning analysis neither abandons reason in favor of undisciplined feelings nor allows a split between science and life. Frankl succeeds where Freud fails because he recognizes that the meaning of *human*, the meaning of *science,* and how each is approached, are all philosophical issues of prime importance in forming an adequate world view.

The juxtaposition of 19th-century science and German romanticism presents an interesting paradox. While science provided a structure, German romanticism's exaltation of the hero exhibited the defiant power of the human spirit, an essential quality of the self recognized and utilized by both Freud and Frankl. The concept of the free spirit came from the literature of German romanticism, which is described by Michel Focault as a "shared archive rather than a school of thought."[58] Freud and Frankl use this archive, digging out the themes that best fit their own understandings of the self. Freud chooses the romantics' philosophy of nature, whereas Frankl turns to their understanding of self-consciousness as an awareness that is primarily spiritual truth. Frankl does not insist that the self must find the *right* spiritual truth; rather, he sees meaning coming from a search for *truths,* examined and tested by each person in his or her place (*Dasein*). He expands Jakob Böhme's dictum, "The self finds itself in what it knows," to "The self finds itself in what it knows *and practices.*" This revision is in harmony with Freud's adaptation of German romanticism.

Freud was attracted to the great figures of the period and to those who followed, especially Johann Wolfgang von Goethe (1749–1832). We know from Freud himself that what he admired the most in Goethe was his conquistadorial spirit—a spirit with which Freud identifies and that he calls his own. While Frankl is aware of the philosophical and literary contributions of the great figures of the era, he avoids Freud's identification with any one figure. Freud's attraction to great Biblical, literary, and historical figures—including Moses, Goethe, and Napoleon—is seen by Fromm and others as an example of Freud's elitism. Frankl may go to the other extreme in his admiration and trust in the judgment of "the man in the street."

The Influence of Existentialism and Phenomenology on Freud and Frankl

German romanticism set the stage for the existentialist critique of the self that began with Søren Kierkegaard (1813–1855) and that continues through the latter part of this century. Existentialism's emphasis on alienation, defiance, identity, conflict, and on the range of human hope and despair figures prominently in Freud's and Frankl's philosophical psychology. How each man deals with these existential issues summarizes their similarities and differences.

Existentialism is described by Roger Shinn as the existentialist *posture.* This is echoed by Rollo May, who says that "existentialism is not a system of therapy but *an attitude toward therapy.*"[59] Thus, while the same existential human problems confront Freud and Frankl (including human consciousness, anxiety, decision making, commitment, love, and death), each man's attitude toward these problems is crucial in understanding the differences between psychoanalysis and meaning analysis. Rollo May tells how Binswanger pinpointed the positive and negative contributions of Freud:

> Binswanger gave credit to Freud for having enlarged and deepened our insight into human nature, more, perhaps, than anyone since Aristotle. But he went on to point out that these insights wore "a theoretical-scientific garb that as a whole appeared to me too 'one-sided' and narrow." He held that Freud's great contribution was in the area of *homo natura,* man in relation to nature (*Umwelt*)—drives, instincts, and similar aspects of experience. And as a consequence, Binswanger believed that in Freud's theory there was only a shadowy, epiphenomenal understanding of man in relation to his fellowmen (*Mitwelt*) and that the area of man in relation to himself (*Eigenwelt*) was omitted entirely.[60]

When Binswanger shared these comments with Freud, Freud's response convinced Binswanger that "Freud looked upon our differences as something to be surmounted by empirical investigation, not as something bearing upon the transcendental conceptions that underlie all empirical research."[61] His adherence to a strict empirical procedure prevents Freud from exploring fully the relation of the self to being. As a result, his existential explorations are also truncated. In contrast, Frankl's recognition of the transcendental as the key to the self allows him to go beyond the biological-mechanistic limits of Freud and the nihilism of Jean-Paul Sartre to explore the spiritual existentialism exemplified by Martin Buber and Gabriel Marcel. In a personal conversation with me, Frankl said that he was seen to be closer in thought to Marcel than to any other contemporary philosopher.

Frankl's existentialism is dramatically illustrated by his experiences in the concentration camps of Nazi Germany. As a result, he declares that when all else seems lost, a person can hold on to human freedom through the (existential) defiant power of the human spirit. Our choices come from our attitudes. This is in direct contrast to Freud, who uses the word *being* not as a reference to the locus of human freedom but as an illustration of how the self is psychologically conditioned. For Freud, the self remains *re-active* rather than *pro-active*. In contrast, Frankl recognizes the self as proactive, able to form patterns of thought and action that can result in potential meanings being actualized not only within one's self (*Eigenwelt*) but also in relation to others (*Mitwelt*). Frankl describes the existential act, which underlies all relations, as the basic trust in Being (*Urvertrauen zum Dasein*).[62] Such trust results in our encountering not only the existential "I am," but also the "I ought." Frankl rethinks and enlarges the existential dimension using insights from phenomenology.

Existentialism and phenomenology are closely allied. Each is rooted in European philosophy. Each begins with the self. Each must be measured against the intellectual explorations of the times. Each is a movement, rather than a system or doctrine. What is termed existential phenomenology is distinguished from stark existentialism by the watchword "Back to the things themselves"— that is, a search for the foundations of Being. Existential phenomenology developed in the latter 19th century under the aegis of Edmund Husserl (1859–1938), Max Scheler (1874–1928), and Martin Heidegger (1889–1976). It defined structures as part of its task and affirmed psychology as a tool while fighting psychologism, the reduction of psychology to a natural science. It began its study of Being by examining consciousness. The leaders of phenomenology saw their role as essentially descriptive rather than prescriptive. Thus, while they differed in thought and methodologies, they were content to let such variations remain, recognizing that these were the results of *doing* philosophy rather than just thinking about it. They struggled to find ways to share one world instead of developing a theory about it. As I discuss in more detail in my chapter on Frankl and phenomenology (Chapter 5), psychologists respond in radically different ways to the existential phenomenological movement. This is seen by the reactions of Freud and Frankl, as each *does* philosophy as a practicing psychiatrist.

In the literature about Freud it is surprising to find that there is no indication of the effect that Husserl and the others active in the phenomenological movement had on him personally or professionally. Yet the issues raised by phenomenology—the nature of conscience, relationships to others, everyday knowledge and systemic knowledge—are central to the theory and practice of psychoanalysis. The reason for the lack of conscious and open exploration of existential phenomenology may be rooted in the personality of Freud himself. We know from the biographies of Freud that he banished from his movement anyone whom he felt disagreed with him personally or professionally. He also dismissed unfavorable reviews of his books, reserving to himself the freedom to point out any of his errors or inconsistencies. Daniel N. Robinson notes that psychoanalytic theories are never fully developed and fail to give any systematic account of what determines behavior and feelings. He concludes that the psychoanalytic attempt to explain these is "tautologous when it is explicit, and biographical when it is merely suggestive."[63] At first glance, Freud seems more systematic than Adler and Jung, but "on further examination the relevant data are as hypothetical and interpretive as the hypotheses they are said to support."[64] Essentially, one must approach Freudian psychoanalysis with faith in what may be called the *psychological* self.

Frankl's grounding in classical humanism and his studies of existential phenomenology cause him to reject the psychological self for the fully human self (mind, body, and spirit). In constructing a holistic view of the self, Frankl brings new dynamics and interpretations to existential phenomenology. One of his most important observations is his belief that phenomenology "speaks the language of man's prereflective self-understanding rather than interpreting a given phenomenon after preconceived patterns."[65] Frankl constructs his theory of freedom of the will on this assumption. Freedom of the will belongs to the immediate data of our experience, including the prereflective as well as the reflective. This is important in comparing Frankl with Freud, for while Frankl agrees with Freud that the subconscious self is basic, he calls it the prereflective self and links it to the noetic dimension, rather than to the psychosexual needs. Thus the self is free to rise above the plane of the somatic and psychic determinants of its existence. By the same token a new dimension is opened. The noetic dimension stands in contradiction to the somatic and psychic phenomena, giving a person freedom to recognize values and to act on them.[66] Frankl insists that persons do not receive an identity through a direct search, but by committing themselves first to something beyond them: to values and/or to a worthy cause. He quotes the existential phenomenologist Karl Jaspers (1883–1969): "What man is, he has become through that cause which he has made his own."[67] Frankl's existential phenomenological analysis underscores that we are beings encountering other beings, and in reaching out for others, meanings are fulfilled.

From Psychoanalysis to Meaning Analysis

Frankl believes that Freud's reality principle is, in fact, another wording for the pleasure principle. Paul Ricoeur notes that Freud never relates his reality principle to the struggle of eros (love) and thanatos (death) that he emphasizes in his later writings.[68] Frankl insists that any true reality principle must deal with the struggle between eros and thanatos, as Frankl does in his treatment of the tragic triad of guilt, pain, and death. In the decisions that come out of our struggles with these three, we decide who we are, we decide what we ought to do, and we decide on what we can base our hopes. Speaking from his own experience, Frankl testifies to the fact that a person is not a thing among others. Each person is ultimately self-determining. In the concentration camps, ultimate freedom still remained. "The freedom to take what attitude they [the prisoners] would toward the concrete situation had not been wrested from them; they had themselves withdrawn their claim to use that freedom."[69] Essentially and ultimately, their use of freedom could be traced to what he describes as a spiritual attitude. An essential difference between Freud and Frankl is found in a phrase often quoted by Frankl, "I would not be willing to live for the sake of my 'defense mechanisms,' much less to die for my 'reaction formations.' "[70]

As the founder of the third Viennese school of psychotherapy, Frankl opposes what has been called the irrational and brooding elements of Freudian and neo-Freudian theories.[71] Instead, Frankl offers an approach to the self that welcomes scientific investigation while rejecting "scientism." He insists that the unconscious element of the self is basic and offers promise as well as defeat. Thus we must call upon spiritual resources that are free from dogma and cant if we are to realize fully our human potential. One of the key reasons that Frankl succeeds in presenting a holistic view of the self, which Freud fails to do, is Frankl's ability to recognize and to incorporate into his philosophy key insights from both classical humanism and existential phenomenology in addition to his knowledge of medicine.

Psychoanalysis, which began for Freud as an experiment in the scientific exploration of the self, has become a dogma of psychology. A major achievement of Frankl's is his challenge to Freudianism in psychotherapy, behaviorism in psychology, and positivism in philosophy.

In his famous letter to Wilhelm Fleiss, Freud called himself a conquistador. Instead, he should best be remembered as a battler for those psychoanalytic causes he felt were most urgent in his own time. In this sense Frankl, too, is a battler. But the battleground has moved from the psyche alone to a holistic self—mind, body, and spirit—in search of meaning, as seen in the reassessment and growth of psychology from Freud to Frankl.

— 3 —

The

Kantian

Dimension

TWO THINGS FILL THE MIND WITH EVER NEW AND
INCREASING ADMIRATION AND AWE . . . THE STARRY
HEAVENS ABOVE AND THE MORAL LAW WITHIN.
—IMMANUEL KANT

The failure of 18th-century philosophy to reconcile the concept of human freedom with the mechanistic view of the universe held by 18th-century science prompted David Hume (1711–1776) to ask, How can moral and spiritual freedom occur if all events are part of a mechanistic plan? and How can scientific knowledge be justified as a complete philosophical answer? Hume argues that since all our knowledge is derived from experience, we cannot have *any* knowledge of causality or necessary connections. As a result, we cannot predict any future event from our experience of the present. Inductive reasoning is not possible, therefore, in Hume's view, and as science is based on inductive thought, there is no such thing as scientific knowledge.

Immanuel Kant openly confesses that Hume's questions interrupted his "dogmatic slumbers," and that he found himself faced with the dilemma posed by Hume's skeptical empiricism confronting the dogmatic rationalism of Christian Wolff. Kant's resolution of this philosophical dilemma required nothing less than a revolution in thought, and the impact of this revolution is still evident in modern philosophy. Kant's thought continues to be used and debated by a wide variety of thinkers, including Viktor Frankl.

Kant's Metaphysics and Epistemology

Kant challenges the metaphysics of empiricism—that is, that knowledge must conform to objects. He reverses that hypothesis by asserting that objects must conform to the mind. He might appear, therefore, as a new Ptolemy in philosophy since he seems to put the knower at the center of the universe. Kant, however, saw his reasoning as analogous to that of Copernicus: "Copernicus hypothesized that the complex planetary motions were not real motions, but only apparent motions dependent upon the real motion of the observer. Knowing the real motion of the observer, the astronomer was enabled to foretell... future apparent motions."[1] If Kant is thereby insisting that the human is *the* most significant fact of the universe and that all interpretations of nature must be evaluated according to this tenet, his philosophy might rightly be identified as anthropocentrism. But Kant's view may be more accurately identified as hominocentrism, in which the human has a *role* in the makeup of nature. The Kantian hominocentric approach to the human self is a comprehensive, morally sensitive philosophy that is focused on the person and that moves from metaphysics to epistemology, from epistemology to ethics, and finally from ethics to religion. The Kantian hominocentric approach to philosophy is self-oriented so that all discussions of metaphysics, epistemology, ethics, and religion are humanistically oriented.

Kant begins his examination of epistemology with the nature of the mind. He recognizes that experience provides the empirical basis of knowledge, but he stresses that the *mind* is the active agent of the self that recognizes, organizes, and unifies experience.[2] The distinctive function of the mind is to bring together and to explain experience, and, according to Kant, knowledge comes from the response of the knower to the thing known. Time and space help to accomplish the task as "lenses through which we always see objects of experience."[3] Kant uses the familiar categories of quantity, quality, and modality in constructing a unified understanding of the self, but he introduces two key terms to describe reality: the *phenomenal* and the *noumenal.* The world we experience is the phenomenal; the world we envisage is the noumenal.

Kant's description of the phenomenological is straightforward and easily acceptable; his use of the concept of noumena presents problems. Literally defined, the word *noumenon* means object of thought. Kant is not consistent in the way that he uses the word. Sometimes he appears to see noumena as objects of thought; at other times, he appears to equate noumena with intelligibility (*intelligibilia*).[4] He further complicates matters by using both negative and positive terms in defining *noumenon.* Negatively, noumenon is excluded from any form of intuition that is sensuous. Positively, noumenon is part of intelligibility (or intellect). Apart from these problems of definition, Kant affirms that noumenon is an essential quality of human thought and experience, especially in relation to what he calls the transcendental dimension.

The transcendental dimension focuses on how we think of objects rather than on the objects themselves. This dimension is basic in understanding the nature and application of ideas. Ideas may be seen in the narrow sense as reason, in the wider sense as perception and understanding.

Kant is careful to distinguish the narrow use of ideas by comparing the role of pure reason (*Vernunft*) with that of understanding (*Verstand*). Reason does not deal directly with phenomena; this is the function of understanding. Reason uses the results of such understanding to relate them to a higher principle (the unconditioned). Understanding depends on our sense experience while reason depends on what understanding has done with experience. Judgment acts as the arbitrator between the results of understanding and the conclusions reached by reason. Essentially, reason legislates desire while judgment legislates feeling by balancing thinking and desire.

The question that arises about judgment is whether it has its own a priori principle.[5] Kant's answer has paradoxical elements. He affirms that there is a "transcendental principle of judgment" that must be validated subjectively, concluding that "the law in us must be holy, and the sentence of this law must be just, which means that the penalties of the law must be applied to the actions of men with all exactness . . . *the judge within us is just . . . if only we have the will to listen to his [God's] voice and do not stifle it.*"[6]

For Kant, reason remains an ideal of reason that he never is able to reconcile with his commitment to an empirical method of knowing. He uses logic based on the assumptions of Newtonian physics that do not allow for any a priori thought or perception. He also agrees with the scientific conclusion of his day that every event can be traced to a cause; he believes that there is a cause for all of nature and that the explanation of the mind and its functions is contained within natural law.

Kant has been described as a Spinoza of the mind.[7] If so, he is a Spinoza who subsumes everything under the category of the mind without adequately explaining either the origin of the mind or the nature of its scope. His metaphysical bias and epistemological reductionism become more apparent in his ethics.

The Moral Core in Kant and Frankl

What ought I to do? is the philosophical question that concerns Kant more than any other. His answer to that question has proven to be the most influential and at the same time the most controversial issue in Kant's philosophy of the self. In great part this is due to the way he defines his terms and to his blurring of the boundaries among metaphysics, epistemology, ethics, and religion. Frankl's philosophical psychology reflects the same interests and also poses similar problems of definition and of the crossing of philosophical boundaries. Three words highlighted by Kant in his ethics—*perception, understanding,* and *judgment*—illustrate how he and Frankl define the nature of ethics and how each man deals with the moral core of the self.

In the Kantian schema, perception is essentially *thinking* perception. Kant reminds us that we do not live in a welter of sensations; rather, as our minds come into contact with objects, our minds impose order, which leads to understanding, active judgment, and to action itself. These, in Kant's view, are subsumed by what he calls transcendental apperception. For Frankl, perception is basically *perception through meaning*, which goes beyond our personal rational and empirical impressions. Frankl substitutes *logos*, or ultimate meaning, for the Kantian term *transcendental apperception.*

For Frankl, a way to understand meaning is "to see ultimate meaning as a supertransmitter, a *logos* in the center of the universe sending out meaning signals all the time in all directions. . . . We all have our own little receiver in our conscience, still primitive and unreliable, trying to tune in on those broadcasts, trying to pick up signals."[8] That our "receiver" is primitive and unreliable does not mean it is chaotic; rather it means that our perceptions may be limited and that we can block or distort the messages that seem to be sent to us. In fact, because of this, our knowledge can be flawed and our judgments prove to be fallible.

Other words for perception are *perspective* or *perspicere* (to look through). Frankl reminds us that we need to examine our subjective perspectives and discover what lies behind them.

Perception leads to what Kant conceives of as intuitive understanding; however, understanding does not depend on intuition but rather on the process of thinking that enables intuition to become what Kant calls creative understanding (*intellectus archetypus*) as contrasted with reproductive understanding (*intellectus ectypus*). Creative understanding is self-conscious; reproductive understanding, with its dependence on objects, is devoid of reason.[9]

Instead of using the term *intuitive understanding*, Frankl talks about intuitive *conscience*, a concept that appears to be Kantian at first glance. But while Kant's intuitive understanding focuses on the free investigation of the world, Frankl's intuitive conscience concentrates on the relation of the self to meaning in existential situations. Kant stresses intuitive understanding's relation to practical reason; Frankl highlights intuitive conscience as concerned for a morality that begins when someone makes a decision to act for the sake of another or for something beyond his or her self.

Further, Frankl points out that a suppressed conscience is more detrimental than an erring conscience. He cites Hitler as an example: "I am convinced that Hitler would never have become what he did unless he had *suppressed* within himself the voice of conscience."[10] In other words, for Frankl, the risk of uncertainty is less harmful than the risk of authoritarian assurance. Frankl calls into question any intuitive understanding that demands absolute certainty in judgment.

Frankl, therefore, challenges Kant's conviction that each person can achieve a universal understanding of subject-object relationships through the use of a person's natural conscience. Frankl points out that there is a dimensional ontology that shows that persons may see the same objects in different ways and so the meanings that result may vary. He agrees with Kant that true thought is expressed through *active* judgment, but parts company with Kant by questioning the *quality* of that active judgment.

Four key concepts spell out where and why Kant and Frankl agree or disagree on ethics: (1) duty, (2) will, (3) conscience, and (4) freedom and responsibleness.

Duty

Kant has become known as the philosopher of duty. His sense of the importance of a moral core and its obligations may be traced to the religious piety of his conservative Protestant upbringing. Frankl shares Kant's sense of this, though his convictions spring from a conservative Jewish background. Kant expresses his commitment through an adaptation of the Golden Rule, the moral categorical imperative. Frankl's moral imperative is existential, not categorical, but with echoes of the Jewish Covenant. Kant uses the term *duty* as the operative word while Frankl chooses the term *meaning*.

Frankl recognizes the necessity of the concept of duty as a response to what he calls the demand quality of life, but he sees Kant's view of duty for duty's sake as reductionistic, centering on the law rather than on meaning, which allows freedom and responsibleness. Frankl's view is that the duty-oriented person sees life only as a function. At best, duty, when pursued as a primary goal, can be limiting; at worst, it results in disappointment and failure. If, however, meaning is pursued as a primary goal, duty can ensue. Frankl reminds us that Nietzsche says, "He who knows a 'why' for living, will surmount almost every 'how,' "[11] which includes the unpleasant and painful "hows" that duty sometimes demands.

Kant sees duty within the framework of divine law. Frankl sees duty as a response to what he calls the *Urvertrauen zum Dasein,* the basic trust in Being.[12] Frankl's "trust in Being" is not a blind trust but a belief that persons are given the power by the noetic dimension to transcend those limitations and weaknesses that keep them from being whole. Kant offers the law to protect the person from harm; Frankl offers meaning as an achievable goal through caring for another person or by finding a task worth doing. Frankl puts duty within a framework of meaning and transforms the Kantian categorical command to obey duty into a direction to activate the spiritual dimension of the will.

In his writings, Kant acknowledges, "The categorical imperative does not come to man as a command from outside, which he must obey because he is weak. No, man as a rational being gives himself the imperative, it is his reason. Here reason is sustained by itself, but at the same time by something more."[13] Kant wants duty both ways: as a categorical imperative, which cannot be avoided or debated by the self; but also as a command that comes from within. His position is further complicated by his reliance on the sufficiency of reason to determine duty, on the one hand, and his recognition of a need for "something more" on the other hand. By moving from the priority of reason to the priority of the spirit, Frankl solves these Kantian problems by not giving reason the task of always choosing the right duty, which it cannot sustain, and by showing how openness to the power of the spirit (noös) offers human possibilities that go beyond the limits set by duty. In other words, he claims that the noetic dimension, or the transcendental dimension, provides human possibilities that change the role of the will from the acceptance of duty to the expression of meaning.

The performance of duty depends upon how a person makes a decision through an act of will. It has been said that "defining the will is like defining personality: Everyone knows what it is, but hardly anyone can *say* what it is."[14] Kant says that the will is a unitary faculty having three interrelated aspects: the *source* of ethical incentive (*Wille*), the *power* of ethical incentive (*Willkür*), and the *disposition* of ethical incentive (*Gesinnung*). *Willkür,* or the power of ethical incentive, is the core of personality and responsibleness; as such, it is the key function of the will, flanked by the rational *Wille,* or the source of ethical incentive, and the enduring *Gesinnung,* the dispostion of ethical incentive. Together, these three aspects provide a tripartite rationale for the will.

As the rational source, *Wille* provides the laws or maxims on which *Willkür* is to act. *Wille* is seen by Kant as the law of freedom: it is primarily the law that puts a constraint on *Willkür* to choose the law that expresses moral behavior. Kant argues that despite the constraints placed upon it by *Wille, Willkür* is free to accept or reject *Wille's* rational evidence; otherwise, the assertion that we are moral beings because of the maxims we choose and act upon has no credence. *Willkür* must remain free if it is, as Kant believes, the instrument of transcendental freedom. Kant also believes that a *Willkür* that utterly rejects the maxims of *Wille* would result in a freedom without rationality. He concludes that "of such a freedom we have neither experience nor knowledge."[15]

While Kant's contribution as the philosopher of duty is seminal for modern thought, he leaves three problems regarding the nature of the will that need to be addressed: (1) his dependence on the law as *the* measure of all moral behavior; (2) his inability to thoroughly explain the interrelation of the terms *Wille, Willkür,* and *Gesinnung*; and (3) his denial of the interaction between the noumenal and the phenomenal, which is inconsistent with his acknowledgment that the will does operate in both these areas.

Will

Frankl's exploration of phenomenology and his training in psychology offer another way of dealing with the key problems posed by trying to define the nature of the will and its role in human life. While Frankl affirms the Kantian emphasis on the dimension of life labeled "I ought," he links it to meaning rather than to law and adds scope to the idea of the transcendental that Kant has introduced:

> In the strict sense of Immanuel Kant's transcendentalism, man's trust in meaning would deserve to be called transcendental. If I am allowed for didactic reasons to oversimplify matters, man really cannot perceive things without perceiving them in space and time and applying to them the

category of cause and effect. So far Kant. Now it is my contention that man really could not really move a limb unless deep down to the foundations of existence, and out of the depths of being, he is imbued by a basic trust in the ultimate meaning.[16]

In Frankl's opinion, Kant turns a question of law into a question of fact by showing that humans cannot do without certain categories of reason and morality—they are part of the transcendental aspect of the self. Frankl's significant transmutation of Kant's thought is in moving the emphasis from fulfilling the requirements of morality to a search for meaning from which ethical behavior may ensue. In Frankl's meaning analysis, meaning has both an "ought" and a "will" that are tested by meaningful contact with the world.[17]

But, Frankl believes, we cannot "will to will," as Kant would have it; instead, we must exercise the "will to meaning." Frankl's understanding of the self is based on three concepts: (1) the freedom of the will, (2) the will to meaning, and (3) the meaning of life.[18] Each concept is a corrective to Kantian reasoning.

Freedom of the will challenges the Kantian reduction of the self that proposes either becoming a moralist or escaping into intellectualism. Frankl says:

> The logotherapist is neither a moralist nor an intellectual. His work is based on empirical, i.e., phenomenological analyses, and a phenomenological analysis of the simple man in the street's experience of the valuing process shows that one can find meaning in life by creating a work or doing a deed or by experiencing goodness, truth, and beauty, by experiencing nature and culture; or, last but not least, by encountering another unique being in the very uniqueness of this human being—in other words, by loving him. However, the noblest appreciation of meaning is reserved to those people who, deprived of the opportunity to find meaning in a deed, in a work, or in love, by the very attitude which they choose to this predicament, rise above it and go beyond themselves.[19]

Freedom of the will is freedom to find meaning and, in so doing, to establish what Kant calls a *Gesinnung,* a disposition of the will toward life that is both creative and responsible. Frankl's will to meaning establishes a new sense of being in which both the resources and the challenges of the will are increased through the noetic dimension; thus meaning replaces law as the essential quality of life.

In his discussion of Kant and the nature of the will, John Silber raises a point that is equally applicable to Frankl. Kant does not explore what incentives prompt the will (*Willkür*) to acknowledge and respond to the authority of law and reason (*Wille*) and thus to experience moral feeling. Silber agrees with Kant that such an exploration is inappropriate, for if such conditions or incentives were found then the will would not be free. As Silber reminds us, "When we look for such conditions, Kant argued, we reveal our failure to comprehend the nature of freedom; that is, we fail to 'comprehend its incomprehensibility.' "[20] Similarly, Frankl does not try to explain the a priori search for meaning other than to say that the noetic dimension is the source and power for the search. It remains part of the mystery or incomprehensibility of life. It is illustrated in the nature and the expression of the human conscience, a shared concern of both Kant and Frankl.

Conscience

Conscience plays a vital role in both Kant's and Frankl's ethics, but their understandings of the nature of its role are radically different and indicate a disparity between their respective perceptions of moral behavior. Kant's definition of conscience is terse, legalistic, and assured. For him, conscience is the human instinct to pass judgment on ourselves in relation to whether or not we have thought and acted in accordance with moral law.[21] Conscience has the power to bring us to judgment, even against our will. It is more than prudence. Prudence merely reproaches us for what we have done, while conscience accuses us, judges us, and brings us to moral repentance. Kant alerts us to the fact that there is the "good" conscience and the "bad" conscience. The latter acts from a fear of being caught while the former acts out of respect for the moral law. He concludes that conscience is "the representative within us of the divine judgment-seat: it weighs our dispositions and actions in the scales of a law which is holy and pure; we cannot deceive it, and, lastly, we cannot escape it because, like the divine omnipresence, it is always with us."[22] After describing conscience in terms reminiscent of Francis Thompson's "The Hound of Heaven," Kant still says that "conscience should not lord it over us like a tyrant."[23] He also warns that we should not become melancholy, looking for evidences of misdoing, but, after we have reproached ourselves and turned toward the moral law, we can proceed cheerfully and with the knowledge that our conscience is alive and well.

Frankl's understanding of the role of the conscience is that neither is it the Kantian moral policeman nor is it reduced to a Freudian extension of the superego. For Frankl, conscience is the human intuitive capacity to find out the unique meanings in each situation. Conscience teaches us to pursue meaning rather than virtue. Just as the search for pleasure is self-defeating, so the striving for a good conscience robs us of the chance of achieving it; for in its pursuit, we become Pharisees.[24] Frankl tells us that a really good conscience can never be reached by grasping for it, but solely by doing a deed for the sake of a cause, or for the sake of the person involved, or for God's sake.[25] If the conscience is allowed to deteriorate into a thermometer for taking one's own moral readings, it will atrophy into what Frankl calls superegotistic pseudomorality.[26]

Conscience is creative as well as intuitive, according to Frankl. It has the ability to discover unique meanings that may contradict accepted values as well as the capacity to find meanings where others fail to do so. Frankl's understanding of the dimensions of conscience avoids Kant's reduction of conscience to fear of punishment or even desire to obey. Frankl urges us to go beyond obedience to rules, to listen to the inner voice of our conscience, and to take the risk of acting on what it says: even the possibility of error does not relieve us from the necessity of testing its promptings. The everyday world is the testing place for the promptings of the intuitive conscience. Conscience is more than a way of testing ethical behavior. It is ultimately the instrument for human better-ment as it confronts law, authority, society, and sees new meaning in old truths.

Frankl points out that an error of conscience implies that another person's conscience is right, and by admitting this, we escape the dogmatic assumption of Kant's deontological duty that can neither see nor admit to the possibility of error. Such testing, which takes place among the ambiguities and tensions of life, can be a positive factor, even in the case of a guilty conscience, if that leads to honest self-criticism, increases self-understanding, and encourages self-improvement. Kant's dutiful conscience sees life regulated at every crossing by a red light that tells a person to stop or a green light that says go ahead. In contrast, Frankl's intuitive conscience recognizes that we live in a time of flashing yellow lights that leave the choices of freedom and responsibleness to the individual.

Freedom and Responsibleness

Kant makes the moral categorical imperative both the impetus for freedom and responsibleness and its judge. All of life, especially virtue and happiness, is subordinated to the eternal moral law of the ethical imperative. He provides a formula for freedom and responsibleness by use of the categorical imperative, but the question is whether or not the formula is true.

Kant's insistence on the ethical "ought" affirms that human freedom does exist (the "ought" implies a "can"). He links freedom to practical reason: in its positive form, freedom is the ability to recognize and act in obedience to the moral law. Freedom is not just being free from something, but being respon-sible to the world through our free acceptance of the moral law. Freedom is required if the self is to be accountable, and accountability underscores the fact that we are in the world to be responsible. In other words, the mandate for freedom does not come from our psychological and mental needs, but from the agenda that we receive from the world. Thus there are varied dimensions expressing the whole phenomenology of existence.

Kant describes freedom, "in its negative aspect, [as] . . . an 'independence of everything empirical'; i.e., the freedom *from* the mechanical necessitation of natural laws."[27] Kant's motive is to guarantee our *complete* freedom by cutting us off from all human, physical, and divine influences so that we can act morally with absolute independence. But he ends up confessing that our freedom is ultimately a mystery that transcends human reason. It is in great part a mystery to Kant because he is unable to overcome his essentially dualistic view of human nature. On one hand, he sees the self as (abstractly) rational, cut off from the empirical world including experiential motives, desires, and impulses; as such, the self concentrates on performing what Kant often describes as joyless duty. On the other hand, he conceives the nature of self as wholly sentient, free from all moral constraints, and concentrated on obtaining maximum sensuous satisfactions.[28] This dualistic conclusion of Kant's view of the self tangles his view of freedom into a Gordian knot: he equates virtue with a happiness that comes from obeying the moral categorical imperative through which the objective reality is appropriated to meet the subjective need.

Frankl's holistic view of the self—mind, body, and spirit—avoids the Kantian dualism of the rational and sentient that results in bifurcation. Although the essential stance of Frankl's meaning analysis agrees with much of the Kantian ethical foundation of freedom and responsibleness and shares the aim of escaping mechanistic necessity, Frankl believes that freedom involves not just being free from something but being free *for* those values that we espouse. While freedom has moral qualities, freedom originates in the noetic dimension of the self, not in a moral absolute. In other words, for Frankl, the ethical is an expression of meaning; meaning is not, as Kant emphasizes, an expression of the ethical.

The noetic, or the noölogical, dimension, which Frankl calls the higher dimension because it is inclusive and encompasses other dimensions of the self, provides a transcendent power that enables us to take a stand against all those forces and circumstances that would reduce our humanity. Frankl points out that our freedom is subject to biological, psychological, and environmental limitations, but if we are not free from the conditions that limit freedom of the self, we are transcendentally free to take a stand toward those conditions. For us an "ought" implies a "can"; and it is important for us to determine, in the light of responsibility, what type of freedom is at stake. In this context, Frankl concentrates on the defiant power of the human spirit that is capable of challenging, through the noetic dimension, limitations imposed on the self. But this power is not to be used in an arbitrary way; linked to meaning, freedom must be lived in terms of responsibleness.

Kant's emphasis on accountability and Frankl's emphasis on responsibleness show how each man views the nature of freedom. We are truly free, according to Kant's view, when we choose to be accountable to the moral law or, more precisely, to the moral categorical imperative. Kant gives two formulations of this imperative: *"Act only on that maxim through which you can at the same time will that it should become a universal law"* and *"Act as if the maxim of your action were to become through your will a Universal Law of Nature."*[29] Our accountability to the moral categorical imperative validates the nature and extent of our freedom.

The closest that Frankl comes to Kantian thoughts of accountability is in his discussion of what he calls the demand quality of meaning; that is, both meanings of the moment and ultimate meanings make demands upon us. Frankl speaks of demands as having an expectation quality. Demands placed on us by values should be seen as meanings to be fulfilled more than as duties to be performed. Although Frankl speaks of the moral categorical imperative of logo-therapy, he is not speaking of a categorical obedience to moral law, as outlined by Kant, but as an existential response to *logos,* the word of meaning. Frankl's categorical imperative advises us to *"live as if you were living for the second time and had acted as wrongly the first time as you are about to act now."*[30] Frankl's framework of meaning, which utilizes time in a new way and links freedom to responsibleness, replaces the Kantian strictures of moral law with spiritual qualities of the self, dimensions that transform the relationship between ethics and religion.

Morality, Psychotherapy, and Religion

The relation of morality to religion is an important issue in the philosophy of both Kant and Frankl. As might be expected, the issue receives more analysis from the 18th-century pietistic Christian than from the 20th-century psycho-logically oriented Jew.

Kant's discussion is contained in his celebrated and controversial book *Religion within the Limits of Reason (Religion Innerhalb der Grenzen der Blossen Vernunft).* Written in 1793, when he was 70, it placed Kant in what has been described as a curious position.[31] Kant defends the freedom of each person to judge events for himself or herself on one hand, and stresses the need for obedience to authority (including the church in religious matters) on the other. It is an anomaly that while he varied greatly in his philosophical opinions during his life, his understanding of Christianity remained unchanged from the Protestant pietism in which he had been nurtured. Possibly to his surprise, his stance caused him to be severely criticized by the Prussian state and earned him a letter of displeasure from the king himself. The criticism of the state was leveled at Kant because he had left a loophole in his argument for obeying authority. He noted that while as a cleric a person is bound to orthodox authority, as a student a person remains free to criticize openly and freely. Kant, the son of the En-lightenment, triumphed over Kant, the son of the church. As a result, the king was not amused, and Kant, as a good son of the State, pledged to the king that he would "entirely refrain from all public statements on religion, both natural and revealed, either in lectures or writings."[32] Kant kept his promise until the king's death in 1797 and then published his complete views on religion.

Frankl's basic statement on psychotherapy and religion is found in his book *Der unbewusste Gott.* It was written in 1948, following his release from the Nazi concentration camps and after he had reestablished his psychiatric work in Vienna. The material for the book came from a series of talks that he had given to a small group of Viennese intellectuals after World War II. He authorized the English edition in 1975, which appeared under the misleading title *The Unconscious God. (The God of the Unconscious* would have been the appro-priate title.) In the English edition, Frankl added to the original chapters—which deal with existential analysis, the nature of conscience, and fundamental premises concerning the relation of psychotherapy and religion—a discussion of new research on meaning analysis and noted in the preface that further discussions of the interrelation of psychotherapy and religion are to be found in his books *Psychotherapy and Existentialism* (1968) and *The Will to Meaning* (1969).

While Kant approaches the nature of ethics and religion from a scholarly, philosophical viewpoint, Frankl's psychological analysis combines insights of contemporary existentialism and phenomenology with the rationale of classical humanism to describe ethically sensitized religious consciousness focused on meaning. As a result, Frankl appreciates and uses the Kantian ethical dimension without either falling into the dualism between reason and experience or retreating into the pietism that reduces Kant's concept of the self.

A prime example of how Frankl transmutes Kant is his use of the Enlightenment's appreciation of rationality without making it the *summum bonum* of the self. For Frankl, rationality remains a tool for understanding the nature of *humanitas* along with experience and emotional maturity. Therefore, reason is a vital dimension of the holistic self in the maturing process that leads to meaning. But the rational does not stand alone. It must be balanced by the somatic and emotional aspects of the self; it must be empowered and—at the same time—transcended by the noetic dimension. In other words, the *Aufklärung's* uneasy alliance of the rational and the pietistic is replaced by Frankl with reason empowered and expanded by the noetic dimension, thus enlarging the scope of human freedom and moral responsibility. Kant's pietism reduces morality to religious conformity. In contrast, Frankl's sense of the noös expands morality to a spiritual dimension that transcends religious customs and doctrines.

Part of Kant's problem in coming to grips with the dimension of human experience is his insistence that duty—for him, the core of the moral self—must be deontological. This leads to his belief that true moral duty can be recognized and will be acted upon in obedience to the moral categorical imperative, which in turn causes good will and the realization of the human hope for happiness. Frankl is, at the same time, more realistic and more pragmatic than Kant. For Frankl, happiness can never be guaranteed either by therapy (as in Freud's teaching) or by a religion of duty (as in Kant's teaching). The person seeking happiness is frustrated by the pursuit of happiness itself. The same can be said about duty. Duty for duty's sake—that is, without meaning—is hollow and self-defeating. Happiness can ensue from living out the self-transcendence of human existence: "Once one has served a cause or is involved in loving another being, happiness occurs by itself."[33] The same is true of duty. When the meaning of duty is clear, then the person exercises the will to meaning and duty ensues. The more a person concentrates only on duty, the more such a person misses his or her goal. The doing of duty is impaired to the extent to which it is made either the object of attention or an objective of intention. Frankl calls the first hyperreflection and the second hyperintention. This can be seen both on a personal and on a mass level. He points out that a preoccupation with success (whether it is sexual or ethical) causes preoccupations and apprehensions that bring about precisely that which the person fears. Just as sex is more than mere sex, duty is more than mere duty. Moral thought and behavior depend on the meanings that are behind them. Frankl's existential concept of meaning is an essential corrective to the Kantian moral dimension.

Frankl believes that "meanings refer to unique situations—and the equally unique persons confronting them."[34] While values may be seen and shared universally, meanings are unique and must be seen and appropriated individually. He defines values as "meaning-universals," pointing out that they are subject to cultural changes: "Traditions and values are crumbling. But meanings are not—cannot be—transmitted by traditions because in contrast to values, which are universal, meanings are unique. As such they are transmitted, mediated to one's consciousness, by personal conscience."[35] Where Kant sees complete surety, Frankl sees risk. Frankl says we can never be sure that we are receiving or transmitting the right meaning or—as a result—doing the right duty. He quotes appreciatively Gordon W. Allport's reflection that "we can be at one and the same time half-sure and whole-hearted."[36]

Kant's last words on religion, published after the death of King Frederick II, concentrate on such concepts as moral consciousness, the supreme principle of morality, the good (or dutiful) will, and the kingdom of ends. Although he speaks of reverence to God and service to God, such duty is seen only through obedience to the moral law. Yet he also admits to a divine presence. He believes that the moral law is the one valid path to faith in God, a law that reminds us "that in all our duties we regard God as the universal legislator who is to be reverenced."[37] As a result, Kant's interpretation of religion, including his understanding of God, is essentially reduced to a moralistic and rationalistic level. This is a situation that Frankl is determined to avoid in relating meaning analysis to religion.

Frankl's discussion of the goals, or aims, of psychotherapy and the goals of religion is crucial for understanding the differences between these approaches to the self. While both psychotherapy and religion are concerned, in different ways, with reconciliation and consolation, the aim of psychotherapy is to foster health whereas the aim of religion is to help the person to achieve salvation. Frankl points out that though the aims are dissimilar, what happens in each case may be the same:

> Although religion may not aim at mental health it might result in it. Psychotherapy, in turn, often results in an analogous by-product; while the doctor is not, and must not be, concerned with the patient to regain his belief in God, time and again this is just what occurs, unintended and unexpected as it is.[38]

It may be more a matter of faith than belief. "The more weakly one stands on the ground of his belief, the more he clings with both hands to the dogma which separates it from other beliefs; on the other hand, the more firmly one stands on the ground of his faith, the more he has both hands free to reach out to those of his fellowmen who cannot share his belief."[39] In this sense Frankl is a man of faith. His commitment to unconditioned meaning is an act of faith, though he denies this and calls it an intuition or, more accurately, the intuitive conscience. Further, his will to meaning expresses faith that there is a meaning to life. His therapeutic methods are built on the premises of faith—the faith that we as humans are able to dereflect and to self-transcend. Although the goals of meaning analysis are different from those of religion, both emphasize that the realities of life cause us to take a stand and to make choices that will either add to or detract from our wholeness.

Kant's sense of the moral core as the distinguishing mark of our humanness remains a vital aspect of the levels of meaning described by Frankl: (1) a work worth doing, (2) an encounter with another person that shows caring, and (3) a sense of unconditioned meaning. Frankl assures us that our faith in or intuition of ultimate meaning enables us to face the tragic triad (guilt, suffering, and death) and to turn tragedy into triumph. This comes about through what Frankl calls the higher dimension. This higher, or all-inclusive, meaning encompasses what he calls a metameaning, his operational definition of God as the partner in one's most intimate soliloquies. Frankl is correct in pointing out that such a definition escapes the dichotomy between an atheistic and theistic world view. At first glance, Frankl appears neutral, stressing the need for utmost sincerity and honesty in such soliloquies, but then he concludes, "If God really exists he is certainly not going to argue with the irreligious persons because they mistake him for their own selves and misname him."[40] Certainly Frankl did not make this mistake as he said the Shema ("Hear, O Israel. The Lord our God is One.") in the concentration camps. Frankl's understanding of religion and morality centers on the way each of us uses our intuitive conscience to "sniff out" the meaning in each situation and on what decisions we make regarding our freedom and responsibleness. How we relate the facts of our unique existence to the promise of ultimate meaning is a continual challenge and the supreme test of the dimensions of our humanity.

Karl Jaspers says that there are two kinds of Kantians, "those who settle forever in the framework of his categories, and those who, after reflecting, continue on the way with Kant."[41] Frankl is one of the latter. Like Kant, he constructs a philosophy that emphasizes practical reason. Like Kant, he moves from metaphysics to epistemology and from epistemology to ethics, stressing the self primarily as a value bearer. Like Kant, he wrestles with the relation of value bearing to religion, Frankl, however, goes beyond the Kantian emphasis on ultimate duty (the moral categorical imperative) to ultimate meaning, the full realization of the noetic dimension of the self. One of the perspectives that he develops in his search for meaning is through phenomenology, a philosophical approach noted by Kant but not developed in its existential form until the latter part of the 19th century by Edmund Husserl, Max Scheler, and Martin Heidegger.

— 4 —

Pragmatism Redux: The Humanism of James and Frankl

PRAGMATISM UNSTIFFENS ALL OUR THEORIES, LIM-
BERS THEM UP, AND SETS EACH ONE AT WORK.
—WILLIAM JAMES

At first glance, linking the Boston Brahmin William James (1842–1910) with the Viennese psychiatrist Viktor Frankl may appear incongruous. But a closer look shows that despite differences of nationality, temperament, religion, and time, James and Frankl are bound together by a humanistic philosophy of life that is vital, holistic, and relevant to the needs of the self. The key to this partnership is pragmatism.

Definition and Evolution of Pragmatism

The word *pragmatism* was coined by the American logician Charles Sanders Peirce (1839–1914) from the Greek *pragma*, or deed, to describe a means by which persons might examine, logically and practically, the truthfulness of their ideas. To find out the true meaning of an idea, he taught, we should think about its practical consequences by testing it publicly. James agrees with Peirce that the criterion for truth begins with the individual and that a truthful idea is validated through its practical consequences, but whereas Peirce relies essentially on the testing of truth by scientific method, James relies primarily on testing through moral human experience. As Barbara MacKinnon summarizes it:

> James's pragmatic theory of truth simply put is this—the instrumental truth of an idea is its ability to carry or be of use to us. And how is it of use to us? First of all we consider true whatever will best handle (explain) new experience without too much disruption of old beliefs. Since we need to account for new experience, our old truths need continuously to be revised. Secondly, James suggests that the theory is good and can be held true that will best predict future experiences. Thirdly, he says that the theory is true

that best harmonizes with other experiences and beliefs. Finally, keeping in mind his "will to believe," he also argues that whatever belief leads to a better and more fulfilling life is or can be held as true.[1]

Pragmatism, as practiced by James and Frankl, is a method of discovering what is of value in every human circumstance. It uses the resources of medicine, psychology, philosophy, and religion to help persons evaluate and act on the values that make up their views of life in the world. It is descriptive, not prescriptive. An important clue to understanding pragmatism as defined by James and revised by Frankl is supplied by the observation that a spirit of American philosophy, especially in the case of James, "does not permit the definition of specific programs, but it requires that a mirror be held up before ourselves so that we may see better who we are and who we might be."[2] Frankl, like James, holds up such a mirror and, like James, anchors the mirror in a humanism that involves all of the self. Humanism realizes that it is impossible to remove the human element from even our most abstract ideas; thus to an unascertainable extent our truths are products of the self.[3]

Whether the humanism shared by James and Frankl is labeled pragmatism or radical empiricism, it is a direct outgrowth of their holistic philosophy of life. James and Frankl seek to explore as fully as possible the ethical, psychological, and spiritual dimensions of the self. Both oppose any reductionism in thought or action that would diminish the person. Their radical empiricism enlarges the British formulation of empiricism so that experience has a position equal to logic; the self is understood as becoming as well as being, and the role of reason balances empirically based conclusions.

Commonality in James's and Frankl's Outlooks

The intellectual heritages, interests, and training of James and Frankl are strikingly similar. The James family was oriented as much toward Europe as toward the United States. This was largely due to the wealth, intellectual curiosity, and eccentricity of Henry James, Sr., William's father, who insisted that his family share his enchantment with European life and culture. William James's year of study in Europe when he was 25 deepened his knowledge of German science and philosophy, but his response to the latter was not always positive. At that time, he wrote of Kuno Fisher's essay on the German idealist Gotthold Ephraim Lessing's *nathan der Weise*, "The way these cusses slip so fluently off into the 'Ideal,' the '*Jenseitige*,' the 'Inner', . . . you never saw such a mania for going deep into the bowels of truth, with such an absolute lack of intuition and perception of the skin thereof."[4]

James's and Frankl's professional training followed like paths: medicine, psychology, and philosophy. They are both, by inclination and training, men whose understanding of the nature and practices of the self is centered in classical Western humanism.

A measure of the attractiveness of both James's and Frankl's humanism can be traced to the fact that their philosophies of life were tested by personal crises. James's emotional crises were essentially internal and occurred at various periods from his late 20s to his late 50s. He shared them only in his letters to his family, in his private journals, and "in the disguised 'case history' which he later published in his *Varieties of Religious Experience.*"[5] In contrast to those of James, Frankl's crises were basically external, caused by his persecution by the Nazis, including imprisonment in four concentration camps, and the extermination of all but one other member of his family. His description of his crises has become familiar to millions through his autobiographical book *Man's Search for Meaning.* James and Frankl both see their respective crises as periods of testing of their philosophies of life. James felt that his crises strengthened what he calls the will to believe. He writes that he experienced a moment when he became aware that "there comes a point when one must perform an act of thought and decide where to place one's belief."[6] Instead of the will to believe, Frankl describes the existential moment of choice as the exercise of the defiant power of the human spirit. He stresses that this defiant spirit is the *core* of the human; it is what makes a person fully human. James, in his life if not by his words, agrees.

James's and Frankl's interweaving of their thoughts with the events of their lives reveals three attitudes that are key to understanding their pragmatism: (1) an understanding of a need for a *Lebenswelt* that integrates medicine, psychology, and philosophy; (2) a strong humanitarian concern; and (3) a conviction that they are pioneers in humanistic psychology. The humanitarianism shared by James and Frankl is the logical response of each man's *Lebenswelt.* As they see it, humanitarianism places on a person the sole moral obligation to work for the improved welfare of humanity, including the alleviation of its suffering. In turn, this humanitarian understanding is based on the essential humanism shared by both men.

For James, an adequate *Lebenswelt* must deal with those whom he calls tough-minded and tender-minded. In his book *Pragmatism,* he lists and compares the characteristics of each. The tough-minded empiricist goes by facts; such a person is sensationalistic, materialistic, pessimistic, irreligious, fatalistic, pluralistic, and skeptical. In contrast, the tender-minded person goes by principles; such a person is rationalistic, intellectualistic, idealistic, optimistic, religious, free-willed, monistic, and dogmatic.[7] As James sagely observes, "Most of us have a hankering for the good things on both sides."[8] Meaning analysis recognizes both sides of James's characterizations but affirms that a person should refuse to be categorized as, or reduced to being, either tough-minded or tender-minded.

A *Lebenswelt* does not depend on a special or exceptional revelation. As an example, according to John E. Smith, "For Peirce all reflective thought starts with commonsense and begins not with some privileged idea or perception but rather, as he said, '*in medias res.*' This means that everyone begins where he actually is and attempts to clarify the contents of a stock of beliefs already in hand."[9] Peirce provides the pragmatic starting place for James and Frankl.

James and Frankl—each in his own way—help us to clarify our stock of beliefs by insisting that we examine our attitudes in the midst of living. James observes that truth is "an attribute of beliefs which are attitudes that follow satisfactions."[10] The word *satisfaction* acknowledges that a proposed solution to a problem may be workable without having to be perfect. Thus the quest for a *Lebenswelt* that brings satisfaction is not and should not be a search for perfection but rather a quest for a life of meaning, which may include regenerative change. A turning of the self, or *metanoia,* toward those qualities that make life whole brings satisfaction. This is the mark of the healthy-minded, and the goal of both James's and Frankl's humanistic psychology. James speaks of the "sick soul" when the self becomes dysfunctional. Frankl speaks of a noögenic neurosis that prevents the self from calling on the resources of the noetic dimension to achieve wholeness. In both James and Frankl, the agent of change is the defiant power of the human spirit.

Bernard Brennan describes the James family as outsiders to Boston society. He writes of William James that "although he shone brilliantly in the best New England circles . . . he remained an Irishman among the Brahmins."[11] This is only partially true. While James did reflect a Scotch-Irish temperament, siding with the Irish and the Boers against the English, he was an accepted member of the Boston Brahmin society. Brennan appears to forget that the James family was Protestant Scotch-Irish, readily acceptable to the Brahmins, and not Roman Catholic Irish, like those immigrants who were so virulently resisted at every level of Boston society. What is of equal importance is that the Scotch-Irish immigrant lad William James (James's grandfather), who came to the United States in 1789, became "the wealthiest man in the state of New York except for John Jacob Astor."[12] Thus his grandson Henry James, Jr., writes of his own life and of his brother William's that "the rupture with my grandfather's tradition [of making money] was complete; we were never, in a single case . . . for two generations, guilty of a stroke of 'business.' "[13] R. W. B. Lewis points out that what the descendants of William James did "was to displace the language and the motifs of the money world into other realms of discourse, into theology, philosophy, psychology, literature; and to entangle them with other urgencies of experience."[14]

Viktor Frankl's background was significantly different from William James's. If Boston was a Brahmin stronghold, Vienna was a bastion of Roman Catholic aristocracy. Vienna's anti-Semitism, still evident today, was a more virulent and lasting form of bigotry than was the Yankee intolerance of the Irish in Boston. Although James saw and disagreed with Boston's anti-Irish and anti-Catholic prejudices, he was far from being a target. Frankl, in contrast, was a member of a group targeted for verbal, mental, and physical abuse in the Austrian capital, all of which culminated during the German takeover of Austria when he was 33 years old. Although his father was a court stenographer, a position well respected in the legal milieu of the time, and young Viktor was allowed to take advantage of the educational opportunities of Vienna, anti-Semitism was a constant factor of Frankl's life in Vienna. Yet despite differences in generation, religion, and nation, James and Frankl share a humanitarianism with the same four qualities: sensitivity to the sufferings of others; friendships that cross social and intellectual boundaries; a concern for the victimization of others; and opposition to all that dehumanizes the self.

In his discussion of James's "having the sufferer's sensitiveness to the suffering of others," the biographer Ralph Barton Perry notes: "The presence in James of an irrational compassionateness to which both his ideas and his practice had to accommodate themselves is exemplified by his total inability to drop a case of distress from his mind when once it had been brought to his attention."[15] Without the same hint of compulsiveness that Perry notes in James, Frankl also reaches out whenever he senses that a person may be in distress. For example, when lecturing at Bradley University, Peoria, Illinois, in 1968, he was asked by the Bradley television station if he would be willing to provide a taped interview. Wearied from travel, he at first said no. Then he reconsidered and said yes because there might be people in the audience who had not read his book *Man's Search for Meaning,* who might be thinking of suicide, and who might be prevented from ending their lives if they could hear what he had to say.[16]

James and Frankl oppose the evil that brings about the victimization of others, and neither avoids risk or pain to do so. Ralph Barton Perry reports that "in his day, James was recognized as a worker for human decency and civil rights. He was an internationalist, a pacifist, and a true liberal. He battled against what he called the ambitious and blind passion of the crowd."[17] Admittedly, James acted from an enlightened elitist position, using his intellectual and social influence to bring about change. Frankl, inspired by the socially minded Alfred Adler, fought against the same civic injustices. As a young Jewish socialist, he identified with the disenfranchised working-class boys by establishing youth clubs; and since his concentration camp experiences, he has had a special concern for helping prisoners to find meaning.

James focused on the need for a general understanding of mental hygiene. He worked for a program that would educate public opinion in the treatment of mental illness. In 1909, just a year before his death, he helped to found the National Committee for Mental Health. In that same year, he explains in a letter to John D. Rockefeller why he supports more enlightened treatments of mental diseases:

> During my life as a "psychologist" I have had much to do with our asylums, and I have had so painfully borne in upon me the massiveness of human evil which the term "insanity" covers, and the inadequacy of our arrangements for coping with it, that I long ago registered a vow that if I myself, by Heaven's grace should ever be able to leave any money for public use it should be for "insanity" exclusively.[18]

Frankl's medical ministry is a continuation of James's campaign to inform people about psychological problems and to bring about change in the treatment of those suffering from mental problems. Frankl's most original contribution is in helping people to recognize and treat those who are victims of noögenic neuroses, conditions that were essentially dismissed or ignored until he brought them to light.

One of the strengths James and Frankl have in common is their being more questioners of life than answer-givers. They ask the essential questions of Being, to help people get a hold on life. Their psychiatric and philosophical training enables them to be pioneers in philosophical psychology as they probe the nature of the self in relation to metaphysics, epistemology, ethics, and religion. Frankl reminds us that biology leads to psychology, psychology to philosophy, and philosophy to theology.

The Metaphysical Dimension in James and Frankl

James and Frankl have each been criticized for failing to provide a viable metaphysics for their philosophies. If "a viable metaphysics" means a *system* of metaphysics, the criticism is justified. If, however, "a viable metaphysics" means a metaphysical *dimension,* the critics have erred. James and Frankl intentionally avoid constructing a system of metaphysics, believing that a system would restrict an open search for human identity; instead, they describe a metaphysical dimension as an important factor of their views of life. Their emphases, however, differ: James stresses a metaphysical dimension of *morality;* Frankl underscores a metaphysical dimension of *meaning.* Yet neither James nor Frankl is satisfied with mere morality—that is, acting upon what is accepted as moral. For both men, true metaphysics and morality are the highest expressions of what it means to be human. They are all pervasive. Metaphysics is, according to James, an expression of the entire personality and a zest for life.[19]

At issue is whether their metaphysical approaches can be related to experience. We find that at first our experiences are clear-cut; but when we reflect on them and relate them to the question of Being, uncertainties, paradoxes, and disappointments develop. When we think about what has happened, we start a process of labeling, which establishes categories that prevent a holistic view. Despite our failure to achieve a unity of thought and action, we can still have what can be described as a philosophy of hope. James's metaphysics of hope combines Henri Bergson's (1859–1941) logical principle of continuity (synechism) with Peirce's idea that things arise by chance (tychism), so that "we can help to ameliorate the problems in our universe and that, as plural powers, we can make a difference in promoting good and retarding evil."[20]

As Dooley points out, James's metaphysical reasoning is that "man is responsible for his behavior for he can control his thoughts which in turn control his actions; therefore, man is free."[21] James underscores three conditions that must be met by any adequate philosophy of hope:

1. The ultimate principle must not be one that essentially baffles and disappoints our dearest desires and most cherished hopes.
2. We do not desire that our powers be stimulated, but that our choices and actions be relevant.
3. Our practical nature demands that philosophy banish uncertainty from the future by providing an appropriate guide for action.[22]

The working hypothesis of James's and Frankl's metaphysical humanism is an *agapé*-based, experiential understanding of the self. As Frankl observes, recalling an intense moment in his existence as a death camp inmate, "I grasped the meaning of the greatest secret that human poetry and human thought and belief have to impart: *The salvation of man is through love and in love.*"[23] For James and Frankl, love is the evidence of what it means to be truly human in our interaction with one another. All truths, including love, symbolize a pragmatic metaphysics, which, as James believes, "must be cashed in a human experience which is surprising and replenishing when brought within the focus of reflective awareness."[24] Frankl's metaphysics, like James's, is humanistically grounded, value-oriented, and pragmatically tested with the aim of promoting an experience of Being that James calls healthy-minded. Such a metaphysics requires flexibility, not systematization. Such a metaphysics is open to the future as part of a world-in-the-making. It is a metaphysics that explores the nature of Being, shows us how we as individuals help the process of society, and makes us alert to structures of meaning that will help us to complete freedom with responsibleness.

James is essentially a poet of metaphysics, not a pundit. At one time, he writes, he abandoned the idea of wanting to expand his thoughts on metaphysics because of what he describes as his intellectual higgledy-piggledyism.[25] He wanted to avoid any metaphysical formula that would separate him from the sense that "our own reality, that sense of our own life which we at every moment possess, is the ultimate of ultimates for our belief."[26] Frankl's metaphysical task is the same: to determine meaning in the light of belief-full experience. He focuses on the interaction of mind, body, and spirit (noös) while maintaining what James calls the fluency of human thought and action.

James also uses the idea of the noös, or the noetic dimension, but he never defines it. He sees it only as a valuable yet variable human resource. In contrast, Frankl defines the noetic dimension as the key and a permanent quality of the self: it is a dimension of the self, not just a part. As Joseph B. Fabry explains, "Just as we have a length, breadth, and height that are inseparable, so our body, psyche, and spirit are three inseparable dimensions. If one is disregarded, we do not get a full human being but a shadow, a two-dimensional projection."[27] Frankl's intuitive and pragmatic concept of the self escapes the metaphysical dualism of Plato and avoids James's excursions into psychic research.

James's and Frankl's Theory of Knowledge

The effect of this metaphysical holistic model is illustrated by James's and Frankl's theory of knowledge. Their epistemology affirms life despite the doubts, pain, ambiguities, and paradoxes of existence. It reflects a meliorism that recognizes and encourages human initiative. It also avoids the extremes of pessimism and untested optimism. Yet it gives no guarantees but sees wholeness only as a possibility that requires constant human striving if it is to be realized. Frankl calls this striving the will to meaning. The will is the impetus for the search for meaning, the primary motivation of the self. It is also intensely personal, for meaning is not general but specific and unique. The will to meaning demands that each person determine the shape of his or her own life, including its goals. But a will to meaning does not stand alone. True meaning also requires intelligence and what James calls an intuitive sympathy, a way of relating to others by looking beyond their words and gestures to try to understand who they really are. A person must look behind the masks of others because what is real is often obscured by appearances. Frankl says that we must learn to pick up clues, to "sniff out" the facts, using what he calls an intuitive conscience. We should also pick out persons to serve as models for us of what Being truly means. James uses heroic figures, or persons who change history, as prime examples of the dimensions of the human, though he also refers to the man in the street. He cautions, however, that sentimentalization of the latter may lead to not seeing the person with a realistic eye.[28] (Frankl's trust in the man in the street comes close to the sentimentalization about which James warns.)

While James's and Frankl's meliorism guards against any automatic optimistic outcome of life, their epistemology is essentially teleologically positive. But they achieve a positive view only after wrestling with the negative aspects of the self. James believes that our condition is always the same, unaffected by either situation or time. Thus progress goes on unimpeded and unaided. His view of day-to-day existence reflects a personal optimism that "requires the ability both to relax and to remain energized," and his "ethics of optimism" combines psychology and philosophy to achieve a life of action.[29] Frankl transmutes and refocuses James's pragmatic optimism through what he calls tragic optimism.[30] Tragic optimism deals with pain, guilt, and death. Tragic optimism enables persons to turn suffering into a human achievement and accomplishment; to use guilt as an opportunity to change themselves for the better; to see life's transitoriness as an incentive to take responsible action. This involves seeing life from serious perspectives. Frankl calls it dimensional ontology.

Dimensional ontology changes our focus from the neural and mental aspects of self, emphasized by James, to the noölogical, or noetic, dimension. In so doing, the self is enabled to transcend its psychophysical condition by an existential act of the will to enter a new (noölogical) dimension of freedom and responsibleness. The resulting images and projections that we make enable us, on the one hand, to grasp our wholeness and unity and, on the other hand, to see the discrepancies among our bodily, psychic, and mental processes but still have a sense of meaning. Frankl's existential approach parallels James's life view. Both affirm that life is not basically mental, because life takes place within set time frames, and that what we experience in life is what life essentially is.

James focuses on time as the construct for temporal consciousness in which the "cash value" of human experience takes place. He speaks of the specious present, recognizing that we do not exist only in the present, but that we are also aware of the past and look toward the future. Although he views the specious present as duration, not just as a series of temporal events, James says little about the perception of the passage of time. In contrast, Frankl believes that how we *perceive* time is essential in the search for meaning. Frankl's existential analysis uses time as an important agent in how we think of freedom and responsibleness. We are limited and yet we are also unique. Time reminds us that we must act within set limits; it demands that we set priorities in life. Temporality reminds us that human existence has an irreversible quality. We must constantly decide what we consider meaningful and what we do not. Frankl uses a striking parable to illustrate the self and time:

> For man resembles a sculptor who chisels and hammers the unshaped stone so that the material takes on more and more form. Man works the matter with which fate has supplied him: now creating, now experiencing or suffering, he attempts to "hammer out" values in life—as many as he can of creative or experiential or attitudinal values.
>
> We can also introduce the factor of time into this simile of the sculptor: We need only imagine that the sculptor has a limited span of time at his disposal for completing his work of art—but that he is not informed when his deadline is. Thus he never knows when he is going to be "called away," whether the summons may not come in the very next minute. He is therefore forced to use his time well in any case—lest his work remain abortive.[31]

Frankl concludes, "That time runs out before the work is completed by no means makes it worthless, however."[32] Death reminds us that we must *finish* something in the time allotted to us; the end is part of the bargain of life.[33]

James wants to believe in life after death, but he does not construct a theory about it. Frankl sees death as an organic part of life itself. If life has a meaning, it doesn't matter whether life is long or short; its quality is what is essential. Length will not compensate for lack of quality or purpose. If we decide that life has meaning, then it is crucial how and why we make judgments. James uses Peirce's phenomenological terminology to construct what Henry Samuel Levinson describes as a three-level process for making judgments: the first level sets the self questions, the second level uses commonsense traditions, and the third level assimilates the traditions and gives answers, congruent with our needs, to the questions asked by pure experience.[34] Levinson points out that James thought that this description secured a metaphysics without ontology.[35]

But James's position is essentially an epistemological approach rather than an explanation of the nature of Being. He believes that a sense of reality can be achieved through questioning that examines all truths and tests them by experience, not just by theory. To a large extent Frankl agrees.

Frankl's understanding of knowledge shares five elements that were first proposed by James: (1) reality emerges out of an essential search for intelligibility (meaning); (2) truths are essentially presumptive and need to be validated by life's experiences; (3) traditions need to be critically evaluated; (4) some traditions may be accepted, some rejected, and still others transmuted before they can be used; and (5) the final test of all knowledge is how it is put to use in actions that express freedom and responsibleness. James has been accused, by Josiah Royce and others, of circular reasoning. The same criticism can be made of Frankl. Whether or not their epistemological reasoning is arguably circular, their reasoning is *propitiously* circular in helping us to relate what we know to a life of meaning: (1) it explains that what is called reality or truth is made up of a plurality of independent factors that enable humans to have what Frankl calls dimensional ontology; (2) it affirms that the majority of persons are essentially normally active and wish to pursue healthy lives; (3) it recognizes that persons live in communities that share values and goals; and (4) it views the natural world as generically orderable, despite evidences of corruption and brutality.

Neither James nor Frankl desires or attempts to furnish a complete theory of knowledge. To do so would betray the pluralistic form of their radical empiricism. Instead, they supply a fully thought-out rationale. Their rationale (1) affirms the intelligent use of reason and experience; (2) underscores how the noetic dimension bridges the gulf between God and the world; (3) avoids homeostasis by affirming that the self is both being and becoming; (4) recognizes the interaction between intuition and will; (5) insists that ideas and experience are validated by praxis; (6) links freedom to responsibleness; (7) shows that meaning in life is expressed daily by the self in a variety of ways and situations.

James and Frankl agree that there are two dangers in attempting to relate knowledge to life: the first is intellectualizing apart from experience, and the second is separating experience from serious reflection. When we consider the relation of thought to action, we can see the difference between actual and virtual knowledge. James points out that we know things *virtually* before they are tested by our own experience and by the observations of others. Essentially, he acknowledges an extracognitive source of knowledge. In so doing, he is anticipating the existentialist, psychoanalytical, and contemporary aesthetic forms of epistemology.[36] Frankl, a student of the existential psychoanalytical tradition, locates this extracognitive source in the noös. James relates meaning to the relational or transitional states of consciousness so that meanings become functions of a variety of occurrences that take place in what he calls consciousness.[37] Frankl, by connecting meaning with the noös, sees meaning at the *center* of human consciousness and not at the edge. In so doing, Frankl under-scores and enlarges James's description of our uniqueness because we are value bearers. James is correct in believing that consciousness is in some ways a condition for the existence of moral values, but he never finds a compelling reason for the moral search.[38] In contrast, Frankl does find a compelling reason: the search for meaning. The noös provides a will to meaning that involves answering the questions Why be moral? and Why go on living? The existen-tialist philosopher Karl Jaspers sees the world as a "manuscript written in a code we have to decipher," but Frankl believes that "the world is rather a record that we must dictate."[39] This record comes about only after we answer, time and time again, the questions that life addresses to us; and after we respond, we must accept responsibility for our answers.

James and Frankl see time and eternity involved in our daily decisions. To put it another way, how we decide the question of meaning *today* affects our perceptions of what happened in the past and how we look forward to what may happen in the future. Frankl believes that everything is stored in the past forever.[40] Each person is responsible for deciding which memories from the past should be relived in the present and used in the future. The events that are so chosen reflect what Frankl calls the optimism of the past as well as the *activism* of the future.

We can be passive regarding time or we can be active agents in time; and this depends on how we are ourselves, how we look at others, and how we view the world in which we live. Our motives determine the values and stand-ards we accept or reject. James rejects the pain-and-pleasure motivation theory of the self held by Sigmund Freud:

> It seems as if we ought to look for the secret of an idea's impulsiveness, not in any particular relations which it may have with motor discharge—for *all* ideas have relations with some such paths—but rather in a preliminary phenomenon, the *urgency, namely, with which it is able to compel atten-tion and dominate in consciousness.*[41]

Frankl agrees. He calls such an approach attitudinal modulation. To help a person change from neurotic or sick motivations to healthy ones is a central emphasis of psychological pragmatism.

James gives an example of attitudinal modulation in a story from his student days. He tells of a student who threw himself from a window of one of the college buildings and was almost killed. Another student, a friend of James, passed the window daily and experienced a strong temptation to imitate the other young man's action. Being a Roman Catholic, the student told his spiritual director, who responded, "All right! If you must, you must," adding, "Go ahead and do it." This reaction stopped the student instantly. As James remarks, "This director knew how to minister to a mind diseased."[42] Frankl calls the technique that the director used paradoxical intention (translating an irrational fear into an irrational wish). Of course the counselor knew the young man well enough to exaggerate what the student feared so that the young man would affirm what he really believed. James points out that what we really believe is what is real. James describes this as the will to believe; Frankl transmutes this as the will to meaning. Why did James, 30 years later, tell the story of the student tempted to suicide? One reason may be an unconscious identification by James with those who experience, as he had, what is described as panic fear.[43] Panic fear comes from our failure to affirm ourselves in the practical events of daily life. It comes from our inability to make concrete commitments and follow them through. In James's case, his recognition of panic fear in himself resulted in his exercising what he calls the will to believe.[44] Frankl went through the same sensation of panic fear, though his was brought about by his being a concentration camp victim. He also responded by drawing on the defiant power of the human spirit to avoid panic fear and to deal with his suffering.

James's pragmatism does not probe specifically the meaning of suffering, but James's philosophy of the healthy-minded appears to agree with the following statement by Frankl:

> Meaning is available in spite of—nay, even through—suffering, provided ... that the suffering is unavoidable. If it is avoidable, the meaningful thing to do is to remove its cause, for unnecessary suffering is masochistic, rather than heroic. If, on the other hand, one cannot change a situation that causes his suffering, he can still choose his attitude.[45]

Guilt also demands a modulation of attitudes but in ways that differ from those demanded by suffering. James's writing, including his epochal *Principles of Psychology* (1890), never discuss the nature and the impact of human guilt. This is not surprising, because he also ignores the psychology of the unconscious mind, which is the center of much of a person's guilt feelings. Marcus Peter Ford believes that James's strong rejection of unconscious experience comes from James's commitment to the empirical method.[46] Further, James considers psychology an incomplete science because of its lack of a firm metaphysics, which is a curious position for James to take in view of his failure to provide a metaphysical system for his own work. Although James acknowledges Frederic Myers's description of extramarginal feelings, James relegates them to what he calls fringe events. Frankl locates extramarginal feelings in the unconscious.

Frankl's understanding of the unconscious frees the person from the biological-mechanistic strictures set by such psychiatrists as Sigmund Freud. By substituting the noetic dimension for the psychosexual, Frankl enables the self to see the possibilities of freedom and responsibleness. He moves beyond the Freudian instinctual unconsciousness to a consciousness of what it means to be spiritually alive, to be fully human. This requires complementing depth psychology with what he calls height psychology, which enables the self to recognize and act on the moral expectations of life.

If values are mere expressions of the self's inner life (as taught by Freud and Carl Jung), they lose what Frankl identifies as their *demand quality*. He uses ontoanalysis, with its stress on the freedom of the self, as a corrective to psycho-analysis's description of a person as a fully conditioned and wholly predictable object among other objects. In substituting the noetic dimension for the instinc-tual, Frankl insists that we are not egos driven by the id, seeking to manipulate, to deceive, and to demean ourselves and others. Instead, we are spiritually em-powered beings seeking wholeness, true values, and meaning, who can see guilt constructively as well as negatively.

Guilt can be positive when it keeps us from doing something that is clearly wrong. If we have committed an offense, guilt can motivate us to make amends. Guilt is negative when we imagine an offense for which we are not responsible or feel guilty about something over which we have no control. The noetic dimension helps us to examine and distinguish between valid and invalid guilt feelings and helps us to gain a sense of moral balance. Although guilt reminds us of our imperfections and limitations, it is a sign of our humanness and helps us to avoid hubris and to determine what is ethical.

The Ethics of James and Frankl

James and Frankl agree that the philosopher's task is to identify three kinds of ethical inquiry: the psychological (the origin of our moral ideas), the meta-physical (the meaning of moral terms), and the casuistic (the reason we select values). The last, the casuistic, is the most vital in determining the priority of moral obligations. James and Frankl each eschew any moral system as the definitive answer. James feels that "a moral system has no authority and an ethical judgment no truth unless we acknowledge them sharing in the desires and imperatives which are their sources."[47] Otherwise, a system will rob the individual of freedom, including the prerogative to choose. Frankl agrees. Throughout his writings, Frankl emphasizes that human beings are not things among others but basically self-determining spiritual beings, constituted to be free and responsible. Thus we must fight all that would depersonalize us.[48] For if a system or a categorical rule is imposed, reification (depersonalization) results, and we avoid being responsible for our choices.

Frankl agrees with James that "experience is always owned. It belongs to someone, but the nature of this ownership is not easy to determine."[49] Further, it is a shared experience. James writes of the powers of the "conscious body" that affect the world. The meanings that result depend on how and where each person expresses his or her self (in a material, social, or spiritual way).[50] Frankl's meaning analysis substitutes the term *conscious spirit* for the Jamesian descrip-tion *conscious body,* moving the focus of the self from the neurological to the noetic dimension. James believes that selfhood is based on meaning that can vary with the focus of attention. Frankl, in contrast, sees the noetic dimension providing *essential* meanings that are not dependent upon shifts of attention in a given situation. James sees the noetic dimension's relation to the self as transient and ancillary to the ethical task, whereas Frankl assigns the noetic dimension a permanent and central role. The noös is our essential resource for values and their expression. Whether the term *conscious body* or *conscious spirit* is used, James's and Frankl's moral philosophy reflects an expanded radical empiricism.

James and Frankl, each in his own way, break out of the old Kantian categories of pure reason, practical reason, and, even, judgment to introduce a moral, radical empiricism that recognizes and uses intuitive sympathy as the operative factor in human thought and action. The common source for their understanding of intuitive sympathy is Henri Bergson. They accept his view that intellect, properly used, must be related to the flow of experience. Like Bergson, they are realists who see intuitive sympathy as a fundamental expression of the healthy self. In the spirit of Bergson, James writes, "If you put yourself *in the making* by a stroke of intuitive sympathy with the thing, you would realize that reality *falls* in passing into conceptual analysis: it mounts in living its own undivided life—it buds and burgeons, changes and creates."[51] Frankl expands James's conclusions to connect intuitive sympathy with an enlarged view of conscience. He believes that conscience transcends any narrow conception of what is seen as moral to embrace "an intuitive capacity to find out, to 'sniff out,' the unique meaning or *gestalt* inherent in a situation, 'what is meant' in a specific situation."[52] James and Frankl enlarge Bergson's understanding of intuitive sympathy to include moral choices. James highlights choices that are unexpected (the surds of life over the expected). Frankl emphasizes that *all* choices are based on recognition and use of the noölogical dimension, the uniquely human aspect of the self that enables us to use our intuitive conscience as value bearers in the search for meaning.

James and Frankl oppose any reduction of the human dimension to a purely natural world. In his essay "Is Life Worth Living?" James challenges the naturalism of his friend Chauncy Wright. Wright argues that nature is just as it appears; nothing more, nothing less. He has no need to distinguish appearance from reality because he feels that they coincide in the natural order of things. Wright believes that everything that is seen is as it truly is. Nothing is hidden. Everything is in full view. James disagrees. He believes that most things in life *are* hidden. We must look behind appearances to find causes, in nature and especially in human nature.

James's and Frankl's conviction that we must look behind the words and gestures of others, seeking clues that will help us to discover the realities behind the masks, has implications for their moral theory. For them, ethical truth comes only through testing. We need to search out and evaluate what others see as ethically important, which demands empathy on our part as well as intelligence. James identifies this empathy as sympathy. For him, sympathy is not only sensitivity, consideration, tolerance, and responsiveness, but also a sense of exhilaration. Sympathy reflects a sense of life that is a source of optimism.[53]

James's and Frankl's optimism is teleological. It describes a self that can look forward with discernment and hope. James and Frankl differ, however, in regard to the nature of the human condition that lies behind the optimism. James focuses on the psychological inner struggle to be optimistic about one's existence. At the same time, he believes that the human condition is always the same, in any life and in any age. Frankl's optimism is grounded in his existential view that the human condition is *not* always the same and *should not* be so. The noetic dimension empowers the self to find and apply meaning in every situation. Frankl focuses on a conscience that is both creative and intuitive, allowing persons to discover for themselves unique meanings that may contradict accepted values. Conscience is the essential human creative quality that enables the self to avoid conformism and totalitarianism, the two effects of the existential vacuum.[54]

But creativity, Frankl notes, does not equal infallibility. We search for meaning without ever knowing with certainty that our meanings are absolutely true. The imperfect nature of our humanness calls for us to obey our conscience though it may err. Our sense of our own fallibility helps us to have empathy for others when they fail. Frankl links empathy to tolerance. He reminds us that tolerance does not mean either indifference or conformity to another's belief; rather, it involves our acknowledging another person's right to believe and to obey his or her conscience in a complicated world.[55]

Aesthetic and ethical intuitions are often mixed; thus, there is a need for a reasoning process. James and Frankl balance these intuitions with a moral, reasoned, and intuitive conscience. Their radical empiricism appeals to the mind as well as to the heart. Aesthetics is still subservient to rational, ethical decision—in other words, to an act of the will. Frankl defines the core of the will as the will to meaning. James's analysis of the will has three features that are shared by meaning analysis: (1) "The essential achievement of the will . . . is to *attend* to a difficult object and hold it fast before the mind,"[56] (2) "Our wills are free,"[57] and (3) "Where the will is healthy, *the vision must be right*."[58] James avoids the question of the origin of the willed act, but Frankl does not. He locates the origin of the willed act in the noös, the source of human freedom and responsibleness.

Frankl links intuition to intuitive conscience to keep intuition from becoming some mystical fantasy and to avoid reducing conscience to mere moralism. The intuitive conscience has the power to investigate the world of unique possibilities as an instrument of human progress. It has the strength to stand up to authority, law, society, to all outside influences, and to see old truths in a new light. For James, the power of intuition comes at the intersection of consciousness and reality. Like Heraclitus, and later Husserl, James sees consciousness as an ever-moving stream that never has the *same* experience twice.[59]

Although James and Frankl start with Husserl's emphasis on the importance of the flux of experience, James focuses on the nature of the flux itself, whereas Frankl goes beyond it to anchor the self in the noölogical dimension. For Frankl, the noölogical dimension gives the self the power to deal with the ambiguities and contradictions that occur in life's flux and to exercise the uniquely human capacity to rise above oneself and to evaluate one's own moral behavior. But neither James nor Frankl envisions a moral process that reaches perfection. This striving, which Frankl calls the will to meaning, is susceptible to fallibility as well as to certainty. Therefore, the search for a viable ethic should reflect humility as well as courage. We cannot, and should not, *impose* meanings and values on others. Each person is responsible for how he or she thinks and for what he or she does. Each person must wrestle mentally to find how to translate knowledge into responsible behavior.

It has been said of James that his whole philosophy is an ethics. The same can be said of Frankl and for the same reason. They are both what John Wild describes as noetic voluntarists: those who view moral freedom as grounded in the noetic freedom of the mind.[60] While noetic voluntarists are not tied to any system of belief, their thoughts and actions reflect an orderly process. Although the processes of life vary according to each person's disposition and needs, there are five constant hallmarks in noetic voluntarism:

First, life is based on choice or consent. Each person must *choose* which path to take. Life is making decisions regarding the self, whomever and wherever a person may be. Being is truly realized, as Heidegger points out, through *Dasein* (being there). James Edie reminds us that "the first definition of freedom which James accepted (from Renouvier), namely, 'the sustaining of a thought *because* I choose to when I might have other thoughts,' contains in germ the whole of his later theory."[61] This definition is also seminal for Frankl. How a person focuses on what is important determines the self's future thought and action. This is illustrated in logotherapeutic counseling by Dr. Elisabeth Lukas's admonition to her clients not to stand among the flowers and water the weeds.[62]

Second, life is experiential. How a person interprets experience tells whether that person's soul is, in James's terms, a sick one or healthy-minded. James and Frankl see experiential crises as times of testing and, above all, as opportunities for change and growth.

Third, experience and reason are allies in creating and maintaining noetic freedom. We interpret experience. We test as we choose. The wise person selects and selects again. Reason uses the mind to pick out those impressions that will best aid the self to achieve meaning.

Fourth, freedom must be linked to responsibleness. Meaning analysis teaches that we are not only free from something but that we are also free *for* something.

Fifth, exercising freedom demands courage. There is a strong element of the heroic in James's and Frankl's philosophies of the self. This element of the heroic should not, however, be confused with bravado. James, for instance, is aware of the conflicts of the "morbid-minded" and the need for a person to call upon the noetic dimension, as well as intellectual resources, to become healthy-minded.

James's and Frankl's Religious Explorations

James never spells out a therapeutic process for achieving healthy-mindedness as Frankl does in meaning analysis. Instead, James writes about the "More" of life and its relation to "over belief," which we apprehend simply by adjusting our perspective. In so doing, he moves from ethics to the areas of religion and theology. Frankl follows a similar course when he discusses the noetic dimension as ultimate meaning. If pragmatism is a method of discovering what is of value in every situation, it is understandable that James and Frankl should explore ultimate value in terms of theology. Their respective religious explorations result, however, in the least well-defined and most controversial aspects of their philosophies of the self.

James's attempts to explain the linkage of the More to over belief end in a mixture of unfocused mysticism and a form of theism that is questionable at its best. Whereas James believes that we can be moral without being religious, he turns to religion to provide what he calls a *strenuous* mood to be achieved only through the presence of God. He moves from discussing an ethics that meets our daily needs to a focus on an ethics of infinite and mysterious obligation. Such an ethics of obligation results in the infusion of energy, perseverance, and courage, and people so energized can help religion continue to be victorious over irreligion. Despite this ebullient stance, James deliberately makes the connection between ethics and religion vague because, for him, religion is a vague response to a vague human need. James's attempts to deal with religion can be characterized by two battles that he was trying to carry on at the same time: he was opposing the scientific materialism of his age, and he was denying the idealists' description of God as the Absolute or Oversoul. Speaking out of his own desire for a pragmatic faith, he concludes that if one *needs* God's presence then it must be true.

While biographers disagree about the source of James's need to write about religion, his book exploring religious experience and mysticism, *The Varieties of Religious Experience,* written eight years before his death, has been called the most famous of all American treatises on religion. Famous as the book may have become, it did not escape the criticism of George Santayana (1863–1952):

> Seeing James one day after his *Varieties of Religious Experience* had come out, Mr. Santayana crossed the street and said to him with a friendly smile, "You have done the religious slumming for all time." "Really?" answered James genially; "That is all slumming, is it?" "Yes," was the answer, "all." In repeating this James chuckled to himself: "Santayana's white marble mind."[63]

Although James rejects the religious limitations of the "white marble mind," he offers a mystical interpretation of religion that is far removed from his earlier pragmatic reasoning. As Gerald Myers comments, "His philosophy of religion is indeed intriguing, but it is certainly not pragmatic."[64]

James's personal hunger for assurance of the unseen universe turned him from metaphysics, ethics, and religious philosophy to concentration on psychical research. This drew criticism from James's colleague, the idealist Josiah Royce. In 1909, after James had visited the internationally notorious Neapolitan medium Eusapia Paladino, Royce circulated this jingle:

Eeny, meeny, miney mo,
Catch Eusapia by the toe,
And if she hollers then you know
James's theory is not so.[65]

Although James wandered from his essential task—the philosophical interpretation of religion and a description of why it is the most important function of the self—he succeeded in presenting an original mixture of philosophy and religion that remains popular and a source of inspiration for many people. Using the More as a focus, he pioneered making an essential link between mystical experience and psychology through the psychological understanding of the subconscious. Frankl explores more fully the link between religion and psychology. His understanding of the noetic dimension avoids the vagaries and inconsistencies of James's *Varieties* by providing a theology of hope that is pragmatic rather than utopian; psychologically oriented rather than mystical; and focused on the tragic triad rather than on connections with the greater universe or the next life.

Like James, Frankl says that how we act depends on what we believe and that faith must be tested in experience. But Frankl avoids the religious errors of James by offering a noetic dimension or spiritual environment that keeps religious thought open while still insisting on its moral core. Frankl outlines a progression of human thought free of dogma: "Thus biology is overarched by psychology, psychology by noölogy, and noölogy by theology . . . the lower dimension is included in the higher one; it is subsumed in it and encompassed by it."[66] For Frankl, theology is essentially existential. Whereas philosophy discusses the structure of Being, existential theology focuses on the meaning for us of Being. If we have no sense of meaning, we also have no reason to make choices. Frankl believes that one who remains open to it can experience ultimate meaning or what Martin Buber calls the I-Thou relationship.

Paul Tillich (1886–1965), the leading Protestant theologian of the 20th century and himself a refugee of Hitler's Germany, writes that every creative philosopher is a hidden theologian. Tillich, in effect, could be speaking for Frankl when he concludes that "[a person] is a theologian in the degree to which his existential situation and his ultimate concern shape his philosophical vision."[67] As such a theologian, Frankl believes that meaning is greater than logic, because meaning gives the self the power to grasp and shape life in all its dimensions, as well as to overcome guilt, to manage suffering, and to find the courage to face death. Whether we define God as Frankl's ultimate meaning or as Tillich's ultimate concern, our relationship to God is existential. God is not an ideal but a presence. Frankl believes that beyond religious forms—prayers, rites, and examples of prophets and saints—there is a faith that is childlike in the truest and best sense of that description. This faith is also existential because each person must decide in each moment how to express this trust in a life of meaning.

A Humanistic Theory of Meaning

Four general features emerge from James's and Frankl's humanistic theory of meaning. First, it is empirically realistic, phenomenological, open, and non-reductive. Second, it is situational, allowing for a plurality of choices while still maintaining a value orientation. Third, it is future-oriented, yet also knowl-edgeable about the past and defiantly realistic concerning the present. Essentially James sees, as does Frankl, that the human search for meaning is characterized by the defiant power of the human spirit. Each envisages this defiant power working through the structures of the world to help us actualize ethical values and norms. Fourth, James's and Frankl's humanism appeals to an intuitive conscience. An intuitive conscience links freedom, championed by James, to responsibleness, underscored by Frankl. An intuitive conscience is an important instrument of a humanistic pragmatic understanding of life.

The work of James and Frankl is seminal, not final. Both see themselves as pioneers. In a memorandum written just a month before his death in 1910, James said of his work, "Call it 'Beginning of an introduction to philosophy.' Say that I hoped to round out my system, which now is too much like an arch built only on one side."[68] In 1980, Viktor Frankl said in his address to the First World Congress of Logotherapy:

> I concluded my first book by stating that Logotherapy "is a no-man's land. And yet—what a land of promise!" This was 35 years ago. In the meantime, the "no-man's land" had become inhabited. Proof thereof is this congress. And your papers prove also that the "promise" is on the way to being fulfilled.[69]

The arch that James began is still being finished. Frankl's "no-man's land" is still being claimed. The full promise of their pragmatic humanism is yet to be realized.

— 5 —

Phenomenological

Perspectives

PHENOMENOLOGISTS HAVE INDEED CONTINUOUSLY
RECAST THEIR PROPOSITIONS ABOUT THE NATURE OF
CONSCIOUSNESS, EXPERIENCE, KNOWLEDGE, TRUTH
AND INTENTIONALITY, BUT NOW WE SEE THAT THIS IS
NOT A STRUGGLE WITH METHOD, IT IS SIMPLY DOING
PHILOSOPHY.

—ROBERT SOLOMON

The philosophical and psychological theories developed in the late 19th and early 20th centuries gave impetus and direction to a new exploration of phenomenology. This movement, which is called radical or existential phenomenology, introduced a rationale and a methodology that center on how a person acts as well as how a person thinks.

The thought and interaction of three philosophers—Edmund Husserl, Max Scheler, and Martin Heidegger—led to the establishment of existential phenomenology as a vital force in contemporary thought; and the development of existential philosophy and existential psychology, including the meaning analysis of Frankl, bears the imprints of these men.

Husserl and Frankl Compared

Edmund Husserl is the seminal figure in existential phenomenology. The problems that he explored are still challenging contemporary leaders in philosophy and psychology. He sets two goals (which are also basic to meaning analysis): (1) to develop a clear, holistic philosophy of the self; and (2) to legitimize philosophically the work of psychology. From these goals, he develops a threefold agenda:

> To establish a method of defining terms and functions that will prevent philosophical anarchy.

To explain genetically how consciousness takes form in human experience. To develop a "pure psychology" of the phenomena of consciousness while avoiding behaviorism.

Husserl begins his study of terms and functions with the battle cry "Back to the things!" By "the things" he means the sources. Just as Descartes worked to free himself from the constraints of scholasticism, Husserl wants to be free from the bondage of positivism, naturalism (scientism), and psychologism. He wants to establish, through the use of internal logic, a "rigorous science" that is dedicated to expressing our essential humanness and to nurturing it philosophically and psychologically. He wants to discover the essence of humanistic thought rather than any process of thinking. He wants to find new philosophical foundations. In this task, he examines three interrelated factors—foundations (sources), intelligibility, and understanding. Husserl's definitions of these terms and his use of them are of prime importance in the development of existential phenomenology, though some phenomenologists have managed to misunderstand or misappropriate each of them.

Husserl has been accused of being radical in his search for foundations. Radical he is, in the sense of the original meaning of the word *radicalis*—that is, having roots. He is radical in the same way as Descartes, who probed the medieval philosophy of his day and went to the roots of Western thought. Like Descartes, Husserl is an investigator, more a philosophical archaeologist than a philosophical architect. "Rather than building upwards, Husserl digs deeper and deeper, trying at the same time to lay ever firmer foundations for establishing insights."[1]

While Descartes turned first to metaphysics to gain insights, Husserl chooses epistemology. Instead of appealing to pure thought, he investigates the nature of thinking and of knowing to show how relationships and structures of meaning are formed. How do things appear to us? How do we *see* things? Seeing is not naive observation, according to Husserl; it is a multidimensional experience calling upon reason, insight, and above all, intuition. A scholar's wife attending one of Husserl's lectures told him that his phenomenology had given her so many new eyes. Her expression "new eyes" was especially appropriate because intuition, in the strict sense of the word's root, *intuitio,* means to look at. Husserl identifies the basic form of intuition as sensuous and links it with commonsense observation of an object. Commonsense intuition concentrates on the content of what the self selects as important. Commonsense intuition becomes categorical intuition when the self uses the world as a guide. Using the world as a guide does not mean uncritical acceptance of the world, for the self alternates between what Husserl calls world-believing and world-belief eliminating. Such an extension of the self includes making distinctions between seeing (intuition) and thinking (thought). While seeing is essentially commonsense observation, thinking intellectualizes what is observed. Seeing concentrates on the meanings of things that are perceived or imagined; thinking searches for a primary significance behind the meanings. Seeing stresses particulars; thinking wants general concepts. Husserl believes that by starting with seeing we go back to the things themselves, and in so doing, we avoid presuppositions and prejudices that arise from thinking. He is not suggesting that our judgments start at point zero; rather, he is urging, like William James, that we begin philosophizing by trying to eliminate all those presuppositions that have not as yet been tested by experience.

Frankl's search for meaning follows the same phenomenological pattern of seeing and thinking. Like Husserl, he wants the self searching for meaning to be as free of as many prejudices and presuppositions as possible. One of the reasons that Frankl often relies on the insights of the man in the street is his belief that such a person is more ready and able to reflect a commonsense view of life than the intellectual who plays mind games. Frankl, of course, takes for granted that the man in the street understands logic and how to use it—an assumption grounded in Husserl's thought and method.

Husserl's phenomenological understanding of logic analyzes such central concepts as intelligibility, understanding, and meaning. Traditional logic limits its analysis to a purely intellectual level. Husserl's understanding of logic goes beyond that traditional level to show how logic should be used at all levels of experience. But he also believes that lower levels of consciousness contain presuppositions that are capable of blocking meaning more so than the higher levels of intellectual consciousness. It is vital, then, that the level of logic be subjected to analysis. Such analysis takes into account both the functions of the mind and the spirit, which Husserl sees as a stream of vitality.

Husserl sees logic as a science of philosophy, a method to help us deal with phenomena as we experience them. He does not expect logic to be a means to master all of the facts of life. His science of philosophy is essentially a science of consciousness that stresses our attitude (*Einstellung*) as well as our reasoning processes. To help us understand the nature of facts, Husserl introduces a novel process that he calls *epoché* (from the Greek word for abstention). He suggests that to find evidence that is clear, distinct, and rational, we must temporarily set aside the traditions, ideas, and pressures of the world and concentrate on the facts of a situation with a "cleared" consciousness. Husserl does not deny the validity of world judgments; he shifts attention away from them so that the self can focus on the nature of Being instead of on the conditions of being in the world.

Husserl teaches that *epoché* must be accompanied by a second strategy: eidetic reduction. Eidetic reduction has to do with the *meaning* of facts or ideas. Husserl distinguishes between "mixed" and "true" facts. Mixed facts show things as they appear; they are empirically oriented. True facts are transcendent and a priori; they go beyond the empirical realm of things to point to values that are already present in the self but need to be recognized and acted on. Husserl speaks of the transcendental ego, through which we experience a sense of certainty (not a sense of infallibility) that is legitimate, right, and meaningful. And he believes that we use intuition to unearth that certainty.

While Frankl does not use the word *epoché,* he follows Husserl's proposal in encouraging the self that concentrates on the nature of being and on an individual search for meaning. Frankl sees each person's search for meaning as unique and specific. Some neo-Freudians and behaviorists argue that talks of meanings and values are only defense mechanisms, reaction formations, and disguised sublimations. Husserl and Frankl reject these assertions as scientism. As previously noted, Frankl quips that he is not willing to live merely for the sake of his defense mechanisms, nor is he ready to die merely for his reaction formations. Joseph Kockelmans writes, "The phenomenological philosopher finds his starting point in the thought that human experience manifests a meaningful structure. . . . He wants to uncover this structure, rescue it from the multitude of human experience in which it lies buried."[2]

Husserl and Frankl emphasize the transcendental dimension of the self. It is their corrective to the philosophical and psychological reductionism of their times. They each affirm a multidimensional self, seeing a person as containing a number of polarities of thought, action, and emotions. Tensions should be recognized and used creatively—not ignored or seen as unavoidably destructive. Their phenomenological approach accepts that the self is not a finished product but always in the making. A phenomenological depth exists that can be discovered layer by layer, but the self can never be completely understood. Existential phenomenology does not aim at enabling the self to achieve perfection, but at delineating the qualities that best help the self to define its individual meaning.

Husserl uses the term *ideal object* as his goal; Frankl uses the term *meaning.* Both men use a descriptive psychology to avoid the reductionism and dogmatism of neo-Freudians and behaviorists. They offer in place of these naturalistic psychologies (which they see as scientism) a psychological explanation of Being that concentrates on the motives and intentions of the self. This rationale has become one of the bases of what is called the Third Force of psychology—the fully human approach to psychotherapy represented by such therapists as Abraham Maslow, Gordon Allport, and Rollo May.

The essential purpose of the strategy of epoché is positive: to help us find and clarify our essential ideas so that we may return to the world better equipped to deal effectively with ourselves and others. Although he does not use Husserl's terminology, Frankl links epoché to eidetic reduction—that is, encouraging a person to put into brackets temporarily the traditions, ideas, and pressures of the world and to concentrate on finding meaning that is unique and specific to the individual. Frankl calls the power that enables a person to find the meaning behind his or her ideas the noetic dimension. (He avoids using Husserl's term *transcendental ego* because *ego,* as used by Freud, is a psychologically restrictive term.)

Paradoxically, the negative act of bracketing brings about the positive act of renewal. For example, a woman suffering from anxiety, self-doubt, and depression, who was dissatisfied with everything in her life, who felt neglected and misunderstood, and who was filled with self-pity, was encouraged to bracket or abstain from what she felt to be the criticisms and slights of the world. This bracketing of or abstention (dereflection) from her false fears and false expectations of the world helped free her to make her own choice of what facts in her life she should accept and act upon. Epoché (general dereflection) helped her to put aside the "mixed facts," and eidetic reduction (self-transcendence) enabled her to go beyond her neurotic symptoms to examine such basic questions as Why am I here? and Whom can I help? and to rethink and rebuild her life with "pure facts" (meaning) as her guide.[3]

Frankl's therapeutic structure—which includes dereflection, self-transcendence, paradoxical intention, and above all, the modification of attitudes—implements the "pure facts" of meaning analysis: life has meaning under all conditions; we have the will to meaning; we have the freedom to fulfill the meanings of our lives under certain conditions; and we have within reach an empowering factor that is the defiant power of the spirit, whether we call it the transcendental dimension or the noetic dimension.

Husserl's pioneer work in humanistic psychology moved the emphasis of therapy from domination by the analyst to the client's exercise of freedom and responsibleness, in which it is the client's primary responsibility to identify and use the power of the transcendental ego. As Kockelmans notes, "we must be careful . . . not to see the intentionality of consciousness as a mere trait or characteristic of consciousness or consider it as one human characteristic among others. It is by means of a conscious act that an object makes its appearance; it is by means of this act that an object becomes present to an observant soul in a special way."[4] Both Husserl and Frankl couple intention with transcendental reflection. Frankl acknowledges his indebtedness to Husserl and to Husserl's mentor, Franz Brentano:

> The self-transcendent quality of the human reality . . . is reflected in the "intentional" quality of human phenomena, as Franz Brentano and Edmund Husserl term it. Human phenomena refer to and point to "intentional objects." Reasons and meanings represent such objects. They are the logos for which the psyche is reaching out. . . . When the self-transcendence of existence is denied, existence itself is distorted.[5]

The rationale for the self-transcendent quality of existence is rooted in Husserl's phenomenological approach to the self. For him, "phenomenology's great discovery is that the 'I think' is not only referred to by the sciences but is for itself a 'sphere of being' (*ein Seinssphare*) which is subject to an articulated and structured experience."[6] Such a structured experience may differ in quality and form with each philosopher. Husserl stresses *eidetic* reduction as a central phenomenon of life. Frankl focuses on the noetic dimension as the key to the self. Max Scheler emphasizes "the philosophy of the heart."

Scheler and Frankl Compared

The ordering of love is at the center of Max Scheler's philosophy of the heart, which was inspired by Pascal's observation that "the heart has its reasons that reason knows not why" and Pascal's *ordre du coeur* (order of the heart) and *logique du coeur* (logic of the heart). For Scheler, the heart gives the self its moral sense; it is the "microcosm of the world of values." Love has cognitive power; it provides the rationale and the power for the self as a bearer of value. Scheler defines the ordering of love as "the movement wherein every concrete individual object that possesses value achieves the highest value compatible with its nature and ideal vocation; or wherein it attains the ideal state of value intrinsic to its nature."[7] The ordering of love awakens the self to authentic self-love. It is the "mother of spirit and reason itself" and the essence of the world order in which the self is called to participate. Essentially, the ordering of love serves as the source of all individual and social values in the present and in the future. While the body may weaken and the will may flag, spirit-empowered love does not weaken or fail. It remains the essence of the self; it is alive and present, ready to furnish true knowledge, to correct errors, to control passions, and to guide the self.

Scheler begins by insisting that each person must develop his or her own unique metaphysical understanding of self. Every person is a *co-creator* with Being; that is, Scheler envisions an essential harmony that involves God, the self, and the world. The dynamics of this harmony allows human spirit and drive to interact in the exercise of personal freedom and responsibleness, which must be tested in life. The discovery of the nature and role of spirit is not an escape from life but a turning *to* life, to find how spirit (noös) enables the self to be fully human as the bearer of values. Scheler's noölogical method (also central in Frankl's thought) therefore emphasizes that the meaning of being lies in the exploration of spirit. He does away, however, with the old body-spirit dualism, which has haunted philosophy since Descartes, by focusing on the nature of the person *as person*. His noölogical method is realistic, dealing with the events of life rather than the world of ideas. Scheler opens the way to *Daseinanalyse* (understanding existentially the place of the self in the world) rather than the ordering of life by formal rule such as Immanuel Kant's moral categorical imperative. Thus, the human being is free to explore how spirit and body work together in the formation of the person and the person's relationship to the world. In Scheler's noölogical method, expressed phenomenologically, the self is never isolated but remains a vital part of the world.

Scheler views philosophy's task as involving the self in what he calls essential knowledge; and essential knowledge, he feels, comes from a thoughtful, active response to a "loving participation in being." Scheler's philosophy is an ontology of the self verified by the world of experience in which the rational and empirical aspects of life interact with the intuitive.

What distinguishes Scheler from other philosophers of the time is the way in which he relates ethics to his philosophy of the heart. Witnessing the after-effects of World War I on Europe and the subordination, especially in his native Germany, of vital societal values to nationalism and utilitarianism, he comments that "the main thought in Pascal's *ordre du coeur* (order of the heart) and *logique du coeur* (logic of the heart) have been revitalized in our era with its immense *desordre du coeur* (disorder of the heart)."[8]

Just as each person holds individual values and gives them an order of significance in his or her life, so a society may choose to order its collective values. But the values and their order of significance, whether those of a person or of the majority of a nation or community, may become reversed or disordered. This is very likely to happen if the person or the collective society has formed its ethics in response to what Scheler calls *ressentiment*. *Ressentiment* (that is, resentment) is a self-poisoning, autointoxicating state that comes about when an individual or a society strives after skewed values. Repressed hatred or envy or jealousy or greed, for example, might be the seed of *ressentiment*. Because such a feeling is repressed, either due to fear or powerlessness at the time, it rankles; and the person or the society urged on by *ressentiment* begins to skew values in order to achieve satisfaction and justify actions. *Ressentiment* can also result from a misunderstanding of the nature of fate and destiny.

For Scheler, fate is one of the givens of life. It is blind to values and limited to concrete events that are beyond our control. In contrast, destiny is not what happens to us but an integral part of our selfhood. Destiny is tied to how we *respond* to events through the insights that we bring to a situation and how we use the ordering of love. Thus, fate and destiny play important but different roles in how we see ourselves and how we respond to life. As human beings, we can face fate and destiny by using self-transcendence, by calling upon a higher dimension of the self—the spirit.

When Scheler writes of the role of the spirit, he is careful to distinguish between control (*Lenkung*) and guidance (*Leitung*). The spirit *guides*; it does not control. Spirit helps persons understand their intentions so that they can fully make their own choices as to how and where to love. Experience is not something added to life; it is validation of life and necessary for judging the authenticity of the self's intentions and actions. So the conditions that call for freedom of choice and personal responsibleness also permit strife. Intentions are formed and are validated or invalidated by experience as the self freely wrestles with its own impulses and drives.

Strife, Scheler believes, is part of the dynamic quality of life. Strife is essential in Scheler's value theory because of the self-testing it should engender. But how is the self to overcome fate or eschew *ressentiment*?

Scheler and Frankl agree that it is through self-transcendence that the self receives values, perspective, and direction in life. Self-transcendence, Frankl writes, takes place through a task worth doing and/or a person to love. The latter, a person to love, is a restatement, in effect, of Scheler's ordering of love.

Scheler and Frankl's noölogical approach expands the dimensions of conscience. Frankl, using Scheler's understanding of phenomenology, defines conscience as "the intuitive capacity of man to find out the meaning of the situation," which includes "the power to discover unique meanings that contradict accepted values."[9] For Scheler and Frankl, human conscience is the value-centered core of the self that acts on intuition and reflects true freedom and responsibleness.

At first glance, it might appear that Frankl's analysis has no relation to Scheler's philosophy of the heart centered in the ordering of love. But there is a strong kinship. Each begins with an ethical task: the need to awaken the self as a bearer of values through which meaning is achieved. Each also affirms that "conscience, the centerpiece of the noetic dimension, is as much a part of reality as body and psyche."[10] Each points out that while the conscience may speak to the self, the person remains free to respond yes or no to it. Each agrees that to be fully human, the self must be *led* and not *driven*. Scheler's understanding of selfhood agrees with Frankl's emphasis that "our human dimension enables us to reach out beyond ourselves and to make meanings and values an essential part of our existence."[11] Scheler and Frankl are realistically optimistic about the future of the human race, despite Scheler's shock and disillusionment about World War I and its aftermath and Frankl's experience as a survivor of four Nazi concentration camps during World War II. This optimism is expressed in Frankl's monanthropism, "an awareness that we are all members of one humanity regardless of color, religion, and political beliefs."[12]

Both Scheler's and Frankl's philosophies move from a grounding in the noös to how the noetic dimension is applied to lived values. They believe in a teleology that reflects an optimism that is reasoned, experiential, and intuitive. Frankl views society as a major dehumanizing factor; he offers therapy to overcome what he calls the noögenic neurosis caused by society. Scheler offers a remedy centered in sociology. He writes of the human that "before he is an *ens cognitas* (a thinking entity) or an *ens volens* (a willing entity), he is an *ens amans* (a loving entity)."[13] He concludes that "where his 'heart' is attached, there, for him, is the 'core' of the so-called essence of things."[14] Frankl essentially agrees that the less the heart is attached the more the self is dehumanized. Frankl adds another dimension, however, by saying that only the search for meaning can lead to a life where the heart can come to terms with the past, live responsibly in the present, and plan with realistic optimism for the future.

A contemporary philosopher writes that Viktor Frankl's chief contribution has been described as "to call to attention to the fact that man must be understood as a creature who needs meaning to live."[15] He goes on to write that "religiously minded people will find classic themes such as the meaning of suffering appearing throughout his writings in secular vestments. Equally significant are numerous insights from Scheler which Frankl has incorporated into his own theories."[16] Both point to the ordering of love as a concept and as an act that releases the self from its egocentric entrapment and enables it to overcome fate and find the truth and meaning in every situation.

Frankl shares key insights with Scheler in three areas: methodology, ethics, and teleology. William Sahakian sees logotherapy as a form of phenomenology, and states that the phenomenology to which logotherapy is most closely related is that of Max Scheler.[17] He goes to the heart of Frankl's methodology when he points out that not only does Frankl define meaning as Scheler does, but he also agrees with Scheler about the phenomenology of experience.

Heidegger and the Question of Being

The complexity of both his philosophy and his personality make Martin Heidegger (1889–1976) the most controversial of the founding fathers of phenomenology. As a person, he manifests the intellect of a giant and the ethical judgment of a dwarf. His ethical shortcomings are illustrated by his early allegiance to the Nazi regime and by the way he treated his friends and colleagues, especially Husserl. Heidegger was one of the first intellectuals to join the Nazi party. In 1933, after Hitler became the German führer, Heidegger was appointed *rector magnificus* of the University of Freiburg, where he had been teaching for five years. In his rectorial inaugural address, he expressed his enthusiasm for the Nazi movement. After hearing this speech, one of his students commented:

> In comparison to the numerous . . . speeches which professors of equal rank have given since the take-over of power, this philosophical and forceful speech is a little masterpiece. Service in the labor forces and in the armed forces merges with service in the realm of learning in such a way that, at the end of this speech, one no longer knows whether to study Diel's *Pre-Socratics* or to march in the ranks of the Storm Troopers.[18]

In his early days as rector, Heidegger continued openly to support the Nazi party in his speeches and writings, but he soon came to disagree with its fanatical excesses. He resigned his post as rector after a short period; and in the following decade, he was forbidden by the government to publish.

The late 1930s marked the beginning of a dark period for Heidegger. He spent most of his time at his retreat in the Black Forest at Todtnau near Freiburg working on two booklets: "Plato's Doctrine of Truth" and "On the Essence of Truth." After the war, he wrote his well-known essay "Letter on Humanism" and in the 1950s published several works and lectured frequently. Paradoxically, although he was persona non grata in the new Germany, his writings brought him worldwide fame, and people from all over the world came to visit him at his mountain retreat.

Criticism of Heidegger focuses not only on his writings while rector of Freiburg, but also on his treatment of his old teacher and friend Husserl, whom Heidegger abandoned when Husserl, who was partly Jewish, came under fire from the Nazis. Although in 1927 Heidegger had dedicated his monumental *Being and Time* to Husserl, in 1933 he allowed the dedication to be omitted, and he and Husserl remained estranged until the old master died in 1938.

Controversy over Heidegger's pro-Nazi period continues. Some critics feel that Heidegger's politically fascist judgments should disqualify his philosophy from being taught. Despite this criticism, it is nevertheless true that he has had a major influence on leading philosophers, theologians, linguists, and humanistic psychologists for more than half a century. Thus, personality and politics apart, his philosophical contribution to existential phenomenology is unparalleled, especially in the search for the nature of Being.

As a teenager, Heidegger read Franz Brentano's treatise on the meaning of Being in Aristotle (*Von der mannigfachen Bedeutung des Seienden bei Aristotles*). Its theme, the quest for the meaning of Being, determined Heidegger's entire philosophical endeavor. Heidegger took Husserl, a former pupil of Brentano's, as his mentor when he entered the university. He learned the phenomenological method from him and adapted Husserl's views to his own philosophical needs. Later, while teaching at Marburg in the late 1920s, he was also influenced by Scheler, but he was ambivalent toward him, paying tribute to him in the footnotes of his writings while criticizing him in the text. His thought was also affected by two colleagues, the outstanding Protestant theologians Rudolf Bultmann (1884–1976) and Paul Tillich. Each of these men contributed to the substance and structure of Heidegger's concept of Being, while he moved from the descriptive emphasis of Husserl's phenomenology and then to a metaphysical approach to his consideration of the nature of Being.

Heidegger's metaphysical approach shows that there are many ways of speaking of Being. Like Husserl, his first concern is to clarify what we mean and what we say. The process of clarification, as we shall see later, leads Heidegger to go beyond his primary metaphysical goal to explore signification, or meaning. To do so, he introduces a new style and new words in his discussion of the nature of Being.

Heidegger insists that Being is not a thing, nor another entity, nor something that is. Thus, one does not ask What is Being? To do so implies that Being is a substance or an entity. One of the reasons that he has been opposed by other Western philosophers, who see Being as a substance or as a class concept, is his refusal to so limit Being. At the same time, he realizes that it is unsatisfactory to say that Being is either self-evident or indefinable. Like Husserl, and Descartes before him, Heidegger begins with the nature of the self. But while they approach the question of the self by asking What can I know? Heidegger asks What is the ground of my being? Husserl and Descartes start with epistemology; Heidegger starts with metaphysics.

Heidegger uses the German term *Dasein* and its variant *Dersein* to address the question of Being. Literally, the German word *Dasein* means being-there. It emphasizes the limitations of the self; it comprehends that we may find ourselves in a particular situation over which we have no control. Traditional German philosophy used *Dasein* to describe all existence; Heidegger limits the meaning of the term to human existence. For Heidegger, *Dasein* describes not only what the self is but how the self is responsible for the expression of Being. Freedom and responsibleness are therefore part of the self's very being (*ontos*), the distinguishing mark of human existence. Heidegger expresses the word *exists* as *ek-sists* to show that the self stands out from other beings as a particular being who has to decide about Being.[19] By restricting the use of *Dasein* to the human condition, he is not denying the rest of creation; rather, he is stressing the fact that *Dasein* stands for a type of self-consciousness that is able to question the nature of meaning. For Heidegger the humanistic aphorism that the proper study of mankind is man means a metaphysical exploration rather than, as Husserl teaches, only a search for more accurate and complete knowledge.

Despite this basic philosophical departure from Husserl, Heidegger used Husserl's *Logical Investigations* as the groundwork for his own thought. It cleared the way so that he could begin to build his own understanding of the self. He started his studies of the book by Husserl in his first semester of university courses in 1909: "I remained so bewildered by Husserl's work that I continued in the ensuing years to read from it over and over again, without sufficient insight into what captivated me."[20] What Husserl helped him to do was to gain an understanding of a genuine philosophical empiricism and, further, to supply him with the phenomenological tools to practice it. Yet Heidegger was disturbed by the limits that Husserl placed upon consciousness by avoiding ontology. Despite this, Heidegger's study of Husserl's early and later works helped him to understand better "phenomenological seeing" and to incorporate this as a part of his own understanding of *ek-sistenz*.

Heidegger's insistence that metaphysics rather than epistemology is the best philosophical tool to understand the self is the basis of his disagreement with Husserl's phenomenology. It is also the raison d'être for his own existential approach to the self, which he develops in *Being and Time* (*Sein und Zeit*, 1927) and *The Question of Being* (*Zur Seinsfrage*, 1958). Yet as late as 1973, when he gave his last seminar, Heidegger continued to use Husserl's understanding as the way to explore the question of Being. What is essential to recognize in the long and complicated dialogue between the two men is not their differences, but their common search for the nature of Being, including how the self expresses freedom and responsibleness.

Heidegger, by wrestling with the questions Husserl discusses in *Logical Investigations*, accomplishes two tasks: he provides continuity between early and later developments of phenomenology, and he shows the vital relation between the search for knowledge and the search for Being. Just as Husserl is a pioneer in a phenomenology that underscores the importance of how we know, so Heidegger is a pioneer in a phenomenology that focuses on the nature of who we are. Each begins by uncovering (*alethia*) the meaning of self. To do so they use Socratic questioning rather than relying on dogma or system.

Heidegger's use of the Socratic method takes the form of a dialogue between existence and Being. "Because every *Dasein* has to be, and has to decide about its own existence and to understand itself in one way or another, then every *Dasein* is already involved in the question of existence in a very concrete way."[21] Heidegger calls this inescapable question the *existentiell* question to distinguish it from the existential question, which a person may or may not ask about the theoretical nature of existence. The existential question comes out of the *existentiell*: we ask why on the basis of what happens to us. Heidegger emphasizes the *existentiell*, arguing that we are not spectators of Being but participants in it. Through *existentiell* questioning we uncover our being where we are (*Dasein*). We are able to do this because we "ek-sist"; we "stand out" in the sense that we are not just other things in the world but beings able to judge both ourselves and our world. We also have the ability to shape ourselves and our world, but there is no sure way to do this. Husserl and Heidegger agree that life is an unfinished work; we are always "on the way" (*en via*). Living is more a way of seeing than proving. Thus each *Dasein* is a unique expression of a person's own existence. Each person experiences the facts of being, but may or may not deal responsibly with them and with concern for other persons. This is the option that comes with freedom and is acted out in the everyday world. Heidegger calls this experience *existentialia*.

There is a rhythm in Heidegger's dialectic: questioning, choosing, and acting with concern. As John Macquarrie writes, "Thus the world is understood by Heidegger as a vast instrumental system, held together, as it were, by *Dasein's* concern. It is in terms of this concern that things receive their *significance*, as they are incorporated into the world of man."[22] The key word is *significance* or, as Frankl would say, *meaning*. We do not discover what is significant or meaningful apart from others. Community or "being with" is the essential *existentiale* of *Dasein*. Just as we cannot exist apart from the world, we cannot exist apart from others in the world.

To exist with others in the world we need language, and language requires clarification, as Husserl shows in his *Investigations*. Heidegger enlarges Husserl's thesis by distinguishing between discourse and language. Discourse is a living communication among people, whereas language is how discourse is expressed in words and sentences. Heidegger underscores the use of discourse to express *Dasein*. He also redefines Husserl's understanding of logic. For Heidegger, logic does not exist just to clarify what we see at hand, as Husserl teaches; rather, true logic reflects existential analysis, which outlines the options for authentic Being as well as clarifying its nature.

The analysis takes form through the structure that Heidegger gives *Dasein* and begins with the composition of the word itself. Heidegger emphasizes the *Da*, the "there," of *Dasein* to stress Being's *being there*. To describe how Being is in the world, Heidegger chooses three easily misunderstood concepts of existence: *Befindlichkeit* (the placement of the self in life and in the world), *Verstehen* (understanding the dominant purpose of life), and *logos* (discursive reasoning, or *Rede*).

Befindlichkeit has also been translated as "state of mind," as "the sense of one's situation," and as "moodness."[23] Placement heightens our sense of who we are; it also makes us aware that we are "thrown" into the world. This "thrown-ness" requires that each of us judge who we are and where we are. *Befind-lichtkeit* helps us deal with the events of the world when they occur in our lives. To be fully realized, this permanent aspect of Being must be accompanied by *Verstehen* (understanding), which focuses on how we use our placement in life in relation to others through symbiotic or interdependent relationships. Heidegger connects *Verstehen* with *Vor-stehen* (standing before something in order to master it). *Vor-stehen*, Heidegger believes, helps us not only to see that something is logical but also to see what we may become in addition to what we are. It is "thrown possibility through and through."[24] Heidegger calls this experience of human possibility *Entwurf* (projecting).

As *Dasein* guides our present and future *ek-sistenz*, it also provides for personal freedom and responsibleness. Understanding (*Verstehen* and *Vor-stehen*) cannot be imposed from outside; it must be discovered by each person, who examines what has been learned, stands apart from the needs of the self (*ek-sistenz*), interprets what has been seen, and after reflection, communicates what she or he understands. This process requires a discursive and integrative power that Heidegger calls logos.

Heidegger defines logos, which he limits essentially to speech, as the foundation and the enabler of language. As speech, logos makes being-in-the-world possible because speech enables us to communicate our understandings with one another. Heidegger, therefore, narrows the definition of logos first set forth by Heraclitus. Heraclitus sees logos as a means of communication but believes its essential function is to reflect the power of universal reason that determines both the unity and constant change in the universe according to universal law.[25] Succeeding generations of Greek philosophers emphasized those characteristics of Heraclitus's definition that best fitted their own systems. Plato gives priority to the logos as the primary Idea or Form. Aristotle sees the core of logos as Reason or Judgment. For each of these thinkers, logos functions as a unifying and explanatory force based on an essential quality of life (Reason, Judgment, God). Heidegger breaks with this rationale. Instead, he follows Husserl's admonition "Back to the things themselves." As Magda King points out, "*Logos* says: to let something be seen from itself. Phenomenon says: that which shows itself in itself."[26] Philosophy's purpose is to classify, order, and delineate structures. Heidegger thinks to go beyond this leads only to error and confusion.

Frankl's Transmutation of Heidegger's Phenomenology

Frankl's approach to the three aspects of Being's *existentiales* (placement, understanding, and logos) shows how he transmutes the essential methodology of Heidegger's descriptive phenomenology. In so doing, Frankl gives new interpretations to its basic humanistic and existential concerns. If, as Merleau-Ponty believes, phenomenology is the art and activity of bringing truth into being, then meaning analysis is a philosophical psychology that uses phenomenology to bring meaning into being. Frankl's rationale and methodology in the search for meaning illustrate each of the three aspects of Being's *existentiales*.

Placement, Understanding, and Logos

Frankl realistically acknowledges that where a person finds himself or herself is crucial to the mental health of the person. He also points out that a person's sense of a situation may be distorted. Phenomenology teaches that a sense of one's placement (also called affective disposition or moodness by Kockelmans) is that characteristic of Being whereby the self is knowledgeable about its own position and is attuned to the world. Heidegger, commenting on his perception that we are beings "thrown" into our situations, believes that this "thrown-ness" (*Geworfenheit*) causes the person to become aware that life *is* and also that life "has to be" and "that his being has to be realized by himself as a task."[27] In contrast, Frankl's meaning analysis feels that the experience of "thrown-ness" can lead a person into a sense of despair and resentment, which causes the person to blame the situation not only for *where* he or she *is* but also for *who* he or she is as a person, and that it takes more than a "moodness" or an "affective disposition" to reverse this trend of thinking. In Frankl's view, meaning supplies the needed motive and the will to help a person stand apart (*ek-sist*) and to be the master of his or her situation rather than its victim. In other words, a meaning-full sense of placement helps to achieve true understanding.

One of the first steps in psychotherapy is to allow clients to express how they see where they are placed. Through the use of Socratic dialogue, the therapist helps clients to use dereflection and self-transcendence to reach perspective on where they are placed. Like Heidegger, Frankl links understanding (*Verstehen*) with standing before (*Vor-stehen*) as a way to express authentic being-in-the-world. But while phenomenology speaks of the power of understanding as a primordial power to be, Frankl traces such understanding to a primordial *meaning,* through which the power to be is recognized and acted on. The therapist's task is to help the client discover and use such meaning through the noetic dimension of the self. It is this empowering noetic dimension that is primordial, in Frankl's view, rather than understanding, as Heidegger believes. Frankl believes that understanding needs the authenticity and activating power of the noös if one is to both comprehend one's possibilities and see the significance and possibilities of the world as well. The self is constantly involved in the world. Heidegger calls this projecting (*Entwurf*) and sees understanding as its catalyst. While Frankl does not use the term *Entwurf,* he recognizes its imperative:

> Being human is always directed [projected] to something, or someone other than itself, to a meaning to fulfill or another human being to encounter. Like

the healthy eye, which does not see itself, man, too, functions best when he is overlooking and forgetting himself, by giving himself. Forgetting himself makes for *sensitivity,* and giving himself, for *creativity.*[28]

The myriad and often confusing crosscurrents of the world require a way to sort out what is true from what is false. Heidegger identifies logos as the instrument, or means, of helping persons to explain their common viewpoints, since he sees logos as reasoned speech (*Rede*). Frankl also sees the need for logos, but his understanding of logos goes far beyond the limit set by Heidegger. Frankl builds on Karl Buhler's threefold function of language: "First, language allows the speaker to express himself—it serves as a vehicle of expression. Second, language is an appeal addressed by the speaker to the person to whom he speaks. And third, language always represents something, that 'something' of which one speaks."[29] Heidegger disregards this third function of language, while Frankl finds it crucial. To deal with this third function of language, Brentano and Husserl use the term *intentional referent.* As Frankl explains, "All the potential intentional referents together, all those objects which are 'meant' by two subjects communicating with one another, form a structured whole, a world of 'meaning,' and this 'cosmos' of meanings is what may aptly be called the 'logos.' "[30]

In contrast to Heidegger, Frankl returns to logos as the controlling principle of the universe: it is neither a by-product nor a means to an end; it is an end in itself. As Fabry explains, logos as meaning "is at the center of life toward which we all move, consciously or unconsciously."[31] Frankl spells out the difference between his definition of logos and Heidegger's: "The world of meanings and values may rightly be termed *logos.* Then, *logos* is the objective correlate to the subjective phenomenon called human existence. Man is free to be responsible, and he is responsible for the realization of the meaning of his life, the *logos* of his existence."[32] For Frankl, logos is the primordial source, the ground, and the means of Being. When logos becomes ultimate meaning, it is the highest or the divine meaning. Logos, in Frankl's view, gives more than form to communication; it is its substance as well. Logos is not just a tool of Being; it is the essence of Being.

Care and Meaning

Meaning analysis is ontological, ethical, and therapeutic. It symbolizes and enables authentic *Dasein.* When Heidegger moves beyond the communication of Being to its structure, he uses the word *care* (*Sorge*) instead of the word *meaning.* The use of the terms *Sorge* and *meaning* symbolizes the similarities and differences between Heidegger's and Frankl's understanding of existence. *Sorge* is the term Heidegger uses to describe a threefold form of *Dasein*: "First, it is *existential;* *Dasein* must transcend toward the 'power to be.' Second, it is *facticity*; the essential fact of life is that we are 'thrown' into the world. Third, it is *fallen*; an absorption by the world causes us to fall away from our essential Being."[33] He further defines the term *Sorge* by describing its dual meaning as concern for nature at large (*Besorgen*) and solicitude for fellow beings (*Für-sorge*). The priority of our existential nature is expressed primarily through *Fürsorge,* care of others, which calls for the exercise of freedom and respon-sibleness. Care is the instrument for dealing with our facticity, so that we are not absorbed by the world, or at the other extreme, so that we do not ignore the world's valid claims upon our existence. Frankl's meaning analysis goes beyond Heidegger's definition of existential, facticity, and the "fallen-ness" of the human condition in relation to care by providing a theoretic and practical model of the self based on meaning.

Viktor Frankl considers human beings unique in their being, open to the world through the exclusively human dimension of the spirit. This dimension of the human spirit, which he calls the will to meaning, directs us from our own ego needs to an awareness of and caring about the needs of others as they occur. It is essentially *Fürsorge*. Elisabeth Lukas expands on this as follows:

> Meaning is seen as *the actual meaning of a situation*. Meaning contains an objective component which can be perceived subjectively. Meaning is the connecting link between the human being and the world. Meaning, there-fore, is never just a "meaning for me," but is also a "meaning as such." The self-transcending opening of a person toward the world is so great that for the sake of a desirable meaning goal we may forego, if need be, personal happiness. The question as to what we human beings are is no longer answered by "a creature in pursuit of happiness," but "a creature in pursuit of meaning," that is "a meaning to be found in the world."[34]

This is an open model of Being, based on meaning, that goes beyond solicitude or caring to enable us to love others through I-Thou relationships. As Frankl writes, "Unless life in general had a meaning, it would not make sense to speak of the meaning of love in particular."[35]

Human "Fallen-ness"

The full dimensions of meaning are often experienced not in the life of the healthy individual but in the life of the person who is exhibiting "dis-ease" or, according to Heidegger's description, is "fallen." Heidegger describes human "fallen-ness" in terms of *tranquilizing, alienation,* and *scattering.* Each term carries a special meaning for Heidegger and provides a point of comparison between his phenomenology and Frankl's meaning analysis.

Tranquilizing removes the anxieties and tensions of life that call for decision and action; it supplies peace of mind, or equilibrium, at any price. Frankl calls such tranquilization *homeostasis,* pointing out that "homeostasis is a concept borrowed from biology, but which has since been shown to be untenable there . . . only a brain that is functioning pathologically is characterized by the attempt to avoid tensions unconditionally."[36] Frankl sees "a moderate amount, a sound amount, a sound dosage of tension" as necessary to provide the challenges to the self required for healthy living. "If an individual is not challenged by any tasks to complete, and thus is *spared* the specific tensions aroused by such tasks, a certain type of neurosis—noögenic neurosis—may ensue."[37] Thus, in Frankl's view, we should search for tasks, despite the tensions that they may produce; for in the completion of such tasks, we express the will to meaning.

Alienation, the second mark of the "fallen-ness" of *Dasein,* describes the self separated from authentic selfhood and authentic community. Frankl calls this dual condition emotional alienation and social alienation. One leads to the other and takes various forms, depending on the emotional conditions of persons and the situations in which the persons find themselves. For instance, in the Victorian age many persons were sexually repressed by a puritanical society and expressed their psychic and physical frustration through either covert or open rebellion against society. The English philosopher Bertrand Russell (1872–1970) is a prime example of this. After the early death of his free-thinking parents, he was reared by his extremely puritanical and churched grandparents, who epitomized the late Victorian, conservative Tory, bellicose empire-building viewpoint. In reaction, Russell was, during his long lifetime, a crusader for sexual liberation, atheism, and pacifism. It is not unusual for alienation to occur in repressive societies, but Frankl identifies the emotional alienation and the social alienation that have arisen in our day as reaction against a libertine approach to life in which anything and everything is allowed. As a consequence, Frankl notes, "people display an intolerance of instinctual frustration *and* emotional tension; they exhibit 'incontinence' one might say, in that they cannot restrain their emotions, they cannot refrain from expressing them and sharing them with others."[38] Thus they seek groups or organizations that will meet their particular needs. Some groups are political or social, often extreme in their opinions and programs; other groups are therapeutic and provide "encounter sessions" and sensitivity training in which psychically incontinent persons seek to deal with their social and emotional alienation. Frankl warns that these reactions to problems of alienation should not be mistaken for solutions:

> Even if a "reaction" turns out to be curative, the cure is symptomatic, a palliative. Worse, such a cure may well reinforce the disease. So to the issue at hand, the emotions, they cannot be brought about intentionally to begin with. . . . We have to face the fact that there are certain activities that cannot be demanded, commanded, or ordered. . . . They cannot be established at will. . . . Attempts to do so reflect an entirely manipulative approach to human phenomena such as faith, hope, love and will.[39]

Therefore, some of these groups are dealing with hyperreflection and hyperintention. The properly conceived encounter groups go beyond merely fostering the self-expression of their individual members to helping them to achieve self-transcendence, which is the essential key to their reconstruction of their Being.

Scattering, the third aspect of "fallen-ness," is Heidegger's description of the condition in which the possibilities of Being are dictated by the myriad factors outside of a person's life. Frankl describes this condition of scattering as pandeterminism. By pandeterminism, Frankl means any view of the self that does not take into account the essentially human capacity for free choice. Frankl recognizes that we cannot entirely free ourselves from the conditions and ties of other individuals and of society. We are free, however, to take a *stand* by using our will to meaning when confronted by conditions over which we have no control. In Frankl's view, if we avoid taking such a stand, if we give in to the condition of pandeterminism, pandeterminism can lead to reductionism. Reductionism occurs when we allow ourselves to be so determined by circumstances that we are reduced to the subhuman level assigned to things. The human person determines his or her selfhood. Once a person has given way to reductionism, nihilism (no-thingness) is not far behind.

The anthropological and psychological reductionists insist that there is nothing in the human self that cannot be found in other mammals. Frankl tells the following story to illustrate the reductionist fallacy:

> One [parishioner] contended that the other's cat had stolen and eaten five pounds of butter, which the other denied. "Bring me the cat," the rabbi ordered. They brought him the cat. "Now bring me scales." They brought him scales. "How many pounds of butter did you say the cat has eaten?" he asked. "Five pounds, rabbi," was the answer. Thereupon the rabbi put the cat on the scales and it weighed exactly five pounds. "Now I have the butter," the rabbi said, "but where is the cat?"[40]

Frankl concludes, "This is what happens when eventually the reductionists rediscover in man all the conditioned reflexes, conditioning processes, innate releasing mechanisms and whatever else they have been seeking. . . . 'Now we have it,' they say, like the rabbi, 'but where is man?' "[41]

Conscience and Finiteness

To explore the nature of the authentic person, Heidegger focuses on the place of conscience and the meaning of death. Frankl seems to be following the same pattern by highlighting the place of intuitive conscience and the significance of the tragic triad (pain, suffering, and death). The conclusions that they reach, however, regarding the true nature of Being, differ significantly.

Heidegger and Frankl agree that we cannot know the nature of freedom and responsibleness unless we are first aware of our human limitations. For Heidegger, the most dramatic limitation is the ultimate one, our moving toward death. He feels that if there is no awareness of death and if the future is seen to stretch out indefinitely, then the person feels no pressure to make decisions or take responsibility. This denial of the fact of death constitutes an inauthentic existence, which we bolster by such conscious euphemisms as "he [or she] is just away" or "I lost my wife [or husband]." But the recognition that we are all moving toward death is not an invitation to brood or to despair. Heidegger sees the human awareness of death as contributing to the authenticity of Being rather than taking away from it. Death—as the ultimate boundary—causes the self to define its meaning in terms of the time it is allotted and to examine the choices that must be made within that time. For Heidegger, authenticity is basically nothing more than one of the possible ways of being in the world. As we consciously move toward death, our being-in-the-world is seen to have an end, not in the teleological sense of achieving ultimate meaning but as a fact of existence. The hallmark of our realization of being-toward-death is *angst*, most often translated as "dread" or, preferably, as "anxiety". Being-toward-death may cause the deepest angst, but angst is built into the very nature (the *ontos*) of human existence. Angst comes from being-in-the-world: the fact that we are thrown into our individual situations and must make choices within conditions that we did not choose or cause and over which we have little control. Our sense of personal authenticity develops as we express our power to be. The power to be means that we are always ahead of what actually is. As noted earlier, this is what is meant by *Dasein's* ability to project.

Frankl, like Heidegger, believes that the truly authentic self must be aware of its finiteness, but Frankl sees the human experience of finiteness as having three aspects: guilt or failure, suffering, and death. Heidegger sees just one aspect: death. To have the power to be or to have meaning requires, Frankl believes, that we prepare to take a stand against all three aspects that he identifies as the human experience of finiteness. For Frankl, meaning can be found not only in our actions or in our values but also in suffering:

> This is why life never ceases to have and to retain a meaning to the last moment. Even facing an ineluctable fate, e.g., an incurable disease, there is still granted to man a chance to fulfill even the deepest possible meaning. What matters, then, is the stand he takes in his predicament . . . the attitude we choose in suffering.[42]

Frankl points out that we are threatened by our guilt from the past as well as our death in the future. Both are sources of angst, for if death faces us with our mortality, guilt reminds us of our fallibility. But, Frankl writes, instead of leading to despair, "it is . . . the acceptance of this twofold human finiteness which adds to life's worthwhileness, since only in the face of guilt does it make any sense to improve, and only in the face of death is it meaningful to act."[43]

While death sets the boundary of existence for Heidegger, conscience measures what existence ought to be, the authentic self. As Macquarrie notes:

> One of the basic characteristics of existence . . . is that the existent has a relation to himself. He has an idea of himself, and can either be at one with

himself or estranged from himself. He can either attain or fall short. Conscience is the awareness of how it is with oneself.[44]

Heidegger emphasizes that a personal conscience differs from the conscience
of society. He seems to say that the former is authentic while the latter is
inauthentic and even oppressive. In so doing, Heidegger seems to set the
individual against society. But we need to recall that his concept of *Fürsorge*
(being-for) is a basic part of authentic existence, and while conscience may
critique community, it cannot ignore or reject it out of turn. Yet there is an elitist
element in Heidegger's view that borders on arrogance or at least relies on a
mystical sense of being right.

Frankl agrees with Heidegger that conscience is an integral part of our
Being. He describes conscience as "the intuitive capacity of a man to find out the
meaning of a situation. Since this meaning is something unique, it does not fall
under a general law, and an intuitive capacity such as conscience is the only
means to seize hold of meaning Gestalts."[45] Thus intuitive conscience is, by its
very nature, creative, investigative, and yet fallible. It is also caring, trustful, and
honest with itself and others. In these ways, it resembles Frankl's understanding
of love.

Frankl's definition of conscience avoids the ethical Scylla and Charybdis
of legalism and antinomianism. A "good" conscience cannot be pursued for
conscience's sake; for, as Frankl says, when we do so we are no longer justified
in having it.[46] The very fact that we feel we have become good or virtuous makes
us Pharisees, captives of the sin of pride. Just as when we make health our major
concern we may become ill as hypochondriacs, so if we make virtue our major
concern we become unvirtuous in enacting our assumed virtue.

Ethical values are not given once and for all and for all persons. Each value
must be explored on its own merit. When two values collide, we have to ask if
there is not an additional value or an ethical perspective that may change how
we see the first two values. Frankl does not suggest that whatever value we accept
is authentic or true. We must test what we consider ethical by moral traditions
and standards while evaluating the traditions and standards as well. It is necessary,
Frankl advises, that we search for meanings in life so that we can make independent and authentic decisions. This is not an easy task, but as Frankl writes:

> In an age in which the Ten Commandments seem to lose their uncon-
> ditioned validity, man must learn more than ever to listen to the ten thousand
> commandments arising from the ten thousand unique situations of which
> his life consists. As to *these* commandments, he is referred to, and must rely
> on, his conscience. A lively and vivid conscience is also the only thing that
> enables man to resist the effects of the existential vacuum, namely con-
> formism and totalitarianism.... Human freedom is not omnipotence. Nor is
> human wisdom omniscience, and this holds both for cognition and con-
> science. One never knows whether or not it is the true meaning to which he
> is committed.... But if a man is not to contradict his own humanness, he has
> to obey his conscience unconditionally, even though he is aware of the

possibility of error. I would say that the possibility of error does not dispense him from the *necessity of trial.*[47]

The risk of uncertainty is the risk of *Dasein,* the fact of being-in-the-world.

For Heidegger and Frankl, the courage to be enables us to deal with the angst caused by the conditions of life, including the being-toward-death that is the ultimate challenge and ultimate mystery. We do not have the capacity to understand universal order, either by reason or through our intuitive conscience; but our use of the transcendent dimension allows us to *ek-sist,* to stand outside ourselves, to uncover and use the meanings of life with freedom and responsibleness. We are not perfect beings but spiritually imperfect beings in an imperfect world. We are not victims of life but pilgrims of *ek-sistenz.* We are not solvers of the mysteries of life but—to use Heidegger's phrase—we are shepherds of Being.

Husserl, Scheler, and Heidegger, each in his own way, show that an existential, phenomenological approach to life describes how each person experiences the world for himself or herself. The essentials of phenomenology provide a grounding that has proven to be indispensable for the development of existential, philosophical psychology, including meaning analysis. Philosophically, phenomenology rethinks Kant's idea of the orderly succession of life to show how individual reason and the phenomena of the world interact. Phenomenology reintroduces Socratic dialogue to help persons use questioning to discover for themselves the meanings of life. It uses the insights of such process philosophers as Alfred North Whitehead (1861–1947) to show how "becoming" is as necessary for understanding life as "Being." Phenomenology's concern for the nature of truth established the search for truth as an a priori science that uses the transcendental dimension. While attempting to be fully experiential, phenomenology also acknowledges the importance of human intuition as a form of reasoning that is not strictly rational but includes an ordering of love in our relationships with others. It teaches that a bracketing of significant occurrences of life can help us to stand back from our problems in order to clarify the essential issues involved. Psychologically, phenomenology opposes the traditional, mechanistic, and reductionistic dictates of behaviorism. It also corrects the negative and psychosexual psychotherapy of Freud and his followers. Finally, phenomenology helps us to see that we know ourselves most completely when we understand our being-in-the-world. Both philosophically and psychologically, the perspectives of phenomenology prepared the way for the existential postures that developed, including those of Viktor Frankl.

— 6 —

The

Existentialist

Posture

EXISTENTIALISM DOES NOT REPRESENT A FINISHED
PRODUCT OF THOUGHT THAT CAN BE PASSED ON TO
A RECIPIENT; IT REQUIRES INVOLVEMENT AND FRESH
DISCOVERY FROM EVERY LEARNER.

—ROGER L. SHINN

A popular but mistaken impression is that existentialism came full-blown out of the head of Jean-Paul Sartre (1905–1980) just after World War II. As a result, existentialism has been characterized as atheistic, nihilistic, and antirational. This is neither a true nor a complete description. In its classical form, existentialism has a history as old as philosophy itself. In its contemporary mode, it is represented by a wide spectrum of thinkers that includes, in addition to Sartre, Soren Kierkegaard, Friedrich Nietzsche, Martin Buber (1878–1965), and Gabriel Marcel (1889–1973). Edmund Husserl, Max Scheler, and Martin Heidegger are also often grouped with the existentialists, but they are essentially phenomenologists who reflect an existentialist posture. Although there are strong ties between phenomenology and existentialism, they are two branches of a humanistic philosophical tree rather than dual branches of an existential tree.[1]

The exploration of the relation of the person to the stuff of life (*physis*) was the life task of Socrates; he used the questioning, or dialectic, method to help each person discover for himself or herself the meaning of life. The self is not a blank slate (*tabula rasa*) on which ideas, commitments, and requirements are inscribed; rather, each person is a questioning entity trying to correlate who he or she is with what he or she does. Strictly speaking, there is no viable philosophy that does not question the meaning and expression of personal existence. We are by nature existentialists. The history of Western philosophy is marked by a series of existentialist concerns, from Socrates' imperative "Know thyself" to the Stoics' mastery of one's self amid the challenges of life; from Pascal's philosophy of the heart to Descartes's exploration of human doubt;

from Kant's moral categorical imperative to Kierkegaard's existential choice; from Nietzsche's "death of God" to Sartre's death of good faith.

The Subjectivism of Kierkegaard and Nietzsche

The work of Søren Kierkegaard is the first and most dramatic example of what Roger Shinn calls "the existential posture." The full effect of Kierkegaard was not felt for almost a hundred years after his death. Two factors are responsible: Kierkegaard wrote in Danish, which was not translated for years afterward, and Kierkegaard's own neurotic personality resulted in a difficult, convoluted style of writing. As Emmanuel Mounier comments, "I don't know how the Danes got on for a hundred years with a prophet so unattractive to anyone in his right senses as Søren Kierkegaard."[2] Yet this tormented and eccentric man is seen today as one of the most creative and influential voices of modern philosophy. He is at the same time a philosopher, theologian, psychologist, and storyteller. Nathan Scott, Jr., writes of him, "Indeed, when the full import of his legacy begins to be considered, one wants simply to say of this strange, Hamlet-like 'poet'—as one does of Freud—that he *added* something to our modern awareness of how twisted and devious are all the paths in the country of the human heart, added something in the way that only genius can."[3]

Kierkegaard's philosophy begins with his description of "existential thinking." For him, existential thinking faces the concrete events of one's life; it thinks through all the questions that life raises, accepting both the rational and the absurd. It is an engagement of the whole self—mind, body, and spirit—in a passionate exploration of the meaning of Being. Kierkegaard does not deny the existence of objective knowledge, but he wants us to be aware that its claim of objectivity is illusion rather than fact. Further, he believes that we have lost the capacity for subjectivity, and it is the task of philosophy to rediscover it for us.[4] Objective knowledge would have us base thought and behavior on rules that are causally determined. In contrast, subjective knowledge is searched out, experienced, and reasoned *always in relation to the self.* This subjective process denies that knowledge can be "proven" or systematized; rather, it is paradoxical. The philosopher is also a person of faith. Such a person is free to choose the nature of *ek-sistenz,* in the Heideggerian sense as an ability to stand out from or transcend one's self. Freedom is based on personal choice. Such choice—not the mores of civilization, nor the laws of morality, nor institutionalized religion (as opposed to faith)—is the key to the self. All freedom, all truth, all meaning depend on the choices that the individual makes and acts upon.

Kierkegaard's radical concept of subjective knowledge and its resultant and equally subjective ethics have elicited both extravagant praise and equally extravagant criticism. Marjorie Grene provides a prime example of the latter. Her indictment is biting: "Kierkegaard's greatest weakness is not even his shabby Hegelianism or his overindulgence in verbal sleight of hand. *It is the inadequacy of the man himself to bring to fruition the redirection of philosophy that he initiates.*"[5] H. J. Blackham's positive comments on Kierkegaard are a corrective to Grene's opinion. He tells us to take Kierkegaard seriously "up to a point, to the point of publishing and underlining his warning [against systems], but not to the point of presenting everything or nothing."[6]

Nietzsche, as controversial as Kierkegaard, also sees subjective knowledge as the vehicle for testing whether or not truth is valid. He, like his Danish counterpart, attacks the pretensions of the middle class, which Nietzsche sees as a futile attempt to escape total moral bankruptcy by shoring up ethical codes that are hypocritical and ineffective. Nietzsche agrees philosophically with Kierkegaard, but he breaks with him in the matter of theology. Nietzsche thinks that religious maturity comes from the recognition that God is dead rather than, as Kierkegaard believes, from a sole commitment to Christ. But he agrees with Kierkegaard that what is needed is a radical reevaluation of existence.

Nietzsche's reevaluation of existence is not as radical as it first appears. He does not repudiate all Western values; rather, he wants the self to be free to choose those values that the person feels are authentic, whether or not the values are traditional. This choice demands moral courage from a special type of person—a person Nietzsche calls the *Übermensch,* translated and misunderstood as the "superman." As Nathan Scott, Jr., writes:

> The popular image of the Nietzschean superman is an image of a blustering bully with a raised fist and a threatening grimace on his face—a distortion so absurd as not even to be a caricature. For the *Übermensch* . . . far from being an amoral gangster, is the mortal enemy of unscrupulousness and violence, of lawlessness and terrorism. . . . He is, in Nietzsche's account, a rare aristocrat of the spirit.[7]

In effect, the *Übermensch* is a 19th-century version of Socrates' philosopher-king, a guardian of true values; he is not, however, as the Greeks believed, one working in harmony with the gods but one who challenges life in a world in which God is dead. Like the Greek hero, the *Übermensch* is able to say yes to the "sad and suffering world," reflecting *amor fati,* or love of one's fate.[8] Such Nietzschean Stoic heroism requires not "will to life" but "will to power." Nietzsche's will to power is an assertion of a moral necessity rather than an explanation; it is an attitude more than a process. Essentially, it is a call to explore courageously reality as the *Übermensch* encounters it.

Kierkegaard and Nietzsche are the revolutionary heroes of contemporary existentialism. They provide the starting point for the development of existential psychology, including meaning analysis. Like these men, Frankl realizes that the dis-ease of our time is the divorce of thought and life. Existential thinking helps to restore this unity by introducing a robust and intensified humanism. The humanism, or personalism, of existentialism emphasizes the *vita activa* (active life) over the *vita contemplativa* (the contemplative life). This does not mean that reason is denied, as is sometimes charged by the critics of existentialism;

rather, reason takes its place alongside experience, intuition, and the exercise of the will. Existentialism's personalism aims at establishing a holistic philosophy of the self beginning with commitment.

The watchword of the latter part of the 18th century was "Liberty, equality, and freedom," but the slogan was more often romantic than realistic. Kierkegaard and Nietzsche emphasize that personal freedom must be won amid the doubts, tragedies, ambiguities, and paradoxes of life as it is experienced. This experiential and subjective emphasis has caused some to dismiss existentialism as the musing of a gloomy Dane and the ideological vagaries of a mentally disturbed German, who exemplified his own story of a madman who when asked where God had gone called out, "I meant to tell you! *We have killed him*—you and I! We are all his murderers!"[9] Instead, the emphasis of Kierkegaard and Nietzsche on commitment, courage, and credo (faith) is the foundation for a rethinking of the human condition, which is reflected in Frankl's writings.

Commitment, Courage, and Credo

The Socratic "Know thyself" becomes "*Commit* thyself" for Kierkegaard and Nietzsche. Ideas without commitment are at best ineffective and at worst chimeras that haunt us because we fail to realize them. The lives and works of Kierkegaard and Nietzsche show that commitments can be either theistic or atheistic, but for both men, the key to commitment is the discovery and the use of personal freedom in a pluralistic, confusing, and often hostile world.

Commitment is the ownership of life wherever and whenever it is experienced; it is basically a passionate decision that involves the whole self. Commitment is not irrational; it may start in rebellion, but it must end with freedom and responsibleness. Responsibleness, however, cannot be imposed from outside the self, even by a helper such as a therapist; rather, freedom and responsibleness must be exercised in the way each person chooses. As a result, it is not surprising that existentialism has been called "a turbulence set loose in the modern world."[10] But the turbulence is not existentialism but events that cause the self to reexamine existence. Commitments are more often made in times of strife that in times of calm. Commitment was realized by Kierkegaard, Nietzsche, and Frankl in the midst of mental searchings and struggles. Kierkegaard's ultimate commitment is "to will one thing: purity of heart"; Nietzsche's is to an enlightened "will to power"; Frankl's is to "the will to meaning."

James C. Crumbaugh suggests five steps in meaning analysis that may lead the self out of the existential vacuum, which he perceives is at the root of our contemporary dis-ease, to a commitment to meaning. Undergirding each of these steps is the affirmation that life has meaning in all circumstances and that we are given the power to find such meaning through the will to meaning, which Frankl calls the defiant power of the human spirit. Crumbaugh suggests that meaning analysis advises us to (1) choose the way that we look at ourselves and at the world, (2) develop self-confidence, (3) stimulate creative thinking that will help us to achieve our goals, (4) establish encounters with others that will cause us to reach beyond ourselves, and (5) find a task or a cause to believe in and work for.[11]

Kierkegaard and Nietzsche lay the foundations for the understanding of courage or the power to be, which Frankl speaks of as the defiant power of the human spirit. The power to be is not an addition to the human personality but a basic quality of Being itself. Kierkegaard sees such courage as the *religious* courage of the person commited to Christ; Nietzsche sees such courage as the *defiant* courage of the *Übermensch*; Frankl sees such courage as the *meaning-full* courage of all persons, including the "man in the street." Frankl's "defiant power of the human spirit" accomplishes two goals: it gives the self the courage to rise above the negative influences of a person's *external* (social) environment, and it gives the self the courage to rise above the negative influences of a person's *internal* (or psychic) environment. We have the power to stand outside ourselves (*ek-stasis*), Frankl suggests, through dereflection and self-transcendence and often by using humor to do so. This use of humor is found not only in Frankl's writings but in Kierkegaard's and Nietzsche's writings as well. Whereas Kierkegaard uses humor to stimulate his reader and Nietzsche uses ironic stories to shock or outrage, Frankl uses humor as a means of healing. Paradoxical intention is Frankl's best known therapeutic use of humor. In this technique, an irrational fear is expressed as an irrational wish. The humor apparent in the reversal of the situation helps the person to regain needed perspective. As an example, Frankl relates the plight of a client who was mortified because he perspired heavily whenever he had to speak in public. Frankl urged the man that when he next began to perspire to do so profusely: "Sweat buckets and buckets so that the people will be swept out of the room by it!" The young man, highly amused by the absurdity of the advice, was able to dereflect and overcome his phobia.

Dereflection and self-transcendence require courage. The everyday act of courage takes place when we commit ourselves to accomplishing a meaningful task or to helping another person. Commitment and courage do not stand alone; they both depend on an existential credo (faith).

An authentic credo says "I believe," not "I conform"; it is based on personal, firsthand experience. When a credo is codified, it becomes second-hand and loses personal authenticity. In Kierkegaard's and Nietzsche's conceptions, a credo has three characteristics: a credo is *subjective, paradoxical,* and *emphasizes "lived time."* Kierkegaard and Nietzsche, each in his own way, are existential evangelists witnessing that faith is intensely subjective. For them, faith is only known subjectively; any other form of faith must be unmasked as secondhand. A credo must reflect what each individual believes and sees as true. For Kierkegaard, *what* a person believes is less important than *the manner* in which it is believed.[12] Kierkegaard and Nietzsche deny the possibility of objective truth. Something is true only when it works in a particular situation for a particular person. This means, however, that a person must be aware of how subjective truth affects others and must take responsibility for his or her judgment.

Kierkegaard avoids ethical solipsism by defining truth as purity of heart in accord with the imperatives of Christ. Nietzsche is on shakier ground: he endows the *Übermensch* with the wisdom to know and to act on the truth for the good of others. Frankl's credo is also subjective: he urges us to find truth through our intuitive conscience. He admits, however, that in so doing, "we may be wholehearted and half right." In other words, we may mislead as well as be misled. Frankl does not aim at the truth of perfection but at the truth of meaning, expressed by values that we recognize, accept, and act on. He sacrifices ethical infallibility for humility. Frankl escapes Nietzsche's inwardness by reminding us that values must be tested in the marketplace. Although personal experience has priority over the corporate, the social dimension plays an important role in measuring the effectiveness of our values. What we believe may result in our recognizing life's paradoxes more than its certainties.

The very nature of the credo makes paradoxes inevitable. Kierkegaard is the master of the paradox. Faith is triumphant yet requires suffering. Truth is subjective, but its effect is experienced objectively. We are the children of God, yet we sin in thought and action as part of God's family. We are the children of light while moving inescapably toward the dark (death). God is revealed but also hidden. Nietzsche's paradoxes come from his desire to understand the hidden man in a time when "God is dead." Instead of *Tu es vere Deus absconditus* (Verily, thou art the hidden God), he substitutes *Tu es vere homo absconditus* (Verily, thou art the hidden man). Nietzsche's central paradox is that the man whom he exposes, the *Übermensch,* remains the hidden man—often ambiguous, secret, and half-understood in a world in which he may act but which he may never claim. Nietzsche moves from nihilism to the will to power, following the advice of Heraclitus to "follow the call of conscience. Be yourself!" But Nietzsche never clarifies what being one's own self means. He prepares the ground for Sartre's nihilistic statement, "Man's absolute freedom knows no obedience, no service, no humility, no response to Being."[13]

Frankl also recognizes the paradoxical nature of existence, but he escapes both the piety of Kierkegaard and the secular elitism of Nietzsche by focusing, in his search, on meaning. In his discussion of meaning analysis in medical practice, George R. Simms explains Frankl's purposeful focus on meaning: "Without an individually forged meaning and purpose, it becomes impossible to withstand the great and small crises and tragedies which make up so much of daily existence."[14] The same is true for withstanding the paradoxes of life. Frankl deals with the problem of paradox by pointing out that the self is a diversity within unity. He writes that "in the dimension of the body we are imprisoned; in the dimension of the psyche we are driven; but in the dimension of the spirit we are free."[15]

Our freedom includes the ability to recognize the paradoxes of life and how to deal with them. Take, for instance, the paradoxes of the body and aging.

As we become more physically infirm, we may mentally want to do more; we want to be able to channel our energy in ways that we have discovered in the maturing process. Our noetic dimension gives us the power to withstand this paradox of body and aging by using self-transcendence to choose how an aging body may still be an effective agent of the spirit and the psyche.

Whereas Nietzsche writes romantically of "the love of fate," Frankl deals with "the paradox of fate." Sartre says that fate condemns us to be free only to say no. But for Frankl, fate is not a paradox of condemnation but a paradox of freedom that reminds us that while the conditions of fate may limit us, we are free to take a stand regarding its conditions; we are enabled to say yes as well as no. Frankl is aware that his philosophy is not the complete approach to life and its paradoxes. He points to ultimate meaning—as shown in the I-Thou relationship—but leaves it up to each of us to choose what form of ultimate meaning will give us a sense of purpose and health-fullness.

Frankl sees mental health-fullness as an essential characteristic of life with meaning. Hiroshi Takashima points out that Frankl uses the term *psychonoetic antagonism* to show how a mental dis-ease, such as extreme anxiety, can be overcome:

> A person driven by anxieties may become neurotic. However, if helped to see a purpose in life and act accordingly, this same person may overcome the anxieties and avoid becoming neurotic. In this case the noetic power works antagonistically with respect to the psychic power.
>
> But the noetic power can also work synergistically with the psychic power. For instance, when people have emotional drives, say, to excel in sports, their spirit, expressed as responsibility toward team mates or strong motivation to help win a championship, can strengthen their emotional drive.[16]

When applied to dealing with life's paradoxes, noetic power may be used either way. Negatively, psychonoetic antagonism helps us to transcend the paradoxes we do not understand and to go on with the tasks of living. Positively, it helps us to make the paradoxes we accept as part of our *Lebenswelt*. Paradoxes also remind us of the role of time.

Life in Time

Ordinary time is time that we *observe*; lived time is time in which we *participate*. Existentialism stresses the importance of lived time; in so doing, it sets up a dialectic between the person and lived history (*geschichte*). Kierkegaard and Frankl use time to illustrate the fullness of existence, while Nietzsche uses time as an example of vitality. But all three begin with time as the example of the confrontational nature of existence. Shinn argues that the constant confrontation of the self with existence is the first mark of biblical history; thus, "whether in trust or rejection, in devotion or antagonism, existentialism has its origin in biblical faith."[17] This is borne out by the other two marks that Shinn notes: personal existence and the awareness of history and faith in relation to God.

Kierkegaard's description of lived time follows the biblical story of existence in relation to God, but he uses the stories of the personal struggles of the great figures of biblical history to illustrate the existential themes of confrontation, obedience and disobedience, and sin; and he ignores the use of time by the people of God. Thus, while Kierkegaard illustrates lived time by religious history, it is a truncated history that virtually ignores the implications of time for humanity as a whole.

Nietzsche, after rejecting any form of religious history as lived time, champions a combination of enlarged Stoicism and German romanticism. His Stoicism is exemplified by the *Übermensch*, who affirms lived time by not only bearing the necessities of fate but also *loving* them. Nietzsche links this *amor fati* with a form of German romanticism that he calls Eternal Recurrence, arguing that it is "the most *scientific* of all hypotheses."[18] But it is not treated as a hypothesis by Nietzsche; rather, it is treated as a way of dealing with time as it is experienced. Nathan Scott, Jr., notes:

> For a world in which all things are dominated by the iron necessity of repeating themselves in an endless circle, Eternal Recurrence is a world which is radically absurd ... yet, even to such a world, the superman—great stoic that he is—says "Yes," for he (as Nietzsche said in *Beyond Good and Evil*) "has not only learned to accept and come to terms with what was and is, but wishes to have it again as *it was and is,* for all eternity."[19]

Stoicism and a belief in Eternal Recurrence are enabled by the will to power, the expression of time as vitality.

Frankl's meaning-oriented philosophy expands the fullness of Kierkegaard's view of time and refocuses Nietzsche's vitalism. He starts with a corrective to their narrowing the concept of time to existential choice without regard for time past or time that is to be. He calls attention to Erwin Straus's belief that the reality of a person's life (*Werdewirlichkeit*) cannot be considered apart from historical time.[20] Frankl agrees with Straus that when persons repudiate any sense of direction that takes in the past or looks toward the future, they deform their reality, adopting what Straus calls a presentist existence, living only for the moment.[21] Although there are times in which a normal person may take, up to a point, a presentist attitude for a particular reason, to do so as a matter of course or to build a philosophy around it (as in the case of Kierkegaard or Nietzsche) is neurotic.

Authentic human existence is historical existence. We are placed in historical space; we must discover meaning when and where our lives are located. True history is history that has been given meaning by humankind—that is, lived history (*geschichte*). History without meaning is not history but a series of dates (*historia*). Time that is fully lived is lived in three dimensions: past, present, and future. All three dimensions make up what Frankl calls the novel that each individual lives, "an incomparably greater composition than any that has ever been written down."[22] If we live only in the present, we may lose our psychic balance, which calls upon the past and reaches toward the future to balance perspective. Passing time is seen by Frankl as a trustee, not as a thief; because Frankl is convinced that each of us knows somehow that the content of his or her life is somewhere preserved and saved: "Thus time, the transitoriness of the years, cannot affect its meaning and value."[23] This perspective redefines human destiny so that it may be understood as (1) a person's natural disposition, (2) a person's situation (external environment), and (3) a person's position, a combination of disposition and situation, whereby the self takes an attitude to his or her destiny.[24] *Disposition* represents our biological fate, and *situation* is our sociological fate. But *position* is our spiritual destiny, which allows us to choose how we see ourselves in the past, in the present, and in the future. We exercise this choice by self-transcendence. If we think of time only in terms of how it makes us happy or unhappy, we will be trapped by it. But if we see ourselves as stewards of time, enablers of others in time, then we self-transcend and in so doing, escape being trapped by the dictates of our situation. We exercise our wills to realize a new spiritual destiny.

Frankl's view of lived time is a corrective to the views of both Kierkegaard and Nietzsche. Although Frankl has the same intensity of concentration as they do, he substitutes a dedication to meaning for Kierkegaard's narrow religious commitment and for Nietzsche's egocentric dedication to power. Frankl shows how we use time, not through piety or power, but through three types of values: *creative values* (achieving tasks), *experiential values* (knowing another person; awareness of the Good, the True, and the Beautiful), and *attitudinal values* (facing fate with freedom and understanding).[25] Our acting on values equals lived time.

Sartre and Frankl Compared

The fundamental contribution of Kierkegaard's and Nietzsche's existentialism is its insistence that we must deal with the meaning of existence before we explore essence. They further show that the values of human life are not automatic but must be created by the choices that we make for our own lives. We need to remind ourselves that Kierkegaard and Nietzsche are the first voices of existentialism and are the foundation of what became a movement. As such, they are also the innovators of a new way of thinking. The existentialist who most dramatically assumed Kierkegaard's and Nietzsche's mantles of rebellion was Jean-Paul Sartre. Even more than Nietzsche, Sartre caused the thinkers of the 20th century to come to grips with nihilism. His nihilistic philosophy provides a lively challenge to constructive thinking, including Frankl's philosophy of meaning.

The philosophies of both Sartre and Frankl were tested during World War II; Sartre's as a member of the French Resistance movement, and Frankl's as a prisoner of four Nazi concentration camps. These two humanistically trained men, born in the same year (1905), were taken from their chosen professions (one a teacher, the other a psychiatrist) and subjected to the hardest facts of existence. Their understanding of Being was literally tried by fire. Sartre's description of life in the Resistance movement gives important clues to how he came to see life:

> To those who were engaged in underground activities, the conditions of their struggle afforded a new kind of experience. They did not fight openly as soldiers. In all circumstances they were alone. They were hunted down in solitude, arrested in solitude. It was completely forlorn and unbefriended that they held out against torture, alone and naked in the presence of torturers, clean-shaven, well-fed, and well-clothed, who laughed at their cringing flesh, and to whom an untroubled conscience and a boundless sense of social strength gave every appearance of being in the right. Alone. Without a friendly hand or a word of encouragement. Yet, in the depth of their solitude, it was the others that they were protecting, all the others, all their comrades in the Resistance. Total responsibility in total solitude—is this not the very definition of our liberty? This being stripped of all, this solitude, this tremendous danger, were the same for all. . . . Each . . . knew that he owed himself to all and that he could count only on himself alone. Each of them, in complete isolation, fulfilled his responsibility and his role in history. Each of them, standing against the oppressors, undertook to be himself, freely and irrevocably. And choosing for himself in liberty, he chose the liberty of all.[26]

In this paragraph, Sartre uses words and concepts that are basic to his *Weltanschauung*. For instance, his emphasis on solitude, on reliance only upon one's own self, bad faith (*mauvais foi*) as the accurate description of the behavior of humankind, and the use of vengeance to right a wrong are balanced by a commitment to personal freedom and to working in good faith for the freedom of others.

Frankl's experiences in the Nazi concentration camps also give important clues to how his philosophy and psychology of meaning were tested. Like Sartre, he focuses on choice and action:

> The experiences of camp life show that man does have a choice of action. There were enough examples, often of a heroic nature, which proved that apathy could be overcome, irritability suppressed. Man *can* preserve a vestige of spiritual freedom, of independence of mind, even in such terrible conditions of psychic and physical stress.[27]

Frankl, however, differs radically from Sartre by locating the source of freedom of choice in the noetic dimension. Such freedom, Frankl believes, is not just heroic defiance of bad faith, as Sartre suggests, but the use of the essential spiritual part of the self, which is able to deal responsibly with good faith as well as bad faith. Frankl is more realistic than Sartre since he recognizes that good faith for the wrong reasons can be as threatening as bad faith. Bad faith is often easily recognized and frightening; good faith, which is sometimes misplaced, may be convoluted and more difficult to evaluate. Both Sartre and Frankl suffered "blows of fate" at the hands of the Nazis. How each man responded shows his philosophy of Being.

Sartre describes two modes of Being as *être-en-soi* (being-in-itself) and *être-pour-soi* (being-for-itself). Being-in-itself is exactly Being as it is. In contrast, being-for-itself is how a person reacts to the external world. Although being-in-itself has no reflective consciousness, no a priori core of humanity, it can "project" itself. Being-in-itself coupled with being-for-itself equips a person to deal with being-in-place (*être-la* or *Dasein*). These qualities of Being cause Sartre to underscore that each person deals with being-in-place as both free and determined. According to Sartre, from its very beginning existence is paradoxical and even absurd. Although we are free, we are free only to say no. We are rebels against the structures of existence; yet we need structures to exist because, to use Nietzsche's phrase, "God is dead." Our resultant atheism makes us alienated. We use passion; but passion, although it is also a way of seeing, is essentially useless. Sartre recognizes that our response to the world involves our being-for-others (*être-pour-autrui*), but he sees such relations, or more accurately "connections," as being in fact disconnected. The "we" occurs only by accident; and when it does occur, it is essentially threatening to the self. We can relate to each other only in bad faith, and the result is a fraternity of terror. Equality can only exist in a classless society, which Sartre comes to believe is impossible to achieve. This is what Marjorie Grene calls Sartre's "honest but depressing" understanding of Being.[28]

Frankl's view of the self is clearly different from Sartre's. Although he agrees with Sartre that each person is unique and that freedom and responsibleness are the hallmarks of what it means to be human, he radically redefines each of Sartre's terms: being-in-itself, being-for-itself, being-in-place, and being-for-others. For Frankl, Being is essentially prereflective, especially in the case of Being's intuitive conscience, which is the origin of human freedom and responsibleness.

The "I" and the "we" are not adversaries. Frankl, replacing Sartre's dualism of the "I" and the "we," sees the "we" as a test of both good and bad faith and, above all, as a completion of the self. He transmutes Sartre's being-in-place to dialogue or community-in-place. Whereas Sartre is satisfied with saying only that Being *is,* Frankl says that Being is *meaning.* He replaces Sartrean nihilistic ambiguity with human purpose. As a result, true projection becomes true self-transcendence; bad faith is balanced by good faith; solitude is augmented by dialogue; rebellion is replaced by freedom *for* as well as freedom *from*—we can say yes to life as well as no; vengeance gives way to forgiveness. The passion evident in Sartre becomes for Frankl a passion of *philia* (fraternity) or *agapé* (sacrifice); it becomes a way of seeing.

The difference between Sartre's existential analysis and Frankl's meaning analysis is most dramatically seen in their understanding of the relation of values to meaning. Sartre becomes increasingly fearful, distrustful, and essentially imprisoned by his ego; he comes to describe values basically as a matter of taste. He seems driven to reject all middle-class values, though he never succeeds. In the end, Sartre is left with a dread of humanity. In contrast, Frankl avoids both the strictures of middle-class morality and the license of antinomianism. He urges that we use our intuitive conscience to work out with others meanings that reflect values that are universally recognized. Meanings constitute the reason for acting. If such reason is missing, as in the case of Sartre, then "the lesson to be learned from Sartre's existentialism is . . . a hyphenated nothingness; namely, the no-thingness of the human being."[29] Such a being is incapable of either self-determination or self-creation. How Sartre manages to believe in both is puzzling, especially self-creation. Does he mean that the self is a creator out of nothing, like the traditional theologian's belief of God (*Creatio ex nihilo*)? For Frankl, our task is not to invent ourselves but to use meaning to detect the true dimensions of Being.

Buber, Marcel, and Frankl Compared

The search for wholeness of Being has become an essential part of the task of contemporary existentialists and was essential to the thought of Martin Buber and Gabriel Marcel. Martin Buber and Frankl share a similar Jewish heritage. Further, both were trained in the classical European gymnasium. As a result, their views of life combine humanism, existentialism, and a faith rooted in the biblical tradition. Although there are differences in vocabulary and emphases, they share such themes as encounter, communication, the I-Thou relationship, and above all, the concepts of meaning and hope. Frankl's transmutation of the Socratic dialogue is similar to Buber's concept of reality as the "sphere of the between," "the narrow ridge": the meeting of person with person through the interweaving of I-Thou with I-it, as first presented by Buber in 1923.

The difference between I-it and I-Thou is understood in terms of relationships. The world of the I-it takes place in time and space; the world of the I-Thou takes place in relationships as they occur. After being part of a relational event, the Thou changes to an it determined by time and space. The it is transformed into a Thou when it participates in a relationship. Both the I-it and the I-Thou alternate as necessary to life and to aspects of life. The I-it shows us the outer reality of the world; we cannot live without it. The I-Thou shows the inner reality of the spirit and essentially gives us a spiritual perspective that frees us from the dictates of outer circumstances and inner turmoil. Without the I-

Thou, the I (ego) becomes an overwhelming and destructive force; when linked with the Thou, the I, or self, is able, in Frankl's words, to dereflect and to self-transcend.

The French term *presence* describes not a law but a quality of Being that defines our relationships. *Presence,* called the transcendental dimension by Kant and ultimate meaning by Frankl, has three functions for Buber: (1) it enables true (I-Thou) relationships, (2) it assures that meaning is present in a situation, and (3) it enables the person to be responsible in the here and now. For Buber and Frankl, being responsible is to call upon a special, intuitive awareness in confronting what we see, hear, or feel. "Only . . . true to the moment, do we experience a life that is something other than a sum of moments. We respond to the moment, but at the same time we respond on its behalf, we answer for it."[30] Buber and Frankl call for awareness, not perfection. True response is living toward the other person, ready to risk an open dialogue.

Unlike Sartre, Buber and Frankl do not think that we create ourselves; rather, they believe that we are trustees of all creation, including ourselves. This is not just an idea for them; it is an existential reality. Buber says that we are "addressed" through the existential realities that we experience. How we respond to the way that we are addressed determines both how we think about ourselves and how we relate to others. Those threatened by the world of others retreat into an extreme form of individualism, concentrating on protecting the ego. Of all creatures, humans seem to be especially aware of and vulnerable to the dimensions of such a perceived threat; the human being also feels the isolation and despair that come from such a retreat into the self. As a result, "to save himself from the despair with which his solitary state threatens him, man resorts to the expedient of glorifying it."[31] Such a response is not only expedient but also reactive and unrealistic, for such a response is incapable of overcoming either despair or the sense of nothingness that accompanies it.

Another response, equally unsatisfactory, is collectivism. Modern collectivism is when a person tries to escape the need to express his or her freedom and responsibility by blending into the social amalgam. In other words, the self barters its uniqueness for a false security; the result is that the person's fear and sense of isolation are merely numbed, not resolved or overcome. Buber suggests a third alternative to modern individualism and modern collectivism that adds to a person's worth rather than taking away from it. He urges that we see that we are *interdependent*. For Buber, the reality of human existence lies in a living relationship with others: the I-Thou and the I-it completed and fulfilled in the "we." The "we" relationship is not something added to the self but an essential dimension of Being. Buber notes that "what is peculiarly characteristic of the human world is above all that something takes place between one being and another, the like of which can be found nowhere in nature."[32] It separates the human from the subhuman.

Frankl's experiences in the concentration camps validate Buber's conviction of the importance of the "we." When prisoners, threatened by the world of the camp, retreated into the world of the self, they lost all sense of meaning and ended in despair. Similarly, if they allowed themselves to be absorbed by the collectivism of the camp, they became totally dehumanized and lost the will to live. When individuals, however, sought to discover and build I-Thou relationships, even under the most miserable circumstances, they formed a "we" that affirmed rather than denied their Being.

Buber's I-Thou relationship as the paradigm of the fully human self is foundational for the religious existentialism of Marcel and Frankl. It is the basis of human hope. Like Buber, Marcel and Frankl are prophets of hope. Marcel explains the nature of hope by contrasting it with the word *unhope*:

> The word *unhope* coined by Thomas Hardy . . . translated by a neologism *inespoir,* admirably renders that state of the soul apprehended in terms of what may be called its positive negativity. Unhope which is opposed to hope as fear is opposed to desire, is truly a death in life, a death anticipated. . . . It yawns before us as an abyss at certain moments and we are swallowed up by it as in a morass from which we do not possess the courage even of the most elementary kind to will our escape.[33]

In contrast, hope is far more than escape; it is salvation or wholeness, integrally related to fidelity and love. But hope is not a personal right or possession. It is part of the "we." Hope is not simply a hope for one's self but a "spreading of one's hope, keeping its flame a radiance of hope burning around one."[34] This involves fidelity, or faithfulness. For Marcel, such fidelity is the affirmation of Being in the face of denial and despair. He describes it as *creative* fidelity, showing that "the self which fidelity reveals is a self which fidelity *creates*.[35] Such faithfulness goes beyond constancy. "It is the spontaneous and unimposed presence of an I to a Thou. . . . It is a call to which I answer 'present.' In saying 'here' I create my own self in the presence of a thou . . . fidelity is the active perpetuation of presence."[36]

The term *presence* has dimensions in French that are missing in the English understanding of the word, which is to be present, to occupy space. Marcel's term *presence* involves a bond of feeling between one person and another. He points out that when two people become aware that they have shared an experience—they have visited the same place, they have shared the same risks, they have read and enjoyed the same book, or they share a friendship with a third person—a unity is established in which the I and the Thou become the we. These beginnings of being present *to* the other can develop into being *for* the other. True communication can lead to love (*philia*) that reflects creative fidelity. Marcel describes the *philia* that characterizes creative fidelity as a relationship to "someone who stands up to whatever the circumstances may bring; he does not slip away, but we find him there when we are in difficulty."[37]

> I can easily imagine a man who assures me in the best of faith that his inner feelings or dispositions in my regard have not altered; to a certain extent I will believe him; but if I notice that he is not there in a certain circumstance

when his friendship would have been of value to me, I would hesitate to refer to his fidelity. Of course, presence is not to be construed here as externally manifesting oneself to another, but rather as involving a quality which cannot be so easily described in objective terms, of making me feel that he is *with* me.[38]

In other words, creative fidelity is not just doing, but an expression of Being itself.

Marcel uses the term *disponibilité* to describe the availability and interrelation of hope, human fidelity, and love. *Disponibilité* is the disposition that allows communion between persons. "The disponible person is hospitable to others; the doors of his soul are ajar."[39] Frankl's meaning analysis expresses, without using the term, such *disponibilité*. It emphasizes that caring relationships between persons deliver us from being imprisoned by our egos so that we may find and express meanings that are free and responsible.

Both Marcel and Frankl struggle with where and how such faith, hope, and love originate and how these essential qualities of Being are made available to the self. Marcel never reconciles his traditional Roman Catholic belief with his existential philosophical explorations. The word *presence* is a key example of Marcel's dilemma as he seeks to relate it to the traditional Christian definition of God. Kenneth T. Gallagher says that Marcel offers a new "ontological argument" that substitutes presences for concepts. Marcel believes that any attempt to demonstrate the existence of God is futile, because in such an attempt God is treated as an object, a thing about which we can argue; further, God can never be regarded as an idea. God is experienced as *Presence,* not proved theologically. Marcel concludes (and essentially Frankl arrives at the same conclusion) that "if there is an experience of God (and only in this sense can we speak of the existence of God) *that experience must be the point of departure and nothing more.*"[40] *Presence* is meaning, enabling us to find a gestalt that overcomes alienation, despair, and meaninglessness. Marcel emphasizes the importance of incarnation, participation, and the feeling that it is "an honor to be a person." Frankl stresses *Dasein,* dereflection, and self-transcendence. But for both, the model of the self is the same. They describe the self as involved in a spiritual pilgrimage, a person on the way (*en via*), who finds purpose, or meaning, through becoming involved (*engagé*) in causes, through reaching out to others in love, and through searching for ultimate meaning.

Both Marcel and Frankl see faith as a choice, not as a command; faith must be explored, not imposed. Marcel and Frankl use different, but not contradictory, terms to explain the need for the self to discover and activate the spiritual (noölogical) dimension. Marcel focuses on God as the bearer of grace; Frankl concentrates on God as the bearer of ultimate meaning. Whether through grace or ultimate meaning, the spiritual power provided gives us both individual and social purpose. If theology is used at all, it is as the servant discipline of a true *humanitas.* Frankl concludes what Marcel implies: "the only thing I know for sure is that if common values and meanings are to be found . . .

Monotheism is not enough; it will not do. What we need is not only the belief in the one God but also the awareness of the one mankind, the awareness of the unity of humanity. I would call it *mon-anthropism.*"[41]

Marcel and Frankl are best understood as poets of Being. While they are also prophets of the self, their philosophy of life is existentially and symbolically spiritual, focusing on the use of freedom and responsibleness in everyday life. The following obligation that Marcel sets for himself is equally applicable to Frankl: "remaining faithful to what is essential in ourselves, rather than striving to anticipate a future about which we know nothing."[42]

The Personalist Approach to Existentialism

Although it is relatively easy to point out the key writers of late 19th- and early 20th-century existentialism, it is difficult to summarize the concerns and, even more so, the accomplishments of this multifaceted and controversial movement. Each writer strikes his or her own existentialist posture. This individualism is exemplified by the Frenchman Emmanuel Mounier (1905–1950), who was one of the first post–World War II writers to commingle existentialism with personalism. Personalism is a philosophy of concern for the human person in all of the dimensions of the self.[43]

This particular personalist movement was launched in the early 1930s by Mounier, who was best known as a leader of the New Catholic Left and a disparate coterie of intellectuals. The latter included the philosophers Gabriel Marcel, Nicholas Berdyaev, and Jacques Maritain; the painter Georges Roualt, the composer Nicolai Nabokoff; and later, those bright young men who joined *Esprit,* which was the magazine of the movement edited by Mounier. What made this personalist movement different from earlier personalist philosophies was the urgent mission of its young and Catholic leaders to find a third way, a religious way, between capitalism and communism. As John Hellman notes, however,

> Most of the earliest and most important articulations of personalism were by German-educated, militantly anti-communist Russians, Germans and Belgians, who were Russian Orthodox, Jewish, or non-believers. . . . There was rather, as [Charles] Maurras said about Marxism, "something German and Jewish about it," and the defence of the person, at the outset was rooted in Bergson and Nietzsche more than in the gospels.[44]

Existentialism has the same international mix of proponents. Like earlier personalist philosophies, it was strongly influenced by German and Jewish thought. Where existentialism differs from Mounier's personalism is in its emphasizing a *philosophical* rather than a *religious* approach to the self. Therefore, it is not surprising that existentialism captured the philosophical imagination of the intellectual world following World War II. With the exception of the arguments between Sartre and Albert Camus over communism, the existential philosophers stayed out of the political arena. Mounier and his followers, after becoming embroiled in politics before and during the war period, then channeled their energies into providing religious and social perspectives on behalf of the New Catholic Left. As a result, they helped to lay the intellectual groundwork for the Second Vatican Council.

In the late 1940s and early 1950s, a split occurred in the personalist movement: there were those, most notably Jean Cardinal Daniélou, who concentrated on reform of the Catholic church, and others like Marcel, who developed a philosophy of Christian existentialism. Mounier shifted his concern to the latter. His *Existential Philosophies,* first published in 1948, just three years before his death at 42, shows his perceptive grasp of the central theme of existentialism. Existentialist themes or concepts were not new to him, since they came from the same concerns for the self that were held by personalism. In fact, the eight concepts discussed by the personalist Mounier also provide a succinct summary of the concerns of existentialism. These concepts show as well how Frankl reflects an existentialist-personalist understanding of the self: (1) human contingency, (2) the limits of reason, (3) the risk of Being, (4) human instability, (5) alienation, (6) the imminence of death, (7) solitude, and (8) nothingness.

Human Contingency

Mounier points out that the first concept of human contingency poses two questions. The essential question of human contingency, raised by Socrates more than 2300 years ago, is Why is the human self subject to unpredictability?; and the second question is personal: Why am I, a particular person who is here and now in this place, subject to the unpredictability of events?[45] The Christian and the non-Christian existentialists respond to these two questions in different ways. Mounier, as a Christian existentialist, sees human vulnerability to contingency as part of the divine plan of creation, incarnation, and redemption.[46] Heidegger, on the other hand, sees the existence of the self in a particular place and at a particular time and subject to unpredictable events as a stark fact of existence without explanation. We are, in Heidegger's words, "thrown into the world"; we are there (*Dasein*) whenever what happens, happens. Whereas the nihilistic existentialist concentrates on *Dasein* and accepts or emphasizes the hazards and threats of the situation, and Mounier relates these to a divine strategy of redemption, Frankl concentrates on the Being of *Dasein,* the *Being* of being there. Frankl insists that what affects us is not so much the circumstances in which we find ourselves but what values and attitudes we *bring* to the situation. For he points out, "Once we deal with man as the victim of circumstances and their influences, we not only cease to treat him as a human being but also *lame* his will to change."[48] Frankl uses life's transitoriness as an example of the importance of perspective. Usually a person sees only the "stubble field of transitoriness and overlooks the full granaries of the past."[49] In the face of the transitoriness of our lives, we have the opportunity and responsibility "to actualize potentialities, to realize values, whether creative, experiential, or attitudinal."[50] Once we recognize and act on a value, we fulfill a meaning that can never be taken from us despite the vagaries and threats of existence. The self is the victor, not the victim, of transitoriness.

The Limits of Reason

The existentialist view of reason has caused some critics to claim that existentialism sees human thought as wholly irrational. This criticism is due in part to the undue emphasis placed on Sartre's championing the understanding of the absurdity of the human condition and his failure to recognize reason as a means to help restore humanness. In contrast to Sartre, the majority of existentialists, from Blaise Pascal to Gabriel Marcel, have not sought to abolish reason: they have, in fact, emphasized the importance of reason while asking that reason be balanced by experience, intuition, and faith so that one can achieve a true understanding of what it means to be human. They recognize that life is a balance of the rational and the irrational. Someone does not always say, "I believe because it is reasonable." There are times when a person says, "I believe," and the reason that the person believes seems absurd: *credo quia absurdum*. Existential philosophy, in questioning all of life, examines the rational and seemingly irrational aspects of life. As Marcel points out, not everything that seems incomprehensible is absurd: "Nothing is *absolutely* true . . . we can have neither truth nor goodness except in part measure and only when they are mixed with evil and falsehood."[51] Frankl sees reason, as imperfect as it is, as an important tool in the search for meaning. He also sees that reason must be balanced by an "unreflected existentialist act." In this act, intuition must be called upon; and in this sense, intuition, which is prerational and prelogical, becomes an expression of the heart: "I should say your heart has believed in an ultimate *raison d'être* all along. Sometimes the wisdom of our hearts proves to be deeper than the insight of our brains. And sometimes the most reasonable thing is not to try to be too reasonable."[52]

The Risk of Being

The risk involved in being a human being, which may at times call upon us to make the "bounding leap" described by Mounier, is one of the least understood paradoxes of existentialism. The paradox in this is that the self is a being vulnerable to crushing despair at the same time that it is a being capable of calling upon dimensions of sustaining power. This capability of the self is, for Frankl, the way to meaning; for existentialists, this capability of the human self affirms their belief that the human self is self-determined; for Mounier, this power is an impulsion, a being-in-advance-of-self.[53] In one way or another, each is telling us that we *are* our existence: we are not driven but driver, the choice maker of life. And in this choice, we take the risk—or the "bounding leap"—of free persons.

The life-deniers and the life-affirmers of existentialism view that risk differently. Sartre, and others, see taking that risk as leading only to frustration and defeat: time is our enemy, not our friend; the past marks our failures and cannot be changed; the present illustrates the impotence of being, not its power; the future offers only more despair and nothingness. Marcel and Frankl, life-affirmers, see the past as redeemable, the present as an opportunity to live a life of meaning, and the future as offering additional ways to express that discovered meaning.

Human Instability

The instability of human existence may be seen negatively or positively: "I am a frail existent lost in the bitter ocean of infinity; I am the weak and lonely god without whom this spontaneous creation of myself by myself is liable at any moment to sink in the depths of nothingness";[54] or "I am maintained in existence by the action of God; I am continuously subject to His decree."[55] (One of the best known reflections of the latter is Augustine's "My heart is restless until it finds its rest in Thee.") The humanistic existentialist recognizes in the dynamics of human instability an energy that can counteract and hold together the human personality threatened by forces of disintegration.

We make decisions as unstable persons in an unstable world; but, as Fabry notes, while "the necessity to make choices of meaning, values, and priority leads to tensions . . . these are healthy tensions."[56] When we are able and willing to take on the burden of our incompleteness, we acknowledge our finiteness; and this acceptance of finiteness is the precondition to mental health and human progress. The inability to accept finiteness is often a characteristic of the neurotic personality; as Frankl points out: "The homeostasis principle [to achieve complete stability] . . . is by no means a normal phenomenon but rather a neurotic one. It is the neurotic individual who cannot abide the normal tension of life—whether physical, psychic, or moral."[57] Our ability to recognize and to integrate instability as a normal yet challenging aspect of life allows us to find meaning in every situation.

Alienation

Mounier uses the term *estrangement,* but the word *alienation* better describes the separation of the self from others. *Alienation* conveys the sense of being threatened by a hostile environment, of being subject to conditions that are not understood and over which the person has no control. Mounier describes the experience of the latter condition as viscosity—the other reaches out to me not to help but to gain control over my life. The effect on the human being confronted by such determined denials of her or his humanness is a sense of betrayal and despair. And alienation has another face: Marcel calls it unavailability. When a person is told of another's misfortune and responds with sympathetic words, that person may actually feel nothing: in essence, that person is not available for the other. It may be that the person's failure to react comes from a need for self-protection, or a lack of empathy, or a conviction that the situation is hopeless anyway; but whatever the cause, the person is not "present" to the other. So alienation may exist even though it is disguised with platitudes of concern. Marcel writes that in order to overcome alienation, "supernatural life *must*...find a hold in the natural."[58] Frankl calls this height psychology—that is, using the power of the noetic dimension to dereflect and self-transcend. Meaning analysis takes into account the biological, psychological, and noölogical dimensions of human existence and also the suprahuman dimension, which Frankl defines as ultimate meaning. The suprahuman dimension is one that we cannot fully enter "but whose edge we can touch."[59] Such reaching out involves risk—the bounding leap of self-transcendence—but it enables us to become fully human, to become free of the prison of our own ego so that we can be present to the other. In other words, we exchange *indisponibilité* for *disponibilité*, instead of retreating from the other, we choose to be a being-for-another. Alienation is replaced by interdependence, in which the freedom and responsibility of both persons are not only preserved but also enlarged.

The Imminence of Death

The problem of facing death is linked by Mounier to our aiming at the unattainable goal of immortality. Mounier agrees with Pascal, who wrote that all we see reminds us of the restrictions of this life and the little amount of time left for choices to be made.[60] For Frankl, this is a message not of gloom but of hope: "Finiteness must itself constitute something that gives meaning to human existence—not something that robs it of meaning."[61] The fact of death, instead of being a threat, is the impetus to use our lifetimes to the utmost, "not letting the singular opportunities—whose 'finite' sum constitutes the whole of life—pass by unused."[62] Frankl compares a person's position in time to that of a student taking a final examination: "It is less important that the work be completed than that its quality be high. The student must be prepared for the bell to ring signaling that the time at his disposal is ended, and in life we must be ready all the time to be 'called away.' "[63] If we are living a life with meaning, the time of "the summons" is not as important as the choices that we make and the responsibilities that we fulfill in the time allotted to us.

Solitude

The use of solitude determines whether solitude is a tragic state or an active virtue. The synonyms that define solitude—isolation and seclusion—describe someone who is alone, or in Mounier's words, describe "the secret state" of the self. To a certain extent, each person is solitary, a person alone and a hidden being—sometimes made so by circumstances and sometimes by choice. Because we have freedom of choice, we choose individually how we will respond to a situation; and often the words and actions we choose seem to others to be confusing or ambiguous and even paradoxical. Frankl reminds us that human freedom is not freedom *from* conditions but rather the ability to take a stand *toward* conditions.[64] When we use solitude as a retreat from taking a stand, rather than as a time of preparation to make a responsible choice, we are trapped by the situation that threatens us. We turn in upon ourselves, and our fears and resentments overwhelm us. This kind of solitude becomes self-isolation and breeds self-pity. We close ourselves off from the transcendent, which allows us to stand back from ourselves and to examine the situation with which we are faced and to explore its meaning. A healthy solitude—a standing apart from the pressures of others—may be the first step toward achieving the height dimension that enables us to see others and ourselves in terms of ultimate meaning. Frankl writes that "what on the natural plane takes on the appearance of being man's decision might as well be interpreted on the supernatural plane as the sustaining assistance of God."[65] Frankl, as a medical scientist, does not require clients to explore the door opened to them by religion, but he tells how he used solitude as a way of being open to a message of meaning. A Jew, he entered St. Stephen's Church in Vienna and asked for a sign. Should he pick up the American visa ready for him, or should he stay with his family? He knew that the Nazis would probably imprison or kill him. He returned home and found his father weeping over a stone fragment of a carving of the Torah, which had been salvaged from the firebombed ruins of the family's synagogue. The fragment read, "Honor thy father and thy mother." Frankl took this as a sign and remained with his family. In effect, this sign was seen by him as a message of grace. At that moment, Frankl chose to walk through the door of religion, as he did many other times as a concentration camp inmate. For Frankl, however, self-transcendence is not always a conscious act. His experiences harmonize with Mounier's comments: "By definition, transcendence can only be approached through non-consciousness and by means of a gamble, alternating with challenge."[66] The distinction between the conscious and unconscious may be a moot point and unimportant when compared to the distinction between the instinctual and the spiritual.

Nothingness

In his discussion of nihilism, Mounier cites Sartre and shows how such words as *narcissism, deception, distortion, mockery,* and *fraud* dominate the nihilistic picture of the self. When he links Sartre with Heidegger, Mounier highlights such terms as *unresolved anguish, melancholy mind,* and *ontological dolour* to describe their view of the human condition.[67] Frankl goes to the heart of the matter when he defines nihilism, which explains Sartre's caricature of the self and Heidegger's pessimism:

> Nihilism is not a philosophy which says there is only nothing, nihil, and therefore no Being; nihilism is that attitude toward life which says that Being has no meaning. A nihilist is a man who considers Being, and above all his own existence, meaningless. But, apart from this academic and theoretical nihilism, there is also a practical, as it were, "lived" nihilism: There are people—and this is more manifest today than ever—who consider their life meaningless, who can see no meaning in their existence and therefore think it is valueless.[68]

Nihilism, in Frankl's view, holds before us a mirror that distorts our view of the self and makes us see ourselves as either a psychic mechanism or a product of our economic environment.[69] The first case is a distorted image that shows us the "nothing-but-ness" of the self, which is reductionism.[70] The latter case is a distorted image that Frankl calls homunculism.[71] Homunculism is a belittling view of the worth of the self that is fatalistic, reductionistic, and pessimistic and leads to both individual and collective neuroses, which include anxiety neuroses, obsessional neuroses, melancholia, and even schizophrenia.

Frankl feels that psychotherapy may often reflect nihilism, and as a result, the patient is shown a distorted rather than a true image of Being. The ability of the person to deal with the fate or circumstance that is distressing him or her depends on his or her taking responsibility for his or her attitude toward the world view of the self. "On the one hand," Frankl writes, "the patient is not responsible for his obsessional ideas, and on the other hand he *is responsible for his attitude toward these ideas.*"[72] In contrast to a neurotic, who lives his or her life looking backward, the meaning-oriented person finds significance in the present and believes that meaning will be further fulfilled in the future. Lived nihilism is replaced by lived meaning—finding meaning through a task worth doing or caring for another. The misanthropy of nihilism is replaced by the philanthropy of a life of meaning.

The personalist approach to existentialism corrects the extreme subjectivism of the early existentialists and provides a *Weltanschauung* that focuses on the creative, value-oriented, and philanthropic aspects of the human spirit. This enlarged and refocused existentialist posture paved the way for the development of 20th-century humanistic-existentialist psychology, a movement in which Frankl plays a major role.

— 7 —

Frontiers

of

Humanistic Psychology

HUMANISTIC PSYCHOLOGY HAS AS ITS ULTIMATE
GOAL THE PREPARATION OF A COMPLETE DESCRIP-
TION OF WHAT IT MEANS TO BE ALIVE AS A HUMAN
BEING.

—JAMES F. T. BUGENTAL

Viktor Frankl's philosophical model of the self shares the ultimate goal of humanistic psychology: to provide a complete description of what it means to be alive as a human being. The search for meaning is a search for wholeness. To be alive encompasses the ability to take hold of life day by day as well as to find meaning in suffering. Humanistic psychology and Frankl's logotherapy comprise what is known as the Third Force of psychology. Freud's psycho-analysis has been labeled the First Force and behaviorism as the Second Force. Rather than being a concerted philosophical or therapeutic plan, humanistic psychology builds on, to paraphrase William James, a mosaic philosophy of the self that has emerged from the biological, psychological, and sociological insights of the latter half of the 20th century.

Theory and Practice of Humanistic Psychology

Carl F. Graumann sets forth the aims and the structure of humanistic psychology in his carefully constructed definition of it as *"an endeavor to return to, or recover, what is considered to be essentially human."*[1] Humanistic psychologists—who include such men as Abraham Maslow (1908-1970), Ludwig Binswanger (1881-1966), Carl Rogers (1902-1987), Rollo May (1909-   ), Gordon Allport (1897-1967), and Viktor Frankl—see their work as an endeavor, which is still not completed, to rehumanize psychology. They return to a humanistic base to correct what they see as distortions of the self that began but did not end with

Freud. To a certain extent, this stance is a protest, as some critics have charged. Their challenge to Freud and others is, however, a protest in the positive but often forgotten meaning of the word *protestare,* which is to promise or affirm. Thus, while they do not reach complete agreement on how to fulfill this aim, they agree on a personal humanism that sees the self as a unique individual, that affirms each person as a value-bearer, that feels each person is free to choose rather than be driven by inward compulsions or circumstantial pressures, and that insists humans are persons on the way (*en via*), searching for a whole life. Anything less, they believe, is dehumanization, and they object to those psychological theories and practices that allow the self to be reduced or determined.

The search of humanistic psychologists for a philosophy and methodology that reflect a holistic view of the self requires a recovery of the classical meaning of the term *humanism* in place of the theological reduction of the term in the 19th century to "a belief calling itself religious but substituting faith in man for faith in God."[2] The more accurate description is the sensibility of humanism expressed by the poetry of Lucretius, the Stoicism of Marcus Aurelius, the Christian liberalism of Erasmus, Kantain moral reason, the transcendentalism of Emerson and Thoreau, the enlarged empiricism of William James, the prophetic Judaism of Martin Buber, and the creative fidelity of Gabriel Marcel.[3] A return to the concept of the humanistic imagination preserves the vital emphases on transcendence, intuitive conscience, the search for meaning, and the recognition of the religious dimension in the secular: all combined in the study and better understanding of the self.[4] Such humanism is a philosophy of possibilities in which the religious dimension is seen as an instrument of creativity, rather than as a mark of orthodox belief and action. It shares the insight of John Dewey (1859–1952) that "all possibilities, as possibilities, are ideal in character . . . whatever introduces genuine perspective is religious."[5]

The humanistic psychologist sharing Dewey's perspective is challenged to offer a view of life that draws on the resources of a religious humanistic dimension that will give new meaning to moral commitment and responsible action. Herbert W. Schneider outlines such a strategy for a religious humanism that can be adopted by humanistic psychologists: to maintain a dual attachment to their ideas and to the world in which they live; to be humane, shown in human caring; to avoid disinterestedness and isolation; to be responsible.[6]

Present-day humanistic psychologists are just as devoted to delivering the self from the bondage of Freud's biological-mechanistic reductionism and Skinner's behavioral determinism as the Renaissance humanists were to delivering the self from the bondage of Scholasticism. But the humanistic psychologists' focus on the self does not glorify the individual; rather, it aims at restoring the place of the self in the universe as a free and responsible agent. Following William James's perception, they see respect for one's own individuality and for that of others as part of respect for life itself. Humanistic psychology teaches that the individual does not stand alone but uses his or her uniqueness in relation to others: life is communal as well as individual.

Part of the task of humanistic psychology is to provide ways to overcome the inner alienation of the self and the outer alienation from others. Marx saw alienation from others as a class problem, but humanistic psychology views this social alienation as an individual responsibility, which begins wherever a person is placed or, in Heidegger's words, is "thrown into the world." Our inner experiences are resources for our relationships to others. We do not think, dream, and intuit only for our own well-being but also for the well-being of others through I-Thou relationships. If we hoard our thoughts and feelings, such self-isolation will cause us to turn in upon ourselves in a neurotic manner that represents pseudo-individualism, a form of narcissism. Authentic individualism self-transcends by performing worthwhile tasks or by reaching out to others and enables us to free ourselves from the prison of self-absorption and to become truly ourselves. It is our responsibility, Frankl believes, to exercise our freedom and choose authentic individualism. This position denies Graumann's criticism that "humanistic psychologists tend to ignore human activities in concrete meaningful situations in favor of inner experiences and individual capacities."[7] He may have had in mind, as an example, Abraham Maslow, whose hierarchy of values reaches its apex with self-realization. (Frankl reports that Maslow told him that were he to rewrite his hierarchy of values, he would put meaning at the apex.)[8]

The values that we choose and act upon reveal the type of persons that we are. The distinguishing mark of our individual uniqueness is that we are value-bearing beings. Although this view of the self was first emphasized by Aristotle and continued as an essential aspect of philosophical thought through Immanuel Kant, the humanistic psychologist is faced today with a Western society that claims that it is value-free; and this positivistic approach to the self, which avers that genuine knowledge is defined by scientific evidence, currently dominates many of the attitudes in philosophy, psychology, and most noticeably, education. For example, John Charles Cooper points out that it is generally believed in the United States that value-free instruments used to measure human understanding, such as IQ tests, are preferable to those that might deal with values.[9] Cooper indicates that the abandonment of values has come about because there is a lack of agreement on the nature of values. Since William James, humanistic philosopher-psychologists have recognized that values do not come ready-made, nor are they always clear. The values that we determine, and that we may or may not espouse, can be true or false, which in Pascal's words may be "both the grandeur and misery of man." This spiritual pursuit of values and meaning is what James calls the *active* element in all consciousness.[10] He and Frankl see it as the noetic dimension of the self, the quality that makes us authentically human. The adjective *authentically* underscores the effort of contemporary humanism to put existence before essence, to link such qualities as moral choice, humanness, and meaning. These humanistic theories are active behind humanistic psychologists' practical concern with alleviating the human condition.[11]

The practical emphasis of humanistic psychology is seen in such men as Adler, Scheler, Jung, and Fromm, each of whom wrestled with how to balance theory with practice. Allport, Maslow, Rogers, May, and Frankl continue in this tradition. Rather than give theoretical answers, they use a dialogical method to question the nature of the self and to explore new ways of expressing what it means to be fully human. Their method helps them to avoid the romanticism about the nature of being human that dominated early 19th-century literature and philosophy, as well as the pessimistic reaction to such romanticism that occurred later in that same century. Their work may be considered realism, or tragic optimism, or a balance of intelligence and empathy. Empathy is a key quality of humanness; it means participating in the life of another person as fully as individual sensitivity allows: The humanistic psychologist tries "to know not only what a man does . . . but what he refrains from doing; what he dreams of doing, what he fears to do; what he does with exultation, hesitation, guilt, or boredom. An action is not understood unless one discerns what courage went into it, what routine, what integrity or duplicity, what choice."[12] Although these men are oriented toward action, it is not action for action's sake. In the Jamesian sense of action, they are pragmatists, using, to the best of their ability, their intelligence and experience and incorporating the resources of phenomenology and existentialism. The aim of their psychology of the self is to reveal as far as possible the full scope of what it means to be human.

Amedeo Giorgi lists five expressions of humanistic psychology's understanding of the term *human*: (1) uniqueness, (2) action, (3) humanness, (4) humanism, and (5) life as practiced by the humanities.[13] Most contemporary humanistic psychologists emphasize the first three expressions—uniqueness, action, and humanness—in their explanation of the self, but they also use the term *humane* more and more as the world becomes more and more violent and impersonal. Frankl exemplifies this interweaving of uniqueness, action, and humaneness in his description of a life of meaning. He perceives the uniqueness of the self in an individual's ability to find meaning in life through the realization of creative values (achieving tasks), experiential values (experiencing the Good, the True, and the Beautiful), or by experiencing another person in that person's uniqueness (the I-Thou relationship). Our uniqueness is expressed through our actions: "Man has to answer to life by answering for life; he has to respond by being responsible; in other words, the response is necessarily a response-in-action."[14]

How we look at ourselves determines how we look at others—a proposition that is used to support Freud's pleasure principle, Adler's will-to-power, and Frankl's life-with-meaning. The implications of this proposition range from the claims of Freud, that in order to protect his or her own self-esteem a person will experience or even cause something that is considered inhumane, to Adlers's belief that a person may exercise power in an inhumane way out of the same compulsion. In contrast to Freud's and Adler's estimation of the potency of self-need, Frankl believes in the *potential* of self-need to be transformed, through dereflection and self-transcendence, into a self-healing ability to be humanely present to another person. Frankl's understanding of the therapist-client relationship illustrates on a professional level his concept of being present to another: "You cannot individualize too much. However, you not only have to modify the method from person to person but also from situation to situation, that is to say, you not only have to individualize but to improvise."[15] Thus, being present to another does not mean uniformity or stagnation, nor does it mean constancy; rather it is, in Marcel's words, creative fidelity.

Since the first publication in 1946 of Frankl's *Man's Search for Meaning* (*Ein Psycholog erlebt das Konzentrationslager*), each generation has experienced additional psychological needs, so that the boundaries of humanistic psychology are continually being extended. Just as the sexual repression of the Victorian age gave rise to Freud's psychosexual therapy and the unrest of the post–World War I period made Adler's power principle timely, the nihilism that arose in the 1940s created an existential (spiritual) vacuum that called for a meaning-based psychology. Meaning underlies all the theories of humanistic psychologists, but only Frankl makes it the primary philosophical and therapeutic focus of his psychology.

Frankl links into what he calls "the mass neurotic triad," three symptoms of the existential vacuum of our time: depression, aggression, and abuse of drugs and alcohol. This triad, which is evident at every level of society, represents more than a neurosis in the clinical sense; Frankl describes it as "a paraclinical phenomenon . . . a neuroticization of humanity," and is convinced that "the *de-neuroticization of humanity* requires a *re-humanization of psychotherapy*."[16] Rehumanizing psychotherapy includes reexamining the methods of diagnosis and treatment. In the first case, it means trying to identify the motivation of behavior—that is, the reason or cause. Frankl distinguishes between the two: "Reason is always something psychological or noölogical. Cause, however, is something biological or physiological."[17] If meaning, the central reason for human existence in Frankl's view, is ignored or frustrated, then a person may feel content with either pleasure or power; and the pleasure or the power, normal derivatives of meaning, takes the place of meaning. Rehumanization involves more than a "turning-around" (*metanoia*) of a person's behavior or perceptions. It is education to meaning or responsibility. Education to responsibility cannot be superimposed on a person by society, parents, friends, or therapists. It is a commitment to life that each individual freely accepts for himself or herself. Thus, the therapist who deals with a client's neurosis or addiction must relate to the whole person, not just concentrate on the psyche. Frankl points out the dangers of dehumanizing treatment. He cites a number of speakers at a conference on depression and allied states who referred to "the great danger, inherent in shock treatment and drug therapy, that the medical management may become mechanized and the patient cease to be regarded as a person."[18] Frankl adds, "I think that the danger is not so much inherent in shock treatment or drug treatment in themselves as it is in the extremely technological attitude which dominates so many therapists."[19] Dehumanizing treatment reflects an underlying cynicism, Frankl feels, and this attitude not only dehumanizes the patient but also reduces the therapist to a technician. In addition, today's medical training has not prepared medical doctors to deal with the existential vacuum, or noögenic neurosis; and of equal importance, many physicians are themselves affected by it.

Existentialism, Phenomenology, and Humanistic Psychology

Humanistic psychology has been described as all of psychology viewed through a wide-angle lens.[20] Humanistic psychologists—including the Gestalt-oriented Aron Gurwitsch, Alfred Schutz, and Binswanger's mentor Eugène Minkowski—use phenomenology extensively in constructing their therapies. Frankl also uses phenomenology but is more often identified with existential psychologists such as Ludwig Binswanger, Medard Boss (1903–   ), and Rollo May. Some psychologists have introduced *existential humanistic psychology* as a label and a description of a separate discipline of psychology that employs the interaction of existentialism and humanism. One of the advocates of existential humanistic psychology, Thomas C. Greening, believes that it provides a psychological viewpoint that recognizes the contributions of existentialism and humanism while avoiding some of their limitations.[21] Husserl's phenomenology is modified by Scheler and Heidegger in ways that make its existential features even more prominent, so that for some scholars—for example, Thomas Greening—the labels *existentialism* and *phenomenology* are virtually interchangeable. I view existential humanistic psychology as an integral part of humanistic psychology rather than a separate discipline. While contemporary humanistic psychologists vary in their emphases, their humanistic philosophy shows how phenomenology and existentialism affect psychoanalysis today. Further, when phenomenological and existential psychology are within a humanistic framework, the interaction between philosophy and psychology in helping to achieve a life with meaning is evident.

Phenomenological psychology has been defined as "an approach or orientation in psychology consisting of unbiased exploration of consciousness and experience."[22] This definition takes into account the search of Western philosophers since the Greeks to explore consciousness; it also reflects the counsel of Edmund Husserl that the exploration should be unbiased or free from presuppositions. Husserl, like the Greeks, was searching for a theory of the self that was independent of tradition, universally valid, and open to refinement. Husserl's approach, which avoids any presuppositions and accepts as valid only things intuited and facts established by actual experience, underscores the similarities between phenomenology and existentialism: the emphasis on experience over logic, the reliance on only personal subjective views, and the opinion that there is no split between the mind and the body. Husserl's contribution to phenomenology is his insistence on the importance of data we derive from appearances and from phenomena, and how we describe our experiences.

How we describe our experiences takes into account how we perceive an experience or a phenomenon, what is meant by what we perceive, and our intention. Our intention is how we plan to react in view of our experience and our reflection upon it. In essence, consciousness is intentionality. Although other phenomenologists have modified and enlarged Husserl's approach, he provides the essential view of life, which he calls "our world-experiencing life," of contemporary phenomenology.

The term *phenomenological psychology* refers in a narrow sense to a system that follows Husserl's definitions and methods. In the broadest sense, phenomenological psychology is any psychology "which considers personal experience in its subject matter, and which accepts and uses phenomenological description, explicitly or implicitly."[23] This broad definition includes humanistic psychologists who evaluate and use those characteristics or insights from phenomenological psychology that they feel best meet their goals. Misiak and Sexton suggest four characteristics of phenomenological psychology that are applicable in constructing a humanistic psychology, in addition to the phenomenological approach just noted: (1) a goal of understanding the self in all of its aspects, (2) a primary concern for the nature and quality of human experience, (3) a concentration on intentionality while opposing any reductionistic theories of Being, and (4) the use of a holistic approach in the study of psychological problems.[24] All characteristics of phenomenological psychology will not be adopted by all humanistic therapists, but as a representative branch, phenomenological psychology reflects humanistic psychology's openness and willingness to be in dialogue with other orientations. Humanistic psychologists who are influenced by phenomenology and existentialism are able to use insights from each discipline that best express their understanding of the self.

It is understandable that the penetration into psychology of philosophical ideas, including phenomenology and existentialism, should have occurred first among European psychologists. European students, whether concentrating their studies on the sciences or the liberal arts, were trained in philosophy. Those who were attracted by the new science of psychology seemed especially open to thought, including existentialism, that wrestled with the nature of Being. When it first began to take form in Europe after World War II, existential psychology was not presented as a new theory of psychology, nor should it be thought of as such today. Rather, existential psychology is a new perspective, or orientation, that supplements other therapies aimed at the rehumanization of the self. Professor Frederik J. Buytendijk (1887–1974), a Dutch psychologist and one of the first to combine the insights of phenomenological and existential psychology, wrote that the best way to know the self is "to study the dialogue of man with objects and with his fellow-man."[25] First introduced by Socrates as philosophical dialectic, the dialogical method has been one of the most important existential ways of probing the nature and the direction of the humanness of the self.

Both existentialism and phenomenology use the dialogical method suggested by phenomenology. Both are movements within humanistic psychology that are not dependent upon the theories of one person, although each has been influenced by key persons who often disagree. Both stress the uniqueness of the self and resist all attempts to reduce a person's humanity to a function or a trait. Both aim at a holistic, or comprehensive, understanding of the self. Where existentialism and phenomenology part is where the two differ because of the widely separated positions within existentialism that range from the militant atheism of Sartre to the Catholic theism of Marcel. Further, existential psychology appears to be more effectively applicable than phenomenological psychology in the dimensions of personal counseling and psychotherapy. In psychotherapy, a great deal depends upon the experience and personality of the therapist. This perception is a major factor explaining why Frankl is more often labeled an existential psychologist than a phenomenologist. This existential label fails, however, to take into account Frankl's use of insights from phenomenology, as well as pragmatism, as part of his profoundly humanistic psychology of meaning.

Two qualities listed by Misiak and Sexton as central features of existentialism are equally applicable to humanistic psychology as a set of principles that serve as guidelines for clinical treatment: (1) recognition of the ability of the self to use its capacities for authentic existence, and (2) emphasis on the importance of personal freedom and responsibleness. Similarly, the four characteristics of humanistic psychology listed by the American Association for Humanistic Psychology are equally descriptive of existential psychology: (1) the perception of the person as an *experiencing* human being, (2) the expression of the self in creativity, values, and self-realization, (3) the intrinsic dignity and worth of each individual, and above all, (4) the meaning that evolves through the choices that a person makes.[26]

Five Key Humanistic Psychologists

The stated aims and publications of the American Association for Humanistic Psychology show its intellectual richness and the variety of its psychological approaches to the self as it affirms its common goal: the rehumanization of life. The most convincing evidence that refutes the charge that humanistic psychology is superficial and lacks scientific discipline is found in the results of contemporary humanistic psychologists. Thus the following critiques of five key humanistic psychologists illustrate the intellectual vigor, discipline, and timeliness of the humanistic psychology movement.

Abraham Maslow

Abraham Maslow's humanism centers on the self-actualizing person. The 15 characteristics that Maslow lists for such a person include key humanistic qualities such as autonomy, acceptance, creativity, appreciation, self-detachment, and self-transcendence.[27] Maslow's list of qualities is optimistic, but Maslow is a realistic humanist who recognizes that no one is perfect. He believes that those persons who are self-actualizing are those persons who are able to take hold of life. One of his more interesting diagnoses of why some persons fail to realize their potential is what he calls the Jonah complex: "Like Jonah, who ran from the Lord's call but ended up being delivered where he was supposed to go by a whale, we seek to escape from our destinies."[28] For Maslow, our true destiny is to use our potentialities to the fullest—to do otherwise is to retreat neurotically from life, to engage in voluntary self-limitation, to pretend stupidity, and to practice a false humility that will excuse us from self-actualization and growth. Self-actualization when it does occur does not, however, always lead to happiness. Happiness cannot be achieved directly: happiness cannot be pursued; it must ensue from meaning. For Maslow, as for Frankl, meaning is tied to values.

Maslow sets out to use a scientific approach to values, but he does not see the scientific approach in the Freudian sense of a value-free, biological-mechanistic exploration. True science includes a sense of moral being. Scientists choose what they feel will justify their existence just as others do. We do not live in a value-free society; and when we believe that we do, we end up with a culture characterized by meaninglessness, pessimism, and despair. Thus Maslow urges us to construct a comprehensive, integrated synthesis of values that fosters trust and creative interdependence.

It is understandable that Maslow's concern for values leads him to develop a holistic model of the self, which emphasizes mind, body, and spirit. At first glance, his holistic model appears to be identical to Frankl's, but there are crucial philosophical differences between the two models. Maslow sees the spiritual dimension in terms of the peak experience of self-actualization. Further, he describes such a peak experience, which is the ultimate self-realization, "as a fusion of the ego, id, super-ego, and ego ideal, of conscious and unconscious or primary and secondary processes, a synthesizing of pleasure principle with reality principle . . . a true integration of the person at all levels."[29] Frankl, on the other hand, believes that through the spiritual, or noölogical, dimension, the self can find meaning in every circumstance of life, whether the experience represents a peak or a valley. Further, he feels that the noölogical dimension allows the self to transcend the conflicts of the ego, the id, and the superego; and avoiding the limitation of Maslow's self-realization as the human goal, Frankl sees meaning as the fulfillment of true *humanitas*.

Ludwig Binswanger

Freud and Heidegger each influenced Ludwig Binswanger at crucial times in his analytical thinking. Binswanger first met Freud in March 1907 when Binswanger accompanied his mentor C. J. Jung on a visit to Vienna. From that year until

Freud's death 32 years later, Binswanger maintained a correspondence with Freud that was marked by mutual affection and esteem, despite the differences between their respective approaches to psychotherapy.[30] Binswanger's critical yet high regard for Freud is best illustrated by a speech that he gave in 1936 to the Vienna Academic Society for Medical Psychology in which he honored Freud on his 80th birthday.

In his speech Binswanger said that Freud had enlarged and deepened our understanding of human nature possibly more than any other person since Aristotle. But he also noted that Freud's theoretic-scientific model of the self was too one-sided and narrow, limited to the area of the *homo natura,* the man of nature, and his instincts, drives, and similar aspects of experience. Binswanger concluded that Freud's biological viewpoint needs enlarging rather than un-critical acceptance.... Binswanger recognized religious experience as existing in its own right.[31] Freud's response to Binswanger is most telling:

> Your lecture is a pleasant surprise!... I have always confined myself to the ground floor and basement of the edifice. You maintain that by changing one's point of view, one can also see an upper story, in which dwell such distinguished guests as religion, art, etc. You are not the only one to say this; most cultured specimens of *homo natura* think the same thing. In this you are conservative and I am a revolutionary.... I have already found a place for religion, by putting it under the category of "the neurosis of mankind."[32]

Freud told Binswanger that he had failed to convince him of the need to build a multileveled edifice of the self. Freud also wrote, in the same letter, that given time he might "make room in my humble home for those lofty things," but the fact is that he was content to stay with depth psychology and not venture into height psychology. Freud saw himself as a revolutionary while, in fact, he was a reductionist. Frankl, disagreeing with Freud on the same grounds as Binswanger, points out not only that was Freud aware that he had confined himself "to the ground floor and basement of the edifice," but also that Freud "became a victim of reductionism." Frankl sadly comes to the conclusion that "Even a genius [such as Freud] cannot completely resist his *Zeitgeist,* the spirit of his age."[33]

Binswanger goes beyond Freud's psychological model of the self to use Heidegger's idea of *Dasein* (being-in-the-world) as a basis for an *ontological* model of the self. Ontoanalysis (or *Daseinanalyse*) reinstates the humanness of the self, with the I-Thou relationship as the essential expression of Being. Binswanger's holistic model highlights not only the unity of a person seen existentially before any psychoanalytic split into subject and object, but also the relationship between the person and his or her environment. He uses this phenomenological approach to explore important features of the self such as choice, freedom, and caring, which are based on how a person sees and acts upon values. While he accepts Heidegger's assertion that we are "thrown into the world," Binswanger feels that this "thrown-ness" does not relieve us from being responsible for our history, for forming our own communities of concern, and for planning for the future. He does not reject the *homo natura* introduced by Freud but argues that the subjective and spiritual dimensions of *Dasein-analyse* (existence analysis) should supplement the Freudian model.

Frankl pays tribute to Binswanger's efforts to rehumanize the Freudian psychoanalytic concept of the self. He sees the existential understanding of Being, as Binswanger presents it, as important in helping us to understand the basis of human psychosis. Frankl's concern for the meaning of existence led him to consider *existential analysis* as the term that best described his own psychological method, but he soon realized that confusion could arise because of the translation into English of the term. While the German word *Existenzanalyse* describes Frankl's method and the German word *Daseinanalyse* describes Binswanger's approach, the English term *existential analysis* encompasses both, and as a result, the important distinctions between the two are lost. A more careful translation would use the term *Being analysis* for *Daseinanalyse* and *attitude analysis* for *Existenzanalyse*. Being analysis is concerned with a person's loss of a sense of Being, a state of mind that can lead to psychosis. Attitude analysis is concerned with how a person thinks about his or her being, which may lead to a need for therapy. To avoid any confusion about how the term *existential analysis* is understood, Frankl invented the label *logotherapy*, or *meaning therapy*.

Binswanger emphasizes that *Daseinanalyse* (ontoanalysis) concentrates on Being-in-the-world; this is described by Frankl as the a priori structure of *Daseinsgestalten*, the manner of a person's experience of his or her life in the world.[34] Binswanger feels that a gestalt of existence—seen most clearly in love—bridges the gulf between the subjective and the objective. Frankl thinks such reasoning is self-deceptive and that the self is "neither capable of bridging such a gap, nor would such an accomplishment be commendable."[35] Frankl feels that the gulf between the subjective and the objective creates a tension, a noödynamic, that enlivens the spirit of the self, or what Frankl terms the defiant power of the human spirit. Binswanger recognized this aspect of Frankl's therapy when he told Frankl that "compared with ontoanalysis, logotherapy was more activistic, and even more, that logotherapy could lend itself as the therapeutic supplement to ontoanalysis."[36] Frankl agrees, quoting Medard Boss that "Daseinanalysis [ontoanalysis] has nothing to do with psychotherapeutic practice."[37] Thus Binswanger and Frankl see their two methods—so close yet still distinct from each other—as essentially allies, not competitors, in the humanizing process.

Carl Rogers

Carl Rogers is considered one of the persons who furnishes humanistic psychology with its intellectual leadership, along with Abraham Maslow and Rollo May.[38] Although Rogers was born, reared, and educated in the Midwest, he was very aware of the developments of existential psychology in Europe. In his late

40s, he immersed himself in the philosophy of existentialism by reading Søren Kierkegaard and the writings of Martin Buber. His intellectual leadership in humanistic psychology is reflected by his holistic approach to the self and his introduction of a triad of characteristics for the therapist: empathy, genuineness, and an unconditional positive regard for the client.[39] These three characteristics come from a psychotherapeutic eros that is indestructible, or as Carl Rogers says, "nonconditional." Rogers's understanding of the dynamics of the therapeutic relationship reflects his philosophy and psychology of the self.

The phenomenological world of behavior, a value-oriented philosophy, and the humanistic developments in the world of science each play an important role in Rogers's *Weltanschauung*. Rogers tries to understand clients' gestalt as a means of helping them to reach a more realistic sense of their lives, especially in the formation of values. Influenced by the scientist Michael Polanyi, Rogers describes our human wholeness as a "pattern of relationships" that represents a "hidden" reality.[40] In seeking to understand such relationships, Rogers feels that we must concentrate on commitment rather than on methodology. He urges that the behavioral sciences use a phenomenological method as they seek to understand the self so that they can begin to see humans, and perhaps other animals, "from the inside."[41]

Rogers's psychotherapeutic approach to the self is an empathetic combination of phenomenological, existential, and humanistic qualities that interweaves perceptions, beliefs, feelings, and values in an effort to establish a holistic sense of Being. For Rogers, the person is a total organism who must find ways to deal with a changing environment and a myriad of life experiences. Rogers presents an intriguing mixture of humanism and existentialism. He is clearly a humanist when he selects those experiences that aid human growth over those negative factors that may confuse or hinder it. At the same time, he is more existential than humanist in his belief that emotions and feelings predominate over the intellect. His insistence that a true therapeutic relationship can be a growth experience underscores his humanism, while his emphasis on the present over the past is an existentialist posture. This paradoxical mix of humanism and existentialism provides a creative tension in Rogers's work and creates room for discovery and growth.

Rogers's activist psychology shares Frankl's emphasis on the searching and sharing self. This is to be expected since both men were influenced by Adler's *Gemeinschaftsgefühl* and by Scheler's concentrated phenomenological analysis of the forms of love.[42] Rogers focuses on the subjective processes that help a person to achieve self-actualization and feels that experience should be allowed to convey its own meaning. He believes that psychological adjustment comes from an open, assured, and relaxed self that uses experience to replace distorted values with those that are authentic. He concludes that "as the individual gains in self-acceptance, perception of oneself as similar to others increases, and a more congruent self accords better with others' evaluations."[43] Another way to express this is to say that "the individual gradually internalizes the effect he or she has on others and then possesses self-regard."[44] Rogers's raison d'être differs radically from Frankl's position. Frankl feels that meaning, not congruence, is the key to the mentally healthy self. Frankl believes that while acceptance may be found in reaching out to another, essential meaning must come from the spirit of the giver and that it is not dependent on the recipient, although a reciprocal caring also may ensue.

In the final analysis, Frankl does not feel, as Rogers does, that therapy should be centered on the client. Frankl believes that the therapy should concentrate on the meaning of the situation that confronts the client and that the client has the responsibility to make the vital choices that will affect his or her life. But in taking this position, he nevertheless agrees with Rogers that despite any rebelliousness, narcissism, depression, fears, or even hostility on the part of the client, the logotherapist or Rogerian therapist "cares *because of* these traits, since they reflect how much the individual needs to be cared for."[45] For Frankl and for Rogers, the purpose of the therapist is to be a Socratic midwife to the birth of the client's yet-unlived life.

Rollo May

Ohio-born Rollo May taught at the American College in Salonika, Greece, after his graduation from Oberlin College, Ohio, and summer studies with Alfred Adler. A major crisis occurred in his life at this time when he contracted tuberculosis. He was introduced to existentialism through reading Kierkegaard, which led him to continue his studies first at the Union Theological Seminary in New York, where he took a degree in theology, and then at Columbia University, New York, where he earned a degree in clinical psychology in 1949. During his early years as a psychologist, he edited the book *Existence: A New Dimension in Psychiatry and Psychology* (1958). This book introduced European existential philosophy and psychology to the United States and prepared the way for the work of humanistic psychologists in this country.

May's psychological approach to the self illustrates how thoroughly the religious dimension of existentialism, especially the religious thought of Paul Tillich, permeates his work. In effect, his book *The Courage to Create* is a psychologist's companion to Tillich's philosophical treatise *The Courage to Be*. May sets up dichotomies that are not always logical. For instance, he sees a basic conflict between the reality of the self and the potential of the self. For May, reality constitutes emptiness, violence, and meaninglessness, while potential means identity, courage, creativity, love, will, and value. May selects key qualities from the list of human potentials that will help us overcome what he sees as the schizoid world of loneliness, anxiety, apathy, and self-insignificance. May does not take the term *schizoid* to mean a form of hysteria, as it was understood in Freud's time, but "the problem of persons who are detached, unrelated, lacking in affect, tending toward depersonalization, and covering up their problems by means of intellectualization and technical formulations."[46] He admits, however, that conditions such as isolation and alienation from the world are also experienced by so-called normal people as well as those who are designated as pathological. A problem arises, however, from May's dichotomy between reality and potential. If he sees reality's features as schizoid, how can he also call them real? For Frankl, both reality and potential as described by May are expressions of being that must be recognized, understood, and used in the search for meaning. Whereas Frankl emphasizes meaning and is clear in how he defines it, May emphasizes existential courage and creativity and leaves his understanding of both open to interpretation. May's outline of existential analysis in his book *The Discovery of Being* provides a more fundamental description of his therapeutic method than his attempt to track psychologically Tillich's philosophy in his previous book *The Courage to Create*. In *The Discovery of Being*, May discusses six characteristics, or implications, of existential analysis, which explain where and how he agrees with Frankl's meaning analysis: (1) the flexibility and versatility of techniques, (2) the meanings drawn from the client's own immediate life, (3) the significance of *presence,* (4) the identification of means that will destroy the behavior that threatens *presence,* (5) the validation of the client's experience, and (6) the commitment on the part of the client.[47] Frankl, as well as May, welcomes flexibility and versatility in the practice of psychoanalysis. Meaning analysis, like existential analysis, revises and supplements Freudian psychology. Both Frankl and May, as former students of Adler, incorporate Adlerian individualist psychology while going beyond it.

May cites Frankl as an existential therapist who underscores the importance of the therapist's using the immediate situations of the client's life as a modus vivendi of treatment.[48] Frankl advocates a method of questioning the client that echoes the Socratic method of philosophical inquiry and helps the client to uncover his or her needs and potentials. In this method of questioning, the therapist's respect for the client's personal freedom constitutes an important means of helping the client to link that freedom with responsibleness. May quotes Medard Boss, who wrote that "Freud himself was not merely a passive 'mirror' for the patient in analysis . . . but was 'translucent,' a vehicle and a medium through which the patient sees himself."[49] Frankl disagrees with this evaluation. Frankl points out that in Freud's dream analysis the patients did not see themselves but saw instead how *Freud* saw them. The imposition of the opinions of the therapist on the client is a hazard recognized by perspective psychologists. There is a delicate balance to be reached between avoiding such imposition and still being present for the client. Martin Buber's theory of the I-Thou relationship illustrates how a therapist may be present for a client without violating the integrity of the client's own search for Being. Essentially, such a relationship is dialogical and the client is treated as "Thou," a person to be respected and not as an "it" to be coerced or manipulated. Frankl is especially aware that personal traits and methods of a therapist may block healing. He calls the result an iatrogenic neurosis, a neurosis that is caused by the healer. Therapists in the tradition of May and Frankl are alerted to avoid blocks to being present to the client and also to reassure the client when he or she uncovers experiences that are real. Meaning analysts should find the guidelines recommended by Rollo May compatible with their philosophy of therapeutic treatment.

Existential therapy cannot begin until the client, through his or her personal commitment to change or healing, agrees. May reports that when a client comes in and sits down, he often has the impulse to ask not "*How* are you?" but "*Where* are you?"[50] As May points out, that question explores more than just the client's feelings. The therapist is trying to ascertain what attitudes the client has before the therapy session begins. Frankl believes that a person's attitudinal values determine what choices that person feels he or she can make, and these choices include whether or not the person is committed to change. Attitudes affect the direction of the will. The origin, nature, and expression of the will play central roles in both existential analysis and meaning analysis. How May and Frankl explain these roles shows, however, important differences in their philosophies of the self.

Frankl contrasts the *will* to meaning with the *drive* to meaning. If a person is really driven to meaning, that person will want that meaning fulfilled solely to be free of that drive in order to restore a sense of balance. Frankl agrees that existential philosophy is right to point out that personal freedom means that the self is responsible for fulfilling specific meanings important to the person's own life. But Frankl insists that there must be a certain degree of objectivity involved; otherwise, the perceived meaning will not be worth fulfillment. In other words, meaning must be ahead of being; meaning must set the pace of being. As an illustration, Frankl recalls the biblical story of the Israelites following through the desert wastes the Glory of God, which appeared to them as a guiding, luminous cloud:

> Imagine . . . what would have happened if God's presence, the cloud that had dwelled in the midst of the Israelites, rather than leading them the right way, this cloud would have clouded everything, and the Israelites would have gone astray.
>
> In other words, meaning must not coincide with being; meaning must be ahead of being. Meaning sets the pace for being.[51]

Frankl also believes that in addition to having the will to find specific personal meaning, the self is "responsible *before* something, or *to* something, be it society, or humanity, or mankind, or his own conscience . . . or to someone, to God."[52] Thus a will to meaning is not a will to power, nor a will to pleasure, nor even a will to achieve self-actualization. Rather, the will to meaning is a person's use of the resources of the noetic dimension in the search for a higher and ultimate meaning to his or her existence. In essence, it is the will to self-transcend. Frankl's criticism of Rollo May's understanding of the human will lies in May's focus on that will as a will to power or achievement. In Frankl's view, this means willing to will; and Frankl insists that this cannot be done: "Will cannot be demanded, commanded, or ordered . . . and if the will to meaning is to be elicited [clarified], meaning itself has to be elucidated."[53] And Frankl identifies the sources of meaning in a task worth doing, in loving another person, and in joining the self to an ultimate purpose.

May's and Frankl's holistic models of the self emphasize such important human qualities as freedom, responsibility, courage, and above all, *agapé*, which is defined by May as "a love that is devoted to the welfare of the other."[54] But there is a difference in the rationales of the two men that is indicated by the names given to their theories of psychoanalysis: May concentrates on the self's understanding of the *existentiell* of existence and thus supports *existential* analysis; in contrast, Frankl insists that true existence is realized only through the self's perception of the meaning behind the *existentiell* and has therefore established *meaning* analysis.

Gordon Allport

In 1957, during his first lecture tour in the United States, which was sponsored by the Religion in Education Foundation, Frankl was introduced to Gordon Allport by the foundation's director, Randolph Sassnett. Allport provided the preface to Frankl's *Man's Search for Meaning*, which was published two years later by the Beacon Press. Allport was also instrumental in Frankl's being invited to become a visiting professor at Harvard University. Their friendship continued until Allport's death in 1967.

Allport was a personalist psychologist, and his writings focus on the study of the unique and unified individual, which he based on a comprehensive science of the person.[55] His science of the person is fully humanistic and open to dialogue with others who are in search of a holistic model of the self. Allport's theory tries to solve a continuing dilemma of psychology: how to relate the two poles of human existence—the universal experience and the individual experience. Allport's open system begins by concentrating on the nature of human energy. The energized self welcomes the future rather than being dominated by the past. Allport's system is realistic; he realizes that the conflicts of life often prevent a person from making simple choices, and thus he pays special attention to the nature of intentionality, to the need to mature and grow, and to the key roles played by moral and spiritual values.

Allport believes that "personal values are the dominating force in life and all of a person's activity is directed toward the realization of his values."[56] Values guide persons toward commitment, toward the true use of freedom, and toward responsibleness. Values express the self's noölogical dimension. This noölogical, or religious, dimension helps persons to be more than they were in the past. This aids the growth of maturity. Allport's six aspects of maturity spell out the role of a value-oriented consciousness in dealing with the internal and external challenges to the self: (1) a sense of the self that extends to include all the areas of human existence—family, community, education, religion, politics, and so forth; (2) the ability to reach out to others with tolerance and empathy;

(3) self-acceptance that includes understanding of one's own strengths and weaknesses and recognizing that both are under one's control; (4) a realistic view of what one perceives and feels that one can do; (5) the ability to stand outside of one's self and to view one's self, especially with humor; and (6) the ability to find a meaning or purpose that gives life unity despite tensions, ambiguities, and paradoxes.[57]

Allport's philosophical and psychological agreement with Frankl's meaning analysis is illustrated by the attention that Allport pays to the pursuit of meaning in his book *The Individual and His Religion,* which was published seven years before he met Frankl. In a section entitled "Pursuit of Meaning," Allport tries to find a term that will best describe the interacting aspects of desire, temperament, and values that make up the individual. He chooses the label "religious sentiment," admitting that "its flavor unfortunately suggests feeling more than meaning."[58] A few pages later, he uses the phrase "appetite for meaning," which better matches Frankl's "search for meaning." Allport differs from Frankl in trying to work out different rationales and methods for the engagement of the religious sentiment (the noetic dimension) in terms of a Christian framework. But at the end of the book, he aligns himself with an attitude adopted by Frankl; namely, that the religious sentiment, or appetite for meaning, takes many forms as it seeks to overcome the fragmentations of life, or in Frankl's words, to overcome the existential vacuum. Allport points out that "no two people have identical intellectual difficulties or powers, and hence no two reach identical solutions."[59] Thus, "it is the habitual and intentional focusing of experience rather than the character of the experience itself that marks the existence of a religious sentiment [meaning]."[60] Allport links religious sentiment with mature sentiment. Frankl's philosophy of the self agrees. A life of meaning contains a quest and a fulfillment that shows a growing maturity.

While Allport and Frankl recognize that a meaningfully integrated self must be able to self-transcend in facing the sufferings of life, they are equally concerned for the person who needs to take hold of life on a day-to-day basis. Years after he began his friendship with Frankl, Allport wrote the following words, which show their common view of the noölogically oriented concept of the self:

> Man, then, is not a homeostatic creature. He does not seek equilibrium within himself and with the environment. His restlessness is systemic, and too deep-rooted to be drugged by temporary satisfactions. He seeks a more solid formula for living, something that will enable him to surmount alienation and suffering. . . . And so one answer to our question concerning the nature of the human person is that he is a creature bent on enhancing the value-attributes of his experience. Every day each of us is building many self-world relationships. Some of these become more and more meaningful, more appropriate, more urgent. They are what makes life worthwhile.[61]

Allport and Frankl exemplify the humanistic psychologist's concern for the total human condition (mind, body, and spirit) and for how the self can find meaning and express it both internally and in relation to others. The crux of any evaluation of their theories is testing in life. Humanistic psychology is only humane when it is validated by action. Such validation occurs when "the shattered self" is healed.

Frankl's giving of priority to meaning harmonizes with the 1973 statement of the American Association for Humanistic Psychology, which reflects allegiance to meaningfulness.[62] Although humanistic psychology has received a warm reception in North America, evidence does not support the assertion of Royce and Mos that pragmatism is a "peculiarly North American phenomenon."[63] Humanistic psychiatrists use the psychological and philosophical resources of every other continent as well in developing their emphasis on meaning. This is especially true of Frankl. His dialogue on the relation of meaning to the self receives as enthusiastic a reception in the Far East and in South America as it does in Europe and North America. While Frankl's work is described by him and by others as the Third School of Viennese psychotherapy, his scholarship, experience, and openness to other cultures go far beyond his Viennese training. Frankl underscores the "unity in diversity" of humanistic psychology by welcoming other therapies as part of his therapy. He avoids ever claiming that he has the only answer to helping someone achieve a healthy and whole selfhood. A logotherapist cannot tell a person what meaning is; but as Frankl writes, "He can at least show that *there is* a meaning in life, that it is available to everyone and, even more, that life retains its meaning under any conditions."[64]

— 8 —

Healing

the

Shattered Self

THE THEORY OF VIKTOR FRANKL, WHATEVER ELSE
MIGHT BE SAID ABOUT IT, IS SURELY NOT AN INTEL-
LECTUAL EXERCISE. IT WAS BASED ON HIS EXPERI-
ENCES IN NAZI CONCENTRATION CAMPS DURING
WORLD WAR II, HIS LIVING THROUGH ONE OF THE
GREATEST HORRORS VISITED UPON MAN IN MODERN
TIMES. FRANKL TRULY LIVED HIS THEORIES.

—ROBERT A. LISTON

EACH OF US HAS HIS OWN INNER CONCENTRATION
CAMP . . . WE MUST DEAL WITH, WITH FORGIVENESS
AND PATIENCE—AS FULL HUMAN BEINGS; AS WE
ARE AND WHAT WE WILL BECOME.

—VIKTOR FRANKL

In his attempt to find a central point of agreement among existential writers,
Walter Kaufmann notes, "All of them contrast inauthentic life and authentic life . . .
[all believed that] to be serious, *a philosophy has to be lived*."[1] According to
Charlotte Bühler and Melanie Allen, this insistence that a philosophy has to be
lived is the major point of agreement between existential thinkers and humanistic psychologists.[2] This is especially true of Frankl, who is an existentialist-
humanistic psychiatrist. The lasting appeal of Frankl and his message is that he
authentically lived his theories. In a time of meaninglessness, violence, and
dehumanization, his existentially oriented *ministry humane* is uniquely quali-
fied to help heal the shattered self.

A Four-Step Plan for a Ministry Humane

Frankl's *ministry humane* focuses on helping persons to become aware of what it means to be fully human and to recognize and use all the creative forces of life, which go beyond the intellectual theorizing and psychoanalytic techniques that have dominated so much thinking about the self during the past half-century. Frankl asserts that "the potentialities of life are not indifferent *possibilities,* but must be seen in the light of meaning and values."[3] Such meaning and values cannot be imposed; each individual must seek out for himself or herself the meaning of each situation and the implications the present moment may have for the future. A person faces a variety of potentials every time he or she makes a choice, and a person must decide which potential will be actualized and rescued for the future or relegated to nonbeing. Frankl's *ministry humane* avoids both the licentiousness of extreme libertarianism as well as the rigidity of absolute determinism. It gives guidelines for the quality and expression of humanness that go beyond the Socratic search for selfhood to a search for meaning in selfhood. Such meaning is discovered and utilized through self-transcendence: "Self-transcendence is the essence of existence. Existence collapses and falters unless there's a 'strong idea' . . . or a strong ideal to hold on to."[4] The strong ideal, defined by Frankl as meaning, helps a person to rise above the biological and psychological features of existence. Such transcendence gives the self a new mode of being where "the appropriate and adequate approach to existence is not psychological but existential."[5] Self-transcendence is actualized through the noetic, or spiritual, dimension of the self. Although the spiritual dimension is not the whole of the self, it is its genuine dimension; it is what is true and authentic in a human being. The self-transcendent power of the noetic dimension enables the self to gain necessary distance and perspective in three ways: (1) in relation to the environment, (2) in relation to existence, and (3) in relation to a person's expectations of and obligations in the future.

Dereflection is the first step of self-transcendence, whether we are dealing with the environment, with an existential situation, or with our expectations. Dereflection enables us to escape the "ego trap" by helping us to stop what Frankl calls hyperintention and hyperreflection—our focusing solely on what we need, what we want, and what we feel we must have. Dereflection enables us to turn from these demands of the ego and to look about us to see both the needs and the possibilities of the world. Frankl teaches that a truly human being is not self-absorbed but is a person who directs himself or herself toward others by doing a meaningful task and/or caring for another person. Dereflection substitutes a dialogue of encounter and caring for a monologue of self-inflicted hurts, resentments, and guilt. It is a cleansing process, the first movement in the healing of the shattered (yet ego-dominated) self, and is an example of the will to change. But the process of change must include a belief in something that makes life worthwhile, which is the will to faith. The fully human self is belief-full. Frankl uses the term *supra-world* to describe this belief-fullness. Reuven Bulka quotes an analogy of Frankl to illustrate what the supra-world means: "The ground upon which man walks is always being transcended in the process of walking, and serves only to the extent that it is transcended, that it provides a springboard."[6] Self-transcendence is more than a technique; it is an affirmation of a holistic life to be realized in the present and also to be expanded in the future. The *ministry humane* is based on a realistic faith that a holistic self contains a healthy core, the human spirit, from which we can draw strength to defy the obstacles that we may face in our environment, in existential situations, in our psyches and our bodies, and, to paraphrase Reinhold Niebuhr, to change what can be changed, to live positively with what cannot be changed, and to have the wisdom to find meaning in both instances.

Dereflection should be accompanied by attitude modulation if we are to turn our values and beliefs into actualities. A comparison of dereflection and attitude modulation shows their respective roles in a *ministry humane*. Dereflection turns the self from subjective preoccupations with problems to meanings that exist outside the self; attitude modulation changes a negative experience into a positive one. Dereflection helps us to perceive something new in a situation so that we may let go of our old perceptions; attitude modulation helps us to discover new dimensions in something old so that we see in it new potentials. Both dereflection and attitude modulation help us to look beyond what we have been and what we are at present to new possibilities of what we may become. Dereflection helps us to transcend those conditions that injure or limit us, so that we may make new commitments; similarly, attitude modulation helps us to develop courage in the face of illness and other blows of fate, so that we make commitments with integrity. Dereflection enables us to identify avoidable suffering; attitude modulation enables us to change the defeat of unavoidable suffering into personal victory. Dereflection helps us to ignore those aspects of life that should be ignored; attitude modulation give us the perspective to see those things that should be rethought in a new light. Dereflection helps us to mature by forgetting the self; attitude modulation helps us to mature by changing the self.

The use of dereflection and attitude modulation are part of a four-step plan for a *ministry humane*. Dereflection is the first step in therapeutic healing because it concentrates on reducing the unhealthy symptoms that come from hyperreflection. Attitude modulation is a necessary next step because it helps to change the unhealthy attitudes that have produced the symptoms. These two steps prepare the individual for the third step, which is openness to change or healing. This third step is engaged when the neurotic symptoms have been so reduced that they no longer dominate a person's thinking. These symptoms, however, may still be present or may even return to a level of dominance without the fourth step, which includes the search for meanings, commitments, tasks, and goals. This fourth step illustrates the central aim of meaning analysis: a value-oriented education that helps the person to "take hold of life."

The ability to "take hold of life" begins with self-awareness that goes beyond the ego needs of the self. This self-awareness increases both inward knowledge of our drives, our needs, and our aspirations and an outward understanding of what it means to live our lives in relation to others. Frankl's therapy stresses the uniqueness and dignity of human existence that make such awareness possible; in other words, his therapy deals with being human, which is defined by the holistic self. Being human cannot come about through narcissistic self-awareness but—as Heidegger teaches—through Being-in-the-world, which involves an aware and effective consciousness sensitive to the individual's relationships with the world and to the possibilities such relationships have for the individual and for others. Awareness leads to exploration of what these relationships mean and what choices they elicit from each individual.

The exploring, or pilgrim, self is a major feature of Frankl's educational therapy. Life involves the willingness to take risks; and taking hold of life includes the ability to learn from our failures as well as from our successes, even when, in Allport's words, we can be wholehearted and half sure at the same time. The inability to explore results in spiritual and mental homeostasis—a freezing of the self that results in stagnation, frustration, and neurosis. Exploration, on the other hand, leads to situations in which meanings can be discovered and acted upon. Such action results in values being tested and validated in the marketplace. Awareness and exploration are not just metaphysical ideas; for Frankl, they are basically human functions.

Education for Freedom and Responsibility

Frankl reminds us that we exercise freedom in spite of determinism, and so he wants to educate us to use freedom and responsibleness when we make commitments. A commitment that grows from awareness and exploration is a commitment that comes about when we have used our intuitive conscience as an aid in choosing our values in the existential situations of life. The risks and incompleteness of life means that all "truths" are rather near-truths, which means that we should be cautious about accepting them as dogma. The exploration of meaning leading to commitment must be accompanied by what James Lanz calls skill development, which means more than an improvement of technique. This skill involves our being sensitive to our needs and to the needs of others, and our finding authentic ways to meet the needs that are valid and that will lead to a life of meaning. In a 1953 letter, Frankl wrote, "It is said: where there is a will, there is a way; I add, where there is an aim, there is a will."[7]

The central aim of Frankl's educational therapy is to achieve a life of meaning, but he is not a moralist, for, as he says, "moralists give meaning to others. . . . We are, rather, ontologists."[8] As an ontologist, an educator of being, he defines "good" as what fulfills a being and "bad" as what blocks meaning and prevents the fulfillment of the self; he calls this ontologizing morals. Frankl's avoidance of moralism and dogmatism while he stresses values and meaning has made Frankl's a welcome voice at all levels of education, especially among the young.

In a televised interview about value dimensions in teaching, Dr. Huston Smith asked Frankl if values can be taught. Frankl replied:

> I doubt it. At least I would say rather than being taught, values must be lived, and what we can give, for instance, to our students is not a meaning but rather an example, that is to say, the example of commitment to a cause worthy of such commitment . . . science truth, scientific research, etc., and this example we are giving will be watched and witnessed by our students.[9]

This conversation seems to indicate that Frankl is wholly committed to the we-teach-only-by-example school. But in another discussion, about the role of a therapist, he points out that while the therapist's proper procedure is to answer questions with questions that will help clients to find their own answers, the therapist must challenge those systems that reflect reductionism, pandeterminism, and nihilism. Thus the educator or therapist is not a moral traffic cop. When example fails, the counselor cannot remain neutral but must actively help the student or client to explore those values and meanings that can lead to fulfillment rather than to psychic or moral defeat.

Frankl accuses contemporary education of contributing to the erosion of a sense of meaning by offering students a relativistic and subjective image of the self that counteracts the original zest and idealism of youth with its concern for values. Educators have also given young people mixed signals, conflicting styles of education, and have settled for developing skills (sometimes minimally) rather than helping children to see themselves as full human beings. Elisabeth Lukas points out that three areas of education have inhibited the learner's orientation toward values and meanings: (1) the reduction of a sense of accomplishment, (2) the pressures of the group, and (3) the denial or misunderstanding of freedom.[10] Instead of being committed to achievement, Lukas feels, today's education has been geared to underachievement, so that the student will not feel pressured or overworked. As Lukas asks, "How can the young people feel satisfaction with their own work, pride in workmanship, how indeed can they be at all motivated to seek fulfillment in work, even in hobbies, if everything that results in human accomplishment has been devalued into derision?"[11]

With the breakdown of the family, the peer group of the child or the young person at school and at play becomes the legislator of personal behavior or, in other words, the monitor for group conformity: "The group dictates to its members, it pressures and absorbs them."[12] It is ironic that abuses of meaning take place while the cry for freedom increases. But Lukas continues, "The young person's shout for freedom is as loud as their concept of freedom is false."[13] This has occurred because the young have been allowed to confuse freedom with license, instead of linking freedom with responsibleness. As Lukas explains,

"Freedom does not mean *to do what you want* but *to want what is called for.* I do not mean dictated by an outer authority but called for by an inner authority of the conscience which is responsive to what . . . is called 'the meaning of the moment.' "[14]

In a critique of the American educational system, Dr. Bianca Z. Hirsch, a clinical psychologist in the San Francisco public school system, cites a climate of meaninglessness, lack of values, false freedom, and irresponsibleness that produces an existential frustration experienced primarily by the teacher. Just as an inept or disturbed counselor can cause an iatrogenic neurosis (a neurosis from the healer) in the client, so an existentially frustrated teacher can exacerbate the student's dis-ease caused by meaninglessness. Hirsch cites Frankl's description of existential frustration "as a feeling of futility and/or lack of meaning or purpose in life" and points out that such frustration is often the result of conflict between values and actions and a disparity between short-term and long-range goals.[15] There are dehumanizing factors in the educational system that produce a negative environment in the classroom: a sense of mass production; competency-based rather than value-oriented instruction; computerized presentations; confusion regarding the role of the teacher—which is found among school authorities, students, students' families, the public, and teachers themselves; and the conflicts in administrative and disciplinary procedures. All of these contribute to existential frustration, and Hirsch emphasizes that the juxtaposition of a sense of alienation and ambiguity and a lack of consensus among the various segments of the educational community prevent any decrease in the level of existential frustration felt by the teachers and, by implication, by the students as well. The heart of the problem, she feels, is the disparity between the values and commitments of the dedicated teacher and a pseudo-educational atmosphere that contradicts them.

Attitudinal modulation is an essential ingredient for the teacher and the student to find meaning in the educational process. The attitudes that teachers bring to the classroom have far-reaching effects. How teachers see their own lives, either as fragmented by a dehumanizing process or as healed in the midst of such a process, helps the students to be aware of a holistic understanding of life. The teacher who is able to transcend the existential frustrations of much of the educational milieu will find responses from the students that are both challenging and rewarding.

In his article "What Logotherapy Can Learn from High School Students," Dr. Stephen S. Kalmar reports that student essays written for the Viktor Frankl Merit Award in 1982 "contradicted the views so widely repeated in the media that present 'the youth' of today as a mass of selfish, inconsiderate, rebellious, violent, drug-addicted, purposeless people."[16] Although the essays cited many of the same problems discussed by Bianca Hirsch—including overcrowding, impersonalization, lack of motivation in teacher and student, red tape, robotlike administrators, and lack of communication on every level—the students were impressed by what Frankl has to say about the need for each person to find meaning and to accept responsibility for her or his choices.

Frankl's writings speak to the teenager's sense of frustration, mental pain, and especially, preoccupation with death, as seen in the increase in suicides in this age group. Stephen Kalmar comments that it was encouraging to note in the essays that some students who had thought of suicide quoted Frankl's statement that nobody has the right to throw away one's life, and that Frankl's statements about faith caused some students to see their own religious belief in a new light. Although they frequently faulted their schools, parents, or society for failing to help them to achieve maturity, the students nevertheless realized that "it was their own, their inescapable task to solve their problems themselves and to accept the responsibility for their final decisions and attitudes."[17]

The Therapeutic Relationship

Whether within the student-teacher relationship in education or within the client-therapist relationship in psychotherapy, Frankl's *ministry humane* calls for an authentic expression of caring. Garth Wood, an English psychiatrist, parallels Frankl's concern by calling for "a therapeutic friendship." By this, Wood means that the therapist, "unlike the psychoanalyst, whose approach to the patient's emotional life is through such pseudoscientific methods as the interpretation of dreams and word-association games . . . should rely on the institution of friendship to provide . . . knowledge about the individual [the therapists] wish to help. For that is the natural way to get to know somebody. We must be prepared to reveal our own personalities, to give as well as to take."[18] Wood promotes therapeutic friendship through a method called moral therapy that uses the dynamics of conscience to expose neurosis as a myth. While critics question his dismissal of dream analysis and word-association games, Wood is one of an increasing number of humanistic psychologists and psychiatrists who are aiding those in the helping professions to avoid causing iatrogenic neuroses in the lives of their clients.

Very little has been written about the causes and effects of iatrogenic neurosis, which comes from the healer, mentor, or teacher, possibly because the hurting person is considered by some therapists and physicians less as an individual to be healed than as a piece of machinery to be repaired. Elisabeth Lukas lists four personal and professional characteristics for those who aspire to be good therapists and counselors.

First, such persons must be pessimistic and optimistic at the same time. I read "realistic" for "pessimistic" since Lukas notes that in their approach to the client, therapists "have to be aware of possible misinterpretations and must not overestimate their abilities while still taking people as they are and helping them to become what they could be."[19]

Second, therapists must paradoxically explore causes and yet seem to ignore those causes. The therapist must move the client away from or beyond the causes that cannot be changed, especially when dwelling on them causes pain that is nonproductive. Lukas writes that "it is unpardonable even to indicate to a handicapped woman that her handicap is the cause of her failures, although there may well be a connection . . . some connections are better left alone; if too much attention is paid to them, they can paralyze the human spirit that can defy those connections."[20]

Third, therapists must try to understand clients who have never had the chance to develop in a healthy way, but also those who have been offered positive options and have chosen not to use them.[21] As Lukas notes, it is easy to sympathize with the former but more difficult to sympathize with the latter, especially if therapists have themselves overcome negative environments. Increasingly, we see students from affluent families flunk out of school; children of professional families commit suicide; and wives of prominent figures become drug addicted. So-called privileged persons are also subject to the existential neurosis that afflicts us as human beings in our time. In discussing clients from middle-class and upper-class families, Lukas writes that therapists must understand that these clients as well experience unfounded upsets, senseless suffering, and the effects of macabre egoism.

Fourth, therapists must have their own personal value systems yet also accept the value systems of their clients. But there are times when a client who is entangled within either a destructive or a pandeterministic or a reductionist or a nihilistic value system must be challenged. In dialogue with clients, therapists do not either dictate or ignore the values involved but speak from their own experience, allowing the clients to observe what is being said and then to make their own choices. Lukas argues that the genuineness of the therapist must be apparent, but she adds, "It contains a contradiction: we must acknowledge our continuing search for meaning, and also show that we have found fulfillment. This contradiction, too, can be resolved because nobody's search for meaning is ever concluded and fulfillment reached once and for all."[22]

The therapist should be aware of the most frequent mistakes that are made in counseling:

> Concentrating more on the client's "disturbances" than focusing on the areas of the client's life that are healthy;
>
> Seeing the client's experience of "blows of fate" as an unmitigated tragedy;
>
> Making a negative prognosis appear to be a final judgment;
>
> Making a diagnosis without explaining its significance to the client;
>
> Keeping silent when a word or a gesture is needed to reassure the client;
>
> Giving off-the-top-of-the-head interpretations that pay no attention to facts or that reflect unconfirmed hypotheses.[23]

The therapeutic friendship of the counselor in meaning analysis goes beyond just the desire to avoid these mistakes; it is backed by the therapist's positive philosophy of the self that links maturity to values and meaning. Lukas notes:

The main reason for today's desperate search for meaning is not so much a sudden meaninglessness, as [it is] a delayed maturing of our generation, especially compared with our rapidly growing intellectual and technical skills. It also means that every person goes through all three phases: a general search for meaning, the discovery of a single important meaning, and eventually the realization that many meaningful tasks are waiting.[24]

Frankl's emphasis on the self as a value-bearer points out a basic individual and social need that has become increasingly evident. Almost 50 years ago, William Temple (then archbishop of Canterbury) remarked that the world was like a shop into which a person had come during the night and switched all the prices of the items in the window so that nothing was marked with its true value. The succeeding decades since Temple made that trenchant observation have demonstrated how society seems to have gone from bad to worse in losing its moral compass. But Frankl's therapy is based on the conviction that since the intention of human existence is primarily an orientation to values and meaning, it is possible for us to search out the true values of "the items in the window" through our freedom of will and through our intuitive conscience and to express such values and meaning through attitudinal, experiential, and creative actions.

The Uses of Meaning Analysis

Modulations of attitude are always linked to values that reflect how we face what Frankl describes as the tragic triad, the three major threats to the self: guilt, suffering, and death. Frankl's therapeutic understanding of the significance of this triad comes from his agreement with Heidegger that a person never really faces life until that person first confronts the inevitable fact of his or her own death. Frankl believes that the same factor applies in how the person faces guilt and suffering. Freud concentrated on what he saw as the primary concern of his Victorian age—sexual neuroses. Frankl believes that the primary need of persons today is to recognize their noögenic, or spiritual, neuroses, which are caused in large part by their inability to come to grips with the tragic triad. Once a person sees in suffering the prospect of taking a stand against the blows of fate, sees in feelings of guilt the possibility of taking a stand against the dictatorship of the psyche, and sees in the face of imminent death the hope of fulfillment within the transitoriness of life, one is able to find meaning in all that affects the self.

Frankl's understanding of the self in terms of the three values—attitudinal, experiential, and creative—has been called modal analysis, in which he concentrates on the modes of being rather than on the modes of logic. Freud uses the psychobiological understanding of the self as his ontological mode of being. Frankl argues that the modal scope of the self should be enlarged: "For if we want to obtain an appropriate view of human reality in its full dimensionality, we must go beyond both necessities and possibilities and bring in—in addition to the 'I must' and 'I can' the aspects of the total 'I am' phenomenon—that dimension which can be referred to as the 'I ought.' "[25] The "I ought" complements being (the subjective aspect of the self) with meaning (its objective counterpart).[26] Thus Frankl's meaning analysis is psychotherapy that begins with the consciousness of values and with a person's responsibility to find them and act upon them. Frankl maintains a commonsense attitude toward persons as value-bearers; he recognizes that when we act upon our values, this does not mean that we do so free of error. He recognizes that we establish values and meanings in the midst of the doubts, paradoxes, and ambiguities of human existence.

Frankl's meaning analysis may be considered *primary therapy* for three conditions: noögenic neurosis, injury from the "blows of fate," and stress emanating from the human condition. The noögenic neurosis, which originates in the noetic, or spiritual, dimension of the self, may be caused by conflicts of values and conscience and by frustration in finding the ultimate meaning of life. Frankl treats this neurosis by helping the client to find commitments to fulfill, relationships to establish, and values to act upon. In helping a person to deal with the blows of fate, Frankl encourages that person to call upon the resources of the noetic dimension. And to deal with the problems of the human condition, which some experience as a sense of emptiness, boredom, existential frustration, aimlessness, and despair, Frankl turns the person's attention once more to meaning.

Some of the most effective uses of Frankl's meaning analysis are as a *supplementary therapy* that helps persons deal with their somatogenic, psychogenic, and sociogenic problems. Counselors trained in meaning analysis are often able to help persons who have to deal with the deterioration of or injuries to the body and enable them to recognize, appreciate, and build on the parts of the self that are still healthy and intact. Similarly, they can help those who are facing psychogenic problems; for example, the person who comes home after a mental breakdown can be helped to continue the healing process through finding therapeutic friendships and tasks. Meaning analysis counselors can offer similar help to those facing sociogenic problems—for example, helping the recovered alcoholic to reestablish a place in the community. The Frankl-trained therapist can help such persons because behind each person's apparent problem lie deeper questions of how the person can either change the afflicting situation or find a meaningful attitude toward an afflicting situation that cannot be changed. Further, meaning analysis can help the person apply the four steps of Frankl's therapy: (1) gaining distance from symptoms through dereflection, (2) modifying attitudes, which helps to reduce harmful symptoms, (3) becoming open to change, and (4) searching for goals that will help in finding purpose and meaning. Meaning analysis does not focus only on the battered self but also on the self who is searching for meaning in the continuing crises of existence.

The testing of Frankl's therapeutic methods over the last 45 years has caused a quiet revolution in the counseling field. Men and women who need help in overcoming somatogenic, psychogenic, and especially, noögenic neuroses have found that meaning analysis has enabled them to take hold of life in ways that are ignored or denied by other therapies committed to a two-dimensional view of the self. Depth psychology, or Freudian psychoanalysis, which emphasizes the past and sees the self only in terms of needs and drives, has not met their needs. Neither has transactional analysis been able to help them, since, though it encourages the rewriting of personal "scripts" and de-mythologizes Freud, its therapy focuses on the dimensions of the psyche and ignores the noetic dimension. Behavior therapy reduces symptoms and offers changed behavior but fails to offer the person self-understanding. Reality therapy stresses responsibility but does not offer a method for dealing with blows of fate. Gestalt therapy explains to a person the connections between that person's life and the lives of others but veers away from any idea of self-transcendence. Frankl acknowledges that each of these therapies offers valid dimensions. His quarrel with them lies in their failure to recognize the human's spiritual dimension, which he sees as the key to a life of meaning.

The Pastoral Counselor and Meaning Analysis

Technically, Frankl is not a religious writer, and he insists that he is a person who, from personal experience, is speaking from a purely human level. For Frankl, true encounter with reality is based on self-transcendence rather than in mere self-expression: "Specifically, true encounter transcends itself toward the logos."[27] If we accept the definitions and methodology of humanism, including those of religious humanism, which were discussed in Chapter 7, then it seems that Frankl's understanding of humanism as lacking in the dimension of self-transcendence is reductionistic on his part. Frankl, in practice, like the pragmatic humanist William James, "uses" God, not as a psychological crutch but as R. W. Sleeper describes within the humanist approach: "Seeing God as real . . . because he produces real effects. God's *presence* is felt and makes an 'experienceable difference.' "[28]

Vatican Council II symbolized a new freedom within Catholicism to explore a wider spectrum of resources for mental health, pastoral counseling, and cooperation with other religious and secular approaches that are trying to help heal the shattered human self. Frankl's understanding and use of the spiritual dimension of the human being has raised a better understanding of the bridge between psychiatry and theology:

> The more weakly one stands on the ground of his belief . . . the more he clings with both hands to the dogma which separates it from other beliefs; on the other hand, the more firmly one stands on the ground of his faith, the more he has both hands free to reach out to those of his fellow men who cannot share his belief. The first attitude entails fanaticism; the second, tolerance. Tolerance does not mean that one accepts the belief of another;

but it does mean that one respects him as a human being, with the right and freedom of choosing his own way of believing and living.[29]

Frankl does not stand mute before the mystery of existence. He speaks of meaning and transcendence as providing keys to approaching the mystery of life but not as explanations of all of life's dimensions. He is descriptive, not prescriptive, in his understanding of human existence: "Existence never stands before me as an object, before my eyes; it stands, rather, behind my thinking, behind me as a subject. Existence is, in the last analysis, a mystery."[30] In this respect, Frankl is close to the position of Gabriel Marcel, who uses the term *presence* to describe the mystery of Being. In essence, *presence* is a description of the I-Thou relationship discussed by Martin Buber and underscored by Frankl; it is the basic expression of the self, or in Marcel's words, its spiritual reality.[31] When we experience another's presence, that experience can refresh our own being, reveal who we are to ourselves, and help us to become more fully human.[32] While we can recognize and appreciate another's presence, we cannot and should not try to master or control it. The other person is not a problem to be solved but a mystery that we encounter while being in the world. Marcel reminds us:

> We must carefully avoid all confusion between the mysterious and the unknowable. The unknowable is in fact only the limiting case of the problematic, which cannot be actualized without contradiction. The recognition of mystery, on the contrary, is an essentially positive act of the mind, the supremely positive act in virtue of which all this positivity may perhaps be strictly defined.[33]

As understood by Frankl, the self is a mystery that is approached in our search for meaning, which is enriched and enlarged by another's presence. The presence of another helps us find meaning through self-transcendence as we reach out for a task to accomplish or—even more important—toward another to love. Marcel and Frankl involve us in "borderline situations." Such borderline situations involve both the depth and height of human existence that are reached within acts of spiritual faith. Those acts are described primarily in philosophical terms by Marcel and in psychological terms by Frankl. This alliance between philosophy and faith and psychology and humanness sets the tone for cooperation between pastoral counselors and clinical psychologists.

The pastoral counselor and the meaning analyst share common goals: to provide a holistic model of the self and to refute the claims of psychologism, in which a person is seen as the result of instinctive drives and similar organic energies. Psychologism prevents both self-actualization and self-transcendence because it reduces every human experience to a psychological plane. The pastoral counselor's and the meaning analyst's common task is to correct the dehumanization of the self caused by Freud and by his denial of the essential spiritual dimension of the self. While traditional psychoanalysis emphasizes the unconscious drives of the self, Frankl concentrates on the spiritual unconscious. Psychoanalysis aims at bringing *psychic* factors to consciousness; meaning analysis aims at bringing *spiritual* factors to consciousness so that persons become more fully aware of their freedom and responsibleness. Frankl echoes the spiritual dictum that "you shall know the truth, and the truth will make you free." The personality of the self is seen in meaning analysis as a phenomenology of the searching spirit. Frankl writes that "the three constituents of human existence: spirituality, freedom, and responsibility, represent irreducible and ineluctable phenomena of humanity."[34] These are the "existentials" of life, and when they are ignored, any understanding of the self is reduced or warped. Spirituality is discovered phenomenologically, in the immediate self-consciousness of a person, but it is validated by how that person expresses such spiritual awareness. Frankl's therapy examines a spirituality not connected to religious forms or stereotypes. Frankl perceives spirituality as "being with" (*Beisein*) others and with the natural world.[35] In other words, we demonstrate the validity of our spirituality in I-Thou relationships to others, to nature, and to ultimate meaning.

Frankl warns that we must be wary of identifying our intuitive consciousness with our own feelings, dreams, accepted truths, or wishes, and that we must be conscious of the snares of anthropocentrism and anthropomorphism.[36] Anthropocentrism tempts us to believe that we are gods; anthropomorphism tempts us to understand all others, from animals to God, according to how we ourselves perceive and respond. But Frankl is most concerned that we recognize what he terms *monanthropism,* which is "an awareness that we are all members of one humanity, regardless of color, religion, and political beliefs."[37]

A common awareness of our shared humanity is where the spiritual-therapeutic alliance between the pastoral counselor and the clinical psychologist begins. Certainly this has been the case in pastoral theology courses that I have taught. Initially, many theological students feel that unless Frankl meets their religious criteria, his therapeutic philosophy and methods cannot provide even a starting place for a spiritual understanding of the self. Therefore, in my classes in pastoral care, I begin first by asking the students to examine the philosophical and psychological models of the self and to relate these to their expectations as Protestant theological students, who are concerned with the religious dimension. Often they are misinformed about the models presented by Freud, Adler, Jung, B. F. Skinner, and other leading psychologists. They also have scant knowledge about the models of the self provided by Plato, Aristotle, the Bible, the Renaissance, or by contemporary philosophy, especially existentialism. After an appraisal of such models of the self, they discover that Frankl's holistic view of the self provides a satisfactory model for exploring the nature of existence. Donald F. Tweedie, Jr., explains why Frankl appeals to the religious counselor:

> There is an increasing acceptance in evangelical and humanistic circles of the spiritual factor in understanding mental illness. . . . V. E. Frankl has insisted that an adequate understanding of mental and emotional disorder involves the spiritual dimension, but is equally adamant in his assertion that the spiritual factor of personality could not be itself involved in the

pathology. *His reasons are philosophical and based upon the fact that then there would be no core of personal integrity to which to appeal in times of illness. His Logotherapy rests on such a foundation.*[38]

Second, I help the students to see that while the Frankl model has an essential and primary spiritual dimension, it allows the client to choose what form that dimension will take and how it may be used. They come to realize that the majority of those whom they as pastors will counsel desire the freedom to explore for themselves which religious meanings are central in their lives. Frankl allows room for persons to translate his terms in ways that harmonize with their own religious needs. The same is true with their goals. For instance, while Frankl recognizes God as ultimate meaning in his own life, he realizes that others translate the term *God* in various ways and that they respond differently to what they themselves experience as ultimate meaning.

Third, when I introduce students to Frankl's life and tenets, they begin to see that he does not espouse peace of mind but rather a strength of mind, which is possible because of the defiant power of the human spirit. Frankl integrates common sense with his theories of meaning; he is not part of the religious pop-psych movement that began after World War II, which is best represented by the Protestant pastor Norman Vincent Peale and by Rabbi Joshua Liebman (Dr. Peale in a yarmulke).

Fourth, since traditional theological forms and theories apparently are losing ground in helping mainstream Christians to confront the realities of human guilt, suffering, and death, students find that Frankl's understanding of this tragic triad, validated by his own experiences, offers a personally authenticated view of those human experiences. So theological students—who come to understand Frankl's appreciation of religious values, his perception of the balance between freedom and responsibleness and commitment, and above all, his focus on meaning—see that his theories complement the goals of the helping ministries, especially those of religious counselors. Increasingly, religious counselors recognize that one must differentiate between the medieval "cure of souls" and the modern "care of souls," which is the point that Frankl makes in his meaning analysis.

Frankl's methods reflect a style of counseling that harmonizes with the needs of the religious counselor: the style is to help the client take hold of his or her life as soon as possible. Recovery from emotional ills does not require, in Frankl's experience, an in-depth or lengthy review of a client's personal and emotional condition. In the view of meaning analysis, it is more important for the client, as a first step, to recognize the symptoms of the neurosis and to learn how to reduce them even if all the causes of the client's dis-ease are not perfectly identified at that time. Tweedie notes that "the average number of therapeutic sessions per patient at Frankl's clinic is eight. This figure includes those patients . . . who were cured or improved to the degree that no further treatment was required."[39] Changes from unhealthy to healthy attitudes or from unhealthy behavior to healthy behavior need not be gradual. Frankl has demonstrated that many persons can turn around, or change, immediately: religion calls this complete change of direction *metanoia*. The responsibility for change lies individually and socially with the client and not with the counselor. Frankl's practical, open, existential approach to the self emphasizes responsible action to be taken by the client once he or she rethinks his or her value system. His meaning analysis focuses on the person's understanding, or perhaps misunderstanding, of his or her present existence. This complements the efforts of religious counselors to establish not only therapeutic friendships with the persons who come to them for help but also support groups in which those persons can meet others who are also trying to take hold of their lives.

In our time, when so much of our past has been marred by cruelty and wars and our present is still confused and threatened, a viable *Lebenswelt* that confirms our hope for the future is imperative for our mental health and for religious balance. Such looking forward, however, must be free of any ideas of automatic progress, pie-in-the-sky-by-and-by delusions, and naive Pollyanna optimism. Any such viable *Lebenswelt* must, of course, be realized in each of us as individuals; it cannot be imposed upon us by the world. Frankl's therapy approaches individuals in terms of who they can become, not what they believe they have been or are at the moment; and the same conviction that persons are *not* prisoners of the past or of the present is devoutly shared by most religious counselors. They can share Frankl's belief that the spiritual dimension of the human being cannot become ill but only blocked; and as the decisive, constituent dimension of the self, the human spirit of the individual can redeem that person's past, balance the present, and build the future.

For the therapist and for the religious counselor, establishing a therapeutic friendship with someone who comes to them for help is a spiritual task because it involves a dimension of love. Such love is living the experience of another person in all of that person's uniqueness and singularity.[40] Tweedie points out that this relationship "is not such a deep or comprehensive commitment as love in courtship and marriage, nor does it include physical union as a factor. It is essential for the medical ministry in order to enable the physician to meet the existential needs of his patient. Rapport is only possible through love."[41] This therapeutic, loving relationship modifies any incipient or expressed paternalism on the part of the counselor; provides a recognizable covenant between the counselor and the client; and defines the tenor, mutual expectations, and limits of the relationship.

Meaning analysis does not claim to provide all that is needed therapeutically to heal the shattered self. It sees itself as essentially a way to communicate the nature of the holistic self. Its overall purpose is to help the client find reason for belief and trust that it is possible to live humanely and to find meaning in existence no matter what challenges come to the individual. Although meaning analysis opposes any form of reductionism, Frankl does not consider that the theories advanced by Freud and Adler are invalid but rather that they are inadequate because they fail to recognize or accept the noetic dimension of human existence.

Thomas Merton remarks that liberation from our bodies is less vital than liberation from our minds, for we find ourselves entangled in our minds rather than in our bodies. Frankl's philosophy and his methodology focus on helping us to achieve this liberation from the concentration camp of the mind, so that we may exercise our human freedom and responsibleness. Frankl teaches that finding meaning is not a gift but an achievement. His meaning analysis is not a panacea but a noetically empowered therapy sensitive to our all-too-often unheard cry for meaning.

A Comparison of Socrates'
and Frankl's Philosophical
Fundamentals and Methods

SOCRATES (469–399 B.C.) REPRESENTS THE EARLY PHILOSOPHICAL SPECULATIONS OF THE GREEKS, DEVELOPED AND REVISED BY PLATO (427–347 B.C.) AND ARISTOTLE (384–322 B.C.).

VIKTOR E. FRANKL (A.D. 1905–   ), WHILE AWARE OF THE GREEK CONTRIBUTION, REPRESENTS A PHILOSOPHICAL VIEWPOINT THAT IS A MIXTURE OF SECULARIZED JUDAISM, RENAISSANCE THINKING, GERMAN ENLIGHTENMENT, EXISTENTIALISM, PHENOMENOLOGY, AND HUMANISTIC PSYCHOLOGY.

Socrates	*Frankl*
Knowledge is virtue.	Knowledge is a means of achieving a life of meaning.
Virtue is happiness.	Virtue is found in a meaningful task well done and in caring for others.
The self is the seat of moral ideas.	The self is the seat of noös (spirit), soma (body), and psyche (mind). Noös is the key to the self.
Error is due to ignorance.	Error is due to human frailty and the failure to recognize and use the noetic dimension in the will to meaning.

Socrates

Frankl

Socrates	Frankl
In morals, we should advance the individual and then proceed to the self in its corporate relationships.	In morals, we must make our own existential decisions and then apply them to society, aware of their effect on others.
The dialectic (questioning) method is a preferred way to learn.	The dialectic method is used, but may be revised to use paradoxical intention and attitude modification.
Happiness is the greatest good.	A life of meaning is the greatest good.
While aware of our culture (including its pressures and corruption as well as rewards), the self must make its own choices in life.	Position identical to Socrates'.
The soul must be "purged" and released from the prison of the body to progress toward "transmigration" of the soul after death.	The soul is an essential part of the self in interaction with mind and body. No doctrine of afterlife but a sense of Providence and shared humanity.
The moral dimension is a vital element of the self.	The moral dimension is basic to the self, in which responsibility is an essential expression of meaning.
Mind is the true reality.	Meaning through the noetic dimension is the true reality.
The universe is essentially rational.	The universe, despite its ambiguities and conflicts, does have meaning.
We learn from the past and look forward to the future.	Position identical to Socrates'.
An unexamined life is not worth living.	An unexamined life leads to a noögenic neurosis.
Suicide may be an option for the self.	Suicide is never an option. We can find meaning in every situation if we use the resources of the noetic dimension.

From *International Forum for Logotherapy* 11 (Fall/Winter 1988)

Notes

Viktor E. Frankl's books that are available in English are referred to in the notes by the following abbreviations:

MS *Man's Search for Meaning* (New York: Washington Square Press, 1984)

DS *The Doctor and the Soul: From Psychotherapy to Logotherapy* (New York: Vintage Books, 1986)

WM *The Will to Meaning: Foundations and Applications of Logotherapy* (New York: New American Library, 1988)

PE *Psychotherapy and Existentialism: Selected Papers on Logotherapy* (New York: Touchstone Books, 1978)

UG *The Unconscious God: Psychotherapy and Theology* (New York: Simon & Schuster, 1978)

UH *The Unheard Cry for Meaning: Psychotherapy and Humanism* (New York: Washington Square Pocket Books, 1985)

Chapter One

1. Bruno Bettelheim, *Freud's Vienna and Other Essays* (New York: Knopf, 1989), 6.
2. Viktor E. Frankl, interview with Thomas Corrigan, Berkeley, Calif. (Frankl Library and Memorabilia, 1980, audio cassette).
3. Ibid.
4. Peter Gay, *Freud: A Life for Our Times* (New York: Norton, 1988), 224.
5. Vera J. Lieban-Kalmar, "Effects of Experience-Centered Decision Making on Locus Control: Frankl's Purpose in Life Concept, and Academic Behavior of High School Students" (unpublished Ed. D. dissertation, University of San Francisco, 1982), 21.
6. Bettelheim, *Freud's Vienna,* 52.
7. J. A. C. Brown, *The Post-Freudians* (New York: Penguin, 1961), 37.
8. Alexandra Adler, "A Personal Recollection," *International Forum for Logotherapy, 3* (Spring 1980): 35.

9. Gay, *Freud,* 593.
10. Ibid., 618.
11. Ibid., 624.
12. Ibid., 625.
13. Ibid., 628.
14. Ibid., 618.
15. Viktor E. Frankl, "Experience in a Concentration Camp," *Psychology Today* (February 1968), 56–63.
16. Frankl, *UH,* 75, emphasis added.
17. Frankl, Corrigan interview.
18. Frankl, *MS,* 161.
19. Elisabeth Lukas, "Meaningful Education," *International Forum for Logotherapy,* 12 (Spring 1989): 10.
20. Viktor E. Frankl, "Opening Address to the First World Congress: Logotherapy on Its Way to Degurification," in *Analecta Frankliana: The Proceedings of the First World Congress of Logotherapy: 1980* (Berkeley, Calif. Institute of Logotherapy Press, 1980), 8.
21. Irvin Yalom, *Existential Psychology* (New York: Basic Books, 1980), 442.
22. Stephen S. Kalmar, "The Secular Character of Logotherapy," *International Forum for Logotherapy,* 11 (Spring/Summer 1988): 24.
23. Howard Slaatte, "Self-Transcendence: The Existential Key to Logotherapy," in *Analecta Frankliana,* 31.
24. Reuven Bulka, "Logotherapy and Judaism," in *Analecta Frankliana,* 325.
25. Reuven Bulka, *The Quest for Ultimate Meaning: Principles and Applications of Logotherapy* (New York: Philosophical Library, 1979), 74.
26. Reuven Bulka, "Logotherapy," 324.
27. Ibid.
28. Ibid.
29. Ibid., 236.
30. Ibid., 236–37.
31. Bulka, *Quest for Ultimate Meaning,* 98.
32. Ibid., 136.
33. Harold Kushner, *When Bad Things Happen to Good People* (New York: Schocken, 1981), 90.
34. Frankl, *PE,* 25.
35. Bulka, "Logotherapy," 330.
36. Frankl, *DS,* 136.
37. Ibid., 137.
38. Bulka, "Logotherapy," 330.
39. Hiroshi Takashima, *Humanistic Psychosomatic Medicine* (Berkeley, Calif. Institute of Logotherapy Press, 1984), ii–iii.
40. Yasuo Yuasa, *The Body: Toward an Eastern Mind-Body Theory* (Albany, N.Y.: SUNY Press, 1987), 11.

41. Takashima, *Humanistic Psychosomatic Medicine,* 14.
42. Ibid., 15.
43. Frankl, *UG,* 75.
44. Hajime Nakamura, "Basic Features of the Legal, Political, and Economic Thought of Japan," in *The Japanese Mind: Essentials of Japanese Philosophy and Culture,* ed. Charles A. Moore (Honolulu: East-West Press Center, University of Hawaii, 1967), 143.
45. Hideki Yukawa, "Modern Trends of Western Civilization and Cultural Peculiarities in Japan," in *The Japanese Mind,* 62.
46. Ibid., emphasis added.
47. Frankl, *UH,* 31.
48. Frankl, *WM,* 43–44.
49. Teitarō D. Suzuki, "Reason and Intuition in Buddhist Philosophy," in *The Japanese Mind,* 83.
50. Yuasa, *The Body,* 9.
51. Ibid., 9–10.
52. Ibid., 18.
53. Ibid., 66, emphasis added.
54. Ibid., 105.
55. Ibid., 86.
56. Ibid.
57. Frankl, *PE,* 46.
58. Charles A. Moore, "Introduction," in *The Japanese Mind,* 65.
59. Suzuki, *The Japanese Mind,* 99.
60. Hiroshi Takashima, *Psychosomatic Medicine and Logotherapy: Health Through Noö-Psychosomatic Medicine* (Oceanside, N.Y.: Dabor Science Publications, 1977), 15–16.
61. Ibid., 17.
62. Ibid., 89.
63. Sandra A. Wawrytko, "The Noölogical Dimension in Chinese Thought: Confucius and Chuang Tzu Confront the Existential Vacuum," in *Analecta Frankliana,* 275.
64. Ibid., 276.
65. Ibid., 277.
66. Ibid., 283.
67. Douglas A. Fox, "The Confucian Principle of *Cheng Ming* as an Adjunct to Logotherapy," *Analecta Frankliana,* 287.
68. Ibid., 288.
69. Sitansu S. Chakravarti, "Hinduism and Logotherapy," *International Forum for Logotherapy,* 10 (Spring/Summer 1987): 44–45.
70. Wolfgang Jilek and Louise Jilek-Aall, "Logotherapeutic Aspects of the North American Indian Guardian Spirit," *Analecta Frankliana,* 311–22.
71. Ibid., 313.
72. Ibid.

Chapter Two

1. Frankl, *PE,* 7.
2. Gay, *Freud,* 129.
3. Ibid., 604.
4. Ibid., 201.
5. Ibid., 741.
6. Abram Kardiner, "Freud—The Man I Knew and His Influence," in *Freud and the Twentieth Century,* ed. Benjamin Nelson (New York: Meridian, 1957), 49.
7. Viktor von Weizsaecker, "Reminiscences of Freud and Jung," in *Freud and the Twentieth Century,* 66.
8. Erich Fromm, *Sigmund Freud's Mission* (New York: Harper Colophon, 1959), 5.
9. von Weizsaecker, "Reminiscences," 66.
10. Ibid., 62.
11. Ibid., 66.
12. Alfred Kazin, "The Freudian Revolution Analyzed," in *Freud and the Twentieth Century,* 14.
13. Jack J. Spector, *The Aesthetics of Freud: A Study in Psychoanalysis and Art* (New York: McGraw Hill, 1974), 19.
14. Gay, *Freud,* 129.
15. Ibid., 9–20.
16. Spector, *Aesthetics of Freud,* 6.
17. Gay, *Freud,* 413.
18. Frederick Copleston, *A History of Philosophy,* vol. I (New York and London: Doubleday Image, 1985), 162.
19. Joseph B. Fabry, *The Pursuit of Meaning,* new rev. ed. (Berkeley, Calif.: Institute of Logotherapy Press, 1987), 21.
20. Bertrand Russell, *A History of Western Philosophy* (New York: Simon & Schuster, 1945), 162.
21. Abraham Edel, *Aristotle and His Philosophy* (Chapel Hill: University of North Carolina Press, 1982), 262.
22. Ibid., 259.
23. Frankl, *PE,* 74.
24. Sigmund Freud, *The Future of an Illusion,* tr. W. D. Robson-Scott (New York: Doubleday Anchor, 1957), 88–89.
25. Frankl, *PE,* 7–8.
26. Kardiner, "Freud," 52.
27. Peter Gay, *A Godless Jew: Freud, Atheism, and the Making of Psychoanalysis* (New Haven: Yale University Press, 1987), 4.
28. Copleston, *History of Philosophy,* vol. 6, 108.
29. Ibid.
30. Will Herberg, "Freud, the Revisionists, and Social Reality," in *Freud and the Twentieth Century,* 153–54.

31. Ibid., 154.
32. Bruno Bettelheim, *Freud and Man's Soul* (New York: Knopf, 1983), 103–104.
33. Frankl, *UG,* 27.
34. Frankl, *PE,* 54.
35. Philip Rieff, *Freud: The Mind of a Moralist* (New York: Doubleday Anchor, 1961), 54.
36. Gay, *Freud,* 131.
37. Abraham Kaplan, "Freud and Modern Philosophy," in *Freud and the Twentieth Century,* 221.
38. Gay, *Freud,* 399.
39. Rieff, *Freud,* 333.
40. Ibid., 341.
41. Kaplan, "Freud and Modern Philosophy," 220.
42. Frankl, *WM,* 22.
43. Ibid., 17.
44. Copleston, *History of Philosophy,* vol. 6, 312.
45. Ibid., 328.
46. Ibid., 336.
47. Sigmund Freud, "Civilization and Its Discontents," in *Standard Edition of the Complete Works of Sigmund Freud,* vol. 21, ed. James Strachey (London: Hogarth Press, 1955), 128.
48. Fromm, *Freud's Mission,* 119.
49. Frankl, *WM,* 21.
50. Ibid., 150.
51. Frankl, *UG,* 35.
52. Ibid., 36.
53. Ibid.
54. Ibid.
55. Ibid., 37.
56. Frankl, *WM,* 16.
57. Ludwig Binswanger, *Being-in-the-World: The Selected Papers of Ludwig Binswanger,* trans. Jacob Needleman (New York: Basic Books, 1963), 195.
58. Ibid., 60.
59. Rollo May, ed., *Existential Psychology,* 2nd ed. (New York: Random House, 1969), 15, emphasis added.
60. Ibid., 27.
61. Ibid., 28.
62. Frankl, *PE,* 57.
63. Daniel N. Robinson, *Systems of Modern Psychology,* (New York: Columbia University Press, 1979), 236.
64. Ibid., 234.
65. Frankl, *PE,* 2n.
66. Frankl, *WM,* 17.

67. Ibid., 38.
68. Paul Ricoeur, *Freud and Philosophy: An Essay on Interpretation* (New Haven: Yale University Press, 1970), 338.
69. Frankl, *DS,* 97.
70. Frankl, *PE,* 10.
71. Robinson, *Systems of Modern Psychology,* 237.

Chapter Three

1. Lewis White Beck, *Early German Philosophers: Kant and His Predecessors* (Cambridge: Harvard University, Belnap Press, 1969), 473.
2. Samuel E. Stumpf, *From Socrates to Sartre* (New York: McGraw-Hill, 1988), 308.
3. Ibid.
4. Copleston, *History of Philosophy,* vol. 6, 267–68.
5. Ibid., 218.
6. Immanuel Kant, *Lectures on Ethics* (New York: Harper & Row, 1963), 67.
7. James H. Randall, Jr., *The Career of Philosophy,* vol. 2 (New York: Columbia University Press, 1965), 143.
8. Fabry, *Pursuit of Meaning,* 52.
9. Karl Jaspers, *Kant* (New York: Harcourt Brace & World, 1962), 49.
10. Frankl, *WM,* 66.
11. Frankl, *PE,* 103.
12. Ibid., 57.
13. Jaspers, *Kant,* 68.
14. E. James Lieberman, *Acts of Will: The Life and Work of Otto Rank* (New York: Free Press, 1985), 357.
15. Immanuel Kant, *Religion within the Limits of Reason Alone,* tr. & intro. Theodore M. Greene and Hoyt Hudson, with a new essay "The Ethical Significance of Kant's Religion" by John Silber (New York: Harper & Row, 1960), cvi.
16. Frankl, *WM,* 150.
17. Frankl, *PE,* 66.
18. Frankl, *WM,* vii.
19. Ibid., 69–70.
20. Kant, *Limits of Reason,* cxi.
21. Ibid., 135.
22. Kant, *Ethics,* 133.
23. Ibid., 134.
24. Frankl, *PE,* 41.
25. Ibid.
26. Frankl, *WM,* 65.
27. Kant, *Limits of Reason,* lv.

28. Ibid., lxii.
29. Copleston, *History of Philosophy,* vol. 6, 324.
30. Frankl, *MS,* 175.
31. Kant, *Limits of Reason,* xxxii.
32. Ibid., xxxv.
33. Frankl, *UG,* 85.
34. Ibid., 119.
35. Ibid., 120.
36. Ibid., 119.
37. Copleston, *History of Philosophy,* vol. 6, 344.
38. Frankl, *PE,* 33.
39. Ibid., 85n.
40. Frankl, *UH,* 70.
41. Jaspers, *Kant,* 154.

Chapter Four

1.   Barbara MacKinnon, *An Historical Anthology* (Albany, N.Y.: SUNY Press, 1985), 218.
2.   Michael Weinstein, *The Wilderness and the City* (Amherst: University of Massachusetts Press, 1982), 218.
3.   Patrick K. Dooley, *Pragmatism as Humanism: The Philosophy of William James* (Chicago: Nelson-Hall, 1974), 1.
4.   Gay William Allen, *William James: A Biography* (New York: Viking, 1967), 130.
5.   Ibid., 163.
6.   Gerald E. Myers, *William James: His Life and Thought* (New Haven: Yale University Press, 1986), 52.
7.   William James, *Pragmatism,* ed. Bruce Kuklick (Indianapolis and Cambridge: Hackett, 1981), 10.
8.   Ibid., 11.
9.   John E. Smith, *Purpose and Thought: The Meaning of Pragmatism* (New Haven: Yale University Press, 1978), 27.
10. Ibid., 64.
11. Bernard Brennan, *William James* (Schenectady, N. Y.: New College University, 1968), 3.
12. Allen, *William James,* 4.
13. Ibid., 3.
14. R. W. B. Lewis, *The Jameses: A Family Narrative* (New York: Farrar, Straus & Giroux, 1991), 13.
15. Ralph Barton Perry, *The Thought and Character of William James,* vol. 2, (Boston: Little, Brown, 1936), 280.
16. Personal conversation with author, November 1968.
17. Perry, *Thought and Character of William James,* 290.

18. Ibid., 319.
19. Walter Muelder, Lawrence Sears, and Anne Schlabach, eds., *The Development of American Philosophy,* 2nd ed. (Boston: Houghton Mifflin, 1960), 345.
20. Myers, *William James,* 342.
21. Dooley, *Pragmatism as Humanism,* 166.
22. Ibid., 5.
23. Frankl, *MS,* 57.
24. Bruce Wilshire, ed., *William James: The Essential Writings* (Albany: SUNY Press, 1984), xlvii.
25. Paul M. Van Buren, "William James and the Metaphysical Risk," in *American Philosophy and Its Future,* ed. Michael Novak (New York: Scribner's, 1966), 60–86.
26. Myers, *William James,* 279.
27. Fabry, *Pursuit of Meaning,* 20.
28. Myers, *William James,* 408–409.
29. Ibid., 414.
30. Frankl, *MS,* 161–79, for the full discussion of tragic optimism in facing "the tragic triad" of guilt, suffering, and death.
31. Frankl, *DS,* 65–66.
32. Ibid., 66.
33. Ibid.
34. Henry S. Levinson, *The Religious Investigations of William James* (Chapel Hill: University of North Carolina Press, 1981), 179.
35. Ibid.
36. John J. McDermott, *The Writings of William James* (New York: Random House, 1967), xli.
37. Myers, *William James,* 260.
38. Ibid., 402.
39. Frankl, *UH,* 124.
40. Ibid.
41. William James, *The Principles of Psychology* (Cambridge: Harvard University Press, 1983), 1164.
42. Ibid., 1159.
43. Weinstein, *Wilderness and the City,* 75.
44. Ibid., 77.
45. Frankl, *MS,* 172.
46. Marcus P. Ford, *William James's Philosophy: A New Perspective* (Amherst: University of Massachusetts Press, 1982), 19.
47. Myers, *William James,* 404.
48. Frankl, *PE,* 63.
49. John K. Roth, *Freedom and the Moral Life: The Ethics of William James,* (Philadelphia: Westminster Press, 1969), 32.
50. Ibid., 34.

51. Levinson, *Religious Investigations,* 256.
52. Fabry, *Pursuit of Meaning,* 65.
53. Myers, *William James,* 407.
54. Frankl, *WM,* 65.
55. Ibid., 66.
56. James, *Principles of Psychology,* 1166.
57. Ibid., 1157.
58. Ibid., 1143.
59. James M. Edie, *William James and Phenomenology* (Bloomington and Indianapolis: Indiana University Press, 1987), 7.
60. John Wild, *The Radical Empiricism of William James* (New York: Doubleday, 1969), 127.
61. Edie, *William James,* 45.
62. Elisabeth Lukas, *Meaningful Living* (Cambridge, Mass.: Schenkman, 1984), 136.
63. Dickinson S. Miller, "Mr. Santayana and William James," (*Harvard Graduate's Magazine,* March 29, 1921), 358. Quoted by Myers, *William James,* 462.
64. Myers, *William James,* 466.
65. Allen, *William James,* 67.
66. Frankl, *UG,* 13.
67. Paul J. Tillich, *Systematic Theology,* vol. I (Chicago: University of Chicago Press, 1951), 251.
68. Allen, *William James,* 67.
69. Frankl, "Opening Address," 9.

Chapter Five

1. Herbert Spiegelberg, *The Phenomenological Movement: A Historical Introduction,* 3rd and enlarged ed. (The Hague/Boston/Lancaster: Martinus Nijhoff, 1984), 71.
2. Joseph J. Kockelmans, *Edmund Husserl's Phenomenological Psychology: A Historic-Critical Study* (Pittsburgh: Duquesne University Press, 1967), 331.
3. See the discussion in Chapter 8, "Healing the Shattered Self."
4. Kockelmans, Edmund, *Husserl's Phenomenological Psychology,* 290.
5. Frankl, *UH,* 58.
6. Paul Ricoeur, *Husserl: An Analysis of His Phenomenology* (Evanston, Ill.: Northwestern University Press, 1967), 91.
7. Max Scheler, *The Nature of Sympathy* (London: Routledge & Kegan Paul, 1979), 161.
8. Max Scheler, *Formalism in Ethics and Non-Formal Ethics,* ed. Manfred Frings and Roger L. Funk (Evanston, Ill: Northwestern University Press, 1973), xxiii.
9. Frankl, *WM,* 63.
10. Fabry, *Pursuit of Meaning,* 67.
11. Ibid., 17.

12. Ibid., 93.
13. Max Scheler, *Selected Philosophical Essays*, trans. and intro. by David R. Lachterman (Evanston, Ill.: Northwestern University Press, 1973), 110–11.
14. Ibid.
15. William A. Sadler, Jr., *Existence and Love: A New Approach to Existential Phenomenology* (New York: Scribner's, 1969), 284n.
16. Ibid.
17. William S. Sahakian, "Logotherapy for Whom?" in *Logotherapy in Action*, eds. Joseph B. Fabry, Reuven Bulka, and William S. Sahakian (New York and London: Jason Aronson, 1979), 57.
18. P. Hunnerfeld, quoted in Joseph J. Kockelmans, *Martin Heidegger: A First Introduction to His Philosophy*, (Pittsburgh: Duquesne University Press, 1965), 5.
19. John Macquarrie, *Martin Heidegger* (Richmond: John Knox Press, 1968), 8.
20. Martin Heidegger, quoted by Jacques Taminaux, "Heidegger's and Husserl's Logical Investigations," in *Radical Phenomenology: Essays in Honor of Martin Heidegger*, ed. John Sallis (Atlantic Highlands: Humanities Press, 1978), 64.
21. Macquarrie, *Martin Heidegger*, 10.
22. Ibid., 16, emphasis added.
23. Joseph J. Kockelmans, *Martin Heidegger: A First Introduction to His Philosophy*, 64.
24. Ibid., 69.
25. Copleston, *History of Philosophy*, vol. 1, 43.
26. Magda King, *Heidegger's Philosophy: A Guide to Its Basic Thought*, (New York: Macmillan, 1964), 155.
27. Kockelmans, *Heidegger*, 66.
28. Frankl, *UH*, 101.
29. Ibid., 73.
30. Ibid., 74.
31. Fabry, *Pursuit of Meaning*, 16.
32. Frankl, *PE*, 33.
33. Kockelmans, *Heidegger*, 80.
34. Elisabeth Lukas, "Love and Work in Viktor Frankl's View of Human Nature," *International Forum for Logotherapy*, 6, (Fall/Winter 1983): 103–104.
35. Viktor E. Frankl, "On the Meaning of Love," *International Forum for Logotherapy*, 10 (Spring/Summer 1987): 5.
36. Frankl, *UH*, 105–106.
37. Ibid., 107.
38. Ibid., 84.
39. Ibid., 85–86.
40. Ibid., 62–63.
41. Ibid., 63.
42. Frankl, *PE*, 24.

43. Ibid., 30.
44. Macquarrie, *Martin Heidegger,* 32.
45. Frankl, *WM,* 63.
46. Ibid., 41.
47. Ibid., 64–66.

Chapter Six

1. Emmanuel Mounier, *Existential Philosophies: An Introduction* (London: Rockcliff, 1951), 3.
2. Ibid., 4.
3. Nathan Scott, Jr., *The Unquiet Vision: Mirrors of Man in Existentialism* (New York: Collins, 1978), 26.
4. Ibid., 8.
5. Marjorie Grene, *Introduction to Existentialism* (Chicago: University of Chicago Press, 1959), 37, emphasis added.
6. H. J. Blackham, *Reality, Man, and Existence,* (New York: Bantam Books, 1965), 16.
7. Scott, *The Unquiet Vision,* 82.
8. Ibid., 82–83.
9. Friedrich Nietzsche, *Joyful Wisdom,* tr. Thomas Common (New York: Ungarlo, 1970).
10. Roger Shinn, *The Restless Adventure: Essays on Contemporary Expressions of Existentialism* (New York: Scribner's, 1968), 13.
11. James C. Crumbaugh, "Logotherapy: New Help for Problem Drinkers," in *Analecta Frankliana,* 165–66.
12. Mary Warnock, *Existentialism* (London: Oxford University Press, 1970), 10.
13. Ibid., 175.
14. George R. Simms, "Logotherapy in Medical Practice," in *Analecta Frankliana,* 153.
15. Fabry, *Pursuit of Meaning,* 20.
16. Hiroshi Takashima, "The Importance of the Four Dimensions of Human Nature," *Analecta Frankliana,* 101.
17. Shinn, *Restless Adventure,* 54.
18. Scott, *The Unquiet Vision,* 83.
19. Ibid., 84.
20. Frankl, *DS,* 27.
21. Ibid.
22. Ibid., 33.
23. Ibid.
24. Ibid., 80.
25. Ibid., xix.
26. Jean-Paul Sartre, quoted by Grene, *Introduction to Existentialism,* 99–100.
27. Frankl, *MS,* 86.

28. Grene, *Introduction to Existentialism,* 99–100.
29. Frankl, *UH,* 61.
30. Martin Buber, quoted by Blackham, *Reality and Existence,* 225.
31. Ibid., 230.
32. Ibid., 232.
33. Gabriel Marcel, *Creative Fidelity* (New York: Noonday Press, 1964), 54.
34. Gabriel Marcel, *Mystery of Being. Vol. 2: Faith and Reality,* (London: Harvill Press, 1950), 160.
35. Kenneth T. Gallagher, *The Philosophy of Gabriel Marcel* (New York: Fordham University Press, 1962), 69.
36. Ibid.
37. Marcel, *Creative Fidelity,* 154.
38. Ibid.
39. Gallagher, *Philosophy of Gabriel Marcel,* 26.
40. Ibid., emphasis added.
41. Frankl, *UG,* 140.
42. Gallagher, *Philosophy of Gabriel Marcel,* xvi.
43. John Hellman, *Emmanuel Mounier and the New Catholic Left 1930–1950* (Toronto: University of Toronto Press, 1981), 5.
44. Ibid.
45. Mounier, *Existential Philosophies,* 24.
46. Ibid.
47. Ibid., 25.
48. Frankl, *WM,* 74.
49. Ibid.
50. Ibid.
51. Mounier, *Existential Philosophies,* 28.
52. Frankl, *WM,* 95.
53. Mounier, *Existential Philosophies,* 29.
54. Ibid., 31.
55. Ibid.
56. Fabry, *Pursuit of Meaning,* 84.
57. Frankl, *PE,* 47–48.
58. Gabriel Marcel, *The Philosophy of Existentialism* (New York: Citadel, 1966), 46.
59. Fabry, *Pursuit of Meaning,* 150.
60. Mounier, *Existential Philosophies,* 38.
61. Frankl, *DS,* 63.
62. Ibid., 64.
63. Ibid., 66.
64. Frankl, *PE,* 121.
65. Ibid., 29–30.
66. Mounier, *Existential Philosophies,* 42.
67. Ibid., 43, 45.
68. Frankl, *WM,* 121.

69. Ibid., 118.
70. Ibid., 21.
71. Frankl, *PE,* 72.
72. Frankl, *DS,* 188.

Chapter Seven

1. Carl F. Graumann, "Psychology: Humanistic or Human?" in *Humanistic Psychology,* ed. Joseph Royce and Leendert Mos (New York and London: Plenum Press, 1981), 4.
2. Nathaniel S. Lehrman, "Prophetic Jewish Humanism: Historic Worship-Based, Nonsupernatural Humanism," *Religious Humanism,* 20 (Winter 1986): 74.
3. Khoren Arisian, Jr., "The Humanist Imagination," *Religious Humanism,* 1 (Spring 1967): 33–34.
4. Ibid.
5. John Dewey, quoted by George E. Axtelle in "John Dewey's Concept of 'The Religious'; Basis for Religious Humanism?" *Religious Humanism,* (Summer 1967): 67.
6. Herbert W. Schneider, "Moral Strategy and Religious Humanism," *Religious Humanism,* 2 (Winter 1968): 24.
7. Graumann, "Psychology," 14.
8. Viktor E. Frankl, in personal conversation with author, November 1968.
9. John Charles Cooper, "Man and Science," in *Humanistic Psychology,* 103.
10. James, *Principles of Psychology,* 285.
11. Howard C. Coward and Joseph Royce, "Toward an Epistemological Basis for Humanistic Psychology," *Humanistic Psychology,* 114.
12. W. C. Smith, quoted in *Humanistic Psychology,* 130.
13. Amedeo Giorgi, "Humanistic Psychology and Metapsychology," in *Humanistic Psychology,* 26–29.
14. Frankl, *UG,* 243.
15. Frankl, "Opening Address," 6.
16. Frankl, *UG,* 103.
17. Frankl, *WM,* 37.
18. Frankl, *PE,* 37.
19. Ibid.
20. Frank T. Severin, *Discovering Man in Psychology: A Humanistic Approach* (New York: McGraw-Hill, 1973), ix.
21. Thomas C. Greening, *Existential Humanistic Psychology* (Belmont, Calif.: Brooks/Cole 1971), 9.
22. Henryk Misiak and Virginia S. Sexton, eds., *Phenomenological, Existential, and Humanistic Psychologies: A Historical Survey* (New York and London: Grune & Stratton, 1973), 42.
23. Ibid., 40.

24. Ibid., 41.
25. Ibid., 83.
26. Ibid., 116.
27. Robert F. Massey, *Personality Theories: Comparisons and Syntheses* (New York: Van Nostrand, 1981), 341.
28. Ibid., 343.
29. Abraham H. Maslow, *Toward a Psychology of Being* (New York: Van Nostrand, 1962), 191.
30. Massey, *Personality Theories,* 440.
31. Ibid., 444.
32. Ibid., 53.
33. Frankl, *WM,* 27.
34. Frankl, *PE,* 134.
35. Ibid., 135.
36. Frankl, *WM,* 9.
37. Frankl, *PE,* 134.
38. Yalom, *Existential Psychology,* 20.
39. Ibid., 409.
40. Charlotte Bühler, "A Human Life as a Whole as a Central Subject of Humanistic Psychology," *Challenges of Humanistic Psychology,* ed. James F. T. Bugental (New York: McGraw-Hill, 1967), 83.
41. Carl Rogers, unpublished paper quoted by Clark Moustakas, "Heuristic Research," in *Challenges of Humanistic Psychology,* 107.
42. Scheler, *Nature of Sympathy,* 161.
43. Carl Rogers, quoted by Massey, *Personality Theories,* 311.
44. Ibid., 312.
45. Yalom, *Existential Psychology,* 408.
46. Ibid., 56.
47. Rollo May, *The Discovery of Being: Writings in Existential Psychology* (New York: Norton, 1983), 153–69.
48. Ibid., 154.
49. Ibid., 156.
50. Ibid., 163.
51. Frankl, *PE,* 12–13.
52. Ibid.
53. Frankl, *WM,* 44.
54. Yalom, *Existential Psychology,* 414.
55. Massey, *Personality Theories,* 272.
56. Gordon W. Allport, *Pattern and Growth in Personality* (New York: Holt, Rinehart & Winston, 1961), 543.
57. Massey, *Personality Theories,* 284.
58. Gordon W. Allport, *The Individual and His Religion: A Psychological Interpretation* (New York: Macmillan, 1951), 17.
59. Ibid., 18.

60. Ibid., 4–5.
61. Frank T. Severin, *Humanistic Viewpoints in Psychology,* (New York: McGraw-Hill, 1965), 44.
62. Giorgi, *"The Challenges of Humanistic Psychology,"* 23.
63. Royce and Mos, *Humanistic Psychology,* xiii.
64. Frankl, *UH,* 45.

Chapter Eight

1. Charlotte Bühler and Melanie Allen, *Introduction to Humanistic Psychology* (Pacific Grove, Calif.: Brooks/Cole, 1972), 22.
2. Ibid.
3. Viktor E. Frankl, "Beyond Self-Actualization and Self-Expressions," in *Perspectives on the Group Process,* 2nd ed., ed. C. Gratton Kemp (Boston: Houghton Mifflin, 1970), 42.
4. Viktor E. Frankl, "Self-Transcendence as a Human Phenomenon," in *Readings in Humanistic Psychology,* eds. Anthony J. Sutich and Miles A. Vitch (New York: Free Press, 1969), 122.
5. Frankl, *PE,* 74.
6. Reuven Bulka, "The Role of the Individual in Jewish Law," *Tradition,* 13 & 14 (Spring/Summer 1973): 129.
7. Viktor E. Frankl, letter to Magda B. Arnold and John A. Gasson.
8. Viktor E. Frankl, "The Task of Education for an Age of Meaninglessness," in *New Prospects for the Small Liberal Arts College,* ed. Sidney Letter (New York: Teachers College, Columbia University Press, 1968), 57.
9. Viktor E. Frankl, interview with Huston Smith, Berkeley, Calif. (Frankl Library and Memorabilia, July 1984, video cassette).
10. Elisabeth Lukas, "Logotherapy's Message to Parents and Teachers," *International Forum for Logotherapy,* 1 (Winter 1978): 11–12.
11. Ibid., 11.
12. Ibid.
13. Ibid., 12.
14. Ibid.
15. Bianca Z. Hirsch, "Manifestations of Existential Frustration in an American Public School System," in *Analecta Frankliana,* 236.
16. Stephen S. Kalmar, "What Logotherapy Can Learn from High School Students," *International Forum for Logotherapy,* 5 (Fall/Winter 1982): 77.
17. Ibid., 82.
18. Garth Wood, *The Myth of Neurosis in Overcoming the Illness Excuse* (New York: Harper & Row, 1988), 122.
19. Lukas, *Meaningful Living,* 129–130.
20. Ibid.
21. Ibid., 136.
22. Ibid., 139.

23. Elisabeth Lukas, unpublished lecture for *diplomate* candidates, Viktor E. Frankl Institute of Logotherapy, Berkeley, Calif., July 1984.
24. Lukas, *Meaningful Living,* 16.
25. Frankl, *PE,* 54.
26. Ibid.
27. Frankl, *UH,* 82.
28. R. W. Sleeper, "Pragmatism, Religion and *Experienceable Difference,*" in *American Philosophy and the Future,* ed. Michael Novak (New York: Scribner's, 1968), 306.
29. Viktor E. Frankl, preface to *Logotherapy and the Christian Faith: An Evaluation of Frankl's Approach to Psychotherapy* by Donald F. Tweedie, Jr. (Grand Rapids, Mich.: Baker Book House, 1961).
30. Viktor E. Frankl, *Handbuch der Neurosenlehre und Psychotherapie* (Vienna: Urban-Schwarzenberg, 1957), 11.
31. Marcel, *Mystery of Being. Vol. 1: Reflection and Mystery,* 203.
32. Ibid., 250.
33. Ibid., 212.
34. Viktor E. Frankl, *Das Menschenbild der Seelenheilkude* (Stuttgart: Hippokrates Verlag, 1959), 99.
35. Ibid., 58.
36. Frankl, *Handbuch,* 80ff.
37. Fabry, *Pursuit of Meaning,* 6.
38. Donald F. Tweedie, Jr., *The Christian and the Couch: An Introduction to Christian Logotherapy,* (Grand Rapids, Mich., Baker Book House, 1963), 55–56, emphasis added.
39. Donald F. Tweedie, *Logotherapy and The Christian Faith: An Evaluation of Frankl's Existential Approach to Psychotherapy* (Grand Rapids, Mich., Baker Book House, 1961), 107.
40. Ibid., 137.
41. Ibid., 138.

Index

Abraham, 12
Adler, Alexandra, 4
Adler, Alfred:
  Frankl, 2, 3–5, 7
  Freud, 3
  geltungsstreuben, 7
  gemeinschaftsgefühl, 4
  humanistic psychology, 126
  May, 137, 324
  Rogers, 135, 322
  self, 154
  social justice, 66, 154
  theories, 157
  will to power, 127–128, 304
Aesthetics, 36
Agapé (see Love)
  defined, 139
  sacrifice, 113
Alethia, 91
Alienation, 97, 120–121
Allen, Melanie, 142
Allers, Rudolph, 4
Allport, Gordon, 84, 124, 127, 139–141,
  145
  Individual and His Religion, The, 140
  maturity, 139
  meaning, 140
  relationships, 140
  sentiment, 140
  values, 139
Amor fati:
  defined, 104
  Nietzsche, 109
Angst (see Anxiety)
  Being-toward-death, 99
  courage to Be, 101
  defined, 104
Anschluss:
  Freud, 5–6
  Viennese, 5
Anthropomorphism, 154
Anxiety:
  Angst, 99
  Being-toward-death, 99

Anxiety (*continued*)
  courage to Be, 101
Appetite for meaning, 140
Aquinas, Thomas, 39
Aristotle, 20, 30–38, 126, 133, 154
  Golden Mean, 32
  logos, 93
  noös, 32
  pleasure, 31–32
  practical philosophy, 30
  practical reason, 31–32
Association for Humanistic Psychology, 141
Astor, John Jacob, 65
Attitude modulation:
  defined, 72
  educational process, 147
  meaning analysis, 150–151
  ministry humane, 144
Aufklärung (see German enlightment)
Augustine, Saint, 120
Aurelius, Marcus, 125
Austria:
  Anschluss, 5–6
  anti-Semitism, 26
  humanistic curriculum, 27, 33, 42
Awareness:
  axiological, 19
  teleological, 19

Bad faith, 111
Baumgarten, Alexander, 36–37
Befindlichkeit:
  defined, 90
  purpose, 93
  verstehen, 93
Behavior therapy, 152
Being:
  defined, 90
  ek-sists, 91
  intuitive conscience, 112
  meaning, 112
  modes, 99, 101, 112, 145, 154
  prereflective, 112
  self, 91

TO THE OWNER OF THIS BOOK:

I hope that you have found *Vicktor E. Frankl: Life with Meaning* useful. So that this book can be improved in a future edition, would you take the time to complete this sheet and return it? Thank you.

Instructor's name: _____

Department: _____

School and address: _____

_____

1. The name of the course in which I used this book is: _____

_____

2. My general reaction to this book is: _____

_____

_____

3. What I like most about this book is: _____

_____

_____

4. What I like least about this book is: _____

_____

_____

5. Were all of the chapters of the book assigned for you to read?   Yes   No

   If not, which ones weren't? _____

6. Do you plan to keep this book after you finish the course?   Yes   No

   Why or why not? _____

_____

7. On a separate sheet of paper, please write specific suggestions for improving this book and anything else you'd care to share about your experience in using the book.

Optional:

Your name: _____ Date: _____

May Brooks/Cole quote you, either in promotion for *Vicktor E. Frankl: Life with Meaning* or in future publishing ventures?

Yes: _____ No: _____

Sincerely,

William Blair Gould

FOLD HERE

NO POSTAGE
NECESSARY
IF MAILED
IN THE
UNITED STATES

BUSINESS REPLY MAIL
FIRST CLASS   PERMIT NO. 358   PACIFIC GROVE, CA

POSTAGE WILL BE PAID BY ADDRESSEE

ATT: *William Blair Gould*

**Brooks/Cole Publishing Company
511 Forest Lodge Road
Pacific Grove, California 93950-9968**

FOLD HERE